I0131707

iPhone with Microsoft Exchange Server 2010: Business Integration and Deployment

Set up Microsoft Exchange Server 2010 and deploy iPhone and other iDevices securely into your business

Steve Goodman

[PACKT] enterprise 88
PUBLISHING professional expertise distilled

BIRMINGHAM - MUMBAI

iPhone with Microsoft Exchange Server 2010: Business Integration and Deployment

Copyright © 2012 Packt Publishing

All rights reserved. No part of this book may be reproduced, stored in a retrieval system, or transmitted in any form or by any means, without the prior written permission of the publisher, except in the case of brief quotations embedded in critical articles or reviews.

Every effort has been made in the preparation of this book to ensure the accuracy of the information presented. However, the information contained in this book is sold without warranty, either express or implied. Neither the author, nor Packt Publishing, and its dealers and distributors will be held liable for any damages caused or alleged to be caused directly or indirectly by this book.

Packt Publishing has endeavored to provide trademark information about all of the companies and products mentioned in this book by the appropriate use of capitals. However, Packt Publishing cannot guarantee the accuracy of this information.

First published: March 2012

Production Reference: 1130312

Published by Packt Publishing Ltd.
Livery Place
35 Livery Street
Birmingham B3 2PB, UK.

ISBN 978-1-84969-148-2

www.packtpub.com

Cover Image by Siddharth Ravishankar (sidd.ravishankar@gmail.com)

Credits

Author
Steve Goodman

Reviewers
Jeff Guillet
Laercio Simoes
Henrik Walther

Acquisition Editor
Wilson D'souza

Lead Technical Editor
Shreerang Deshpande

Technical Editor
Vanjeet D'souza

Project Coordinator
Joel Goveya

Proofreader
Aaron Nash

Indexer
Monica Ajmera Mehta

Production Coordinator
Aparna Bhagat

Cover Work
Aparna Bhagat

About the Author

Steve Goodman has worked in the IT industry for over 12 years and is currently a Technical Architect at one of the UK's leading IT services providers, working on the design and delivery of Exchange, Active Directory, and Virtualization solutions for organizations across the UK.

When he's not helping companies improve their IT infrastructure, he regularly writes about Exchange, Office 365, and PowerShell topics on his website (`http://www.stevieg.org/`). A multiple MCITP, MCSE, and MCT, Steve was also awarded the MCC Award in 2011 by Microsoft for his contributions to the Exchange community.

I'd like to thank my wonderful wife Lisa, and beautiful daughter Isabelle for all their love and patience throughout the writing of this book; and being there for me when I needed kind words of support.

I'd also like to thank my technical reviewers, Henrik Walther, Jeff Guillet, and Laercio Simoes for their support with this book and their continuing dedication and contributions to the Exchange community.

About the Reviewers

Jeff Guillet is an Exchange 2010 Microsoft Certified Master and MVP. He works as a senior consultant for ExtraTeam, a Microsoft Gold Partner, in Pleasanton, CA. Jeff holds MCITP:Enterprise Administrator, MCITP:Enterprise Messaging Administrator, MCITP:Lync Administrator, and CISSP certifications.

Jeff is the co-author of *Windows Server 2008 Hyper-V Unleashed*. He was the technical editor of the books *Lync Server 2010 Unleashed* and *Windows Server 2008 Unleashed*, and also a contributing author of several books including *Exchange Server 2010 Unleashed*, *Windows Server 2008 R2 Unleashed*, and *Exchange Server 2007 Unleashed*, all books from Sams Publishing.

He also publishes the well-known **EXPTA {blog}**, a technical blog with over one million readers worldwide. Please visit http://www.expta.com for the latest Exchange news.

Laercio Simoes has 20 years' experience in Software Development. A PhD in Electrical Engineering, he graduated from the Singularity University. He has won multiple awards in several entrepreneur contests.

He runs a startup company (http://www.hpcbrasil.com/) and is currently building a medical platform data platform (http://www.flextracker.com.br/).

This is his first book as a reviewer.

> To my wife Gislaine and my kids Maria Clara, Giuseppe, and Miguel.

Henrik Walther is a consultant working with Microsoft Consulting Service (MCS) at Microsoft Denmark. Here his primary working areas is Exchange on-premise and Office 365 solutions for the largest customers in Denmark. He has been in the IT industry for more than 17 years primarily working with Microsoft BackOffice solutions such as Exchange Server. Henrik is usually involved in all phases of the project. More specifically the envisioning, planning, and design phases and often also the deployment and migration phases.

Prior to joining Microsoft, Henrik held the Exchange MVP for eight years and back in 2007, he became a Microsoft Certified Master: Exchange.

In addition to being a consultant at Microsoft, Henrik is a respected Technical Writer. Among other things, he's been on the team that did most of the Exchange 2007 related white papers for Microsoft IT Showcase as well as on the team that created questions for the Exchange 2010 MCP exams. He is currently contracted by Microsoft **TechNet** Exchange Product group to write content for the core Exchange documentation and the TechNet Wiki.

www.PacktPub.com

Support files, eBooks, discount offers and more

You might want to visit www.PacktPub.com for support files and downloads related to your book.

Did you know that Packt offers eBook versions of every book published, with PDF and ePub files available? You can upgrade to the eBook version at www.PacktPub.com and as a print book customer, you are entitled to a discount on the eBook copy. Get in touch with us at service@packtpub.com for more details.

At www.PacktPub.com, you can also read a collection of free technical articles, sign up for a range of free newsletters and receive exclusive discounts and offers on Packt books and eBooks.

http://PacktLib.PacktPub.com

Do you need instant solutions to your IT questions? PacktLib is Packt's online digital book library. Here, you can access, read and search across Packt's entire library of books.

Why Subscribe?

- Fully searchable across every book published by Packt
- Copy and paste, print and bookmark content
- On demand and accessible via web browser

Free Access for Packt account holders

If you have an account with Packt at www.PacktPub.com, you can use this to access PacktLib today and view nine entirely free books. Simply use your login credentials for immediate access.

Table of Contents

Preface

Have you been tasked with getting iPhones into the hands of your business executives, and need to ensure they can reliably and securely access corporate e-mail? This book will teach you what you need to know about getting Exchange 2010 set up and then help you deploy iPhones in a secure and manageable way.

Starting with the basics, you'll learn about what Apple mobile devices have to offer and how they have evolved into devices suitable for business use. If you're new to Exchange Server 2010, you'll learn the basics of Microsoft's world leading messaging suite, before learning how to plan, install, and configure a highly available Exchange environment. You will also understand how to configure Office 365 and learn how both can be configured to apply policies to iPhone, iPad, and the iPod Touch. You'll also learn how to configure advanced features, such as certificate authentication, how to create and deploy configuration profiles for devices, and how to manage your devices once they are in the hands of your users.

After reading this book, you will be confident about introducing Apple mobile devices into your organization.

What this book covers

Chapter 1, Introduction to iPhone with Exchange Server 2010 introduces the Apple mobile device range and Exchange Server 2010 starting with the fundamentals and explaining the concepts used in later chapters.

Chapter 2, Architecture and Implementation Planning covers planning the architecture that you will need in place for Exchange Server. You'll learn about the individual Exchange Server roles and how to plan your underlying infrastructure so it not only allows Apple mobile devices to connect, but meets the needs of your company.

Chapter 3, Exchange Server Configuration for iOS Connectivity follows on from the planning in the previous chapter to walk through the process of installing and configuring a highly available Exchange infrastructure that Apple mobile devices, amongst others, can connect to.

Chapter 4, Office 365 Configuration for iOS Connectivity looks at an alternative approach to configuring and running Exchange Server, by using Microsoft's Office 365. We'll see how this simplifies the implementation process and still allows us to connect and manage Apple mobile devices.

Chapter 5, Creating and Enforcing Policies explores how Exchange Server allows us to control end-user devices, from restricting the features that can be used on Apple mobile devices to ensuring only allowed devices can connect to your Exchange infrastructure.

Chapter 6, Configuring Certificate Based Authentication in Exchange Server 2010 walks through how to configure and manage a small public key infrastructure aimed at improving the security of your Exchange environment through the use of user certificates on Apple mobile devices.

Chapter 7, Provisioning iOS Client Devices introduces the iPhone Configuration Utility, the Apple tool specifically aimed at controlling Apple mobile device features and configuration, along with exploring the methods available to deploy profiles to mobile devices.

Chapter 8, Sharing Mailboxes and Calendars covers a variety of methods that allow you to overcome Exchange limitations for access to shared mailboxes from clients other than Outlook and how to configure advanced features in Exchange Server 2010 allowing users to share individual calendars in a way compatible Apple mobile devices.

Chapter 9, iOS Client Device Management the final chapter, explores the ongoing management tasks associated with a mobile device estate along with how to perform common troubleshooting and auditing tasks.

Who this book is for

This book is aimed at system administrators who don't necessarily know about Exchange Server 2010 or ActiveSync-based mobile devices. A basic level of knowledge around Windows Servers is expected, and knowledge of smartphones and email systems in general will make some topics a little easier. Experienced Exchange Server 2010 administrators will gain most value from chapter five onwards, as these chapters build upon a working Exchange 2010 organization.

Conventions

In this book, you will find a number of styles of text that distinguish between different kinds of information. Here are some examples of these styles, and an explanation of their meaning.

Directories, files, and code in text are shown as follows: "We uploaded the Configuration Profile to the `C:\inetpub\wwwroot` directory".

Any command-line input or output is written as follows:

```
C:\WINDOWS\SYSTEM32\INETSRV\APPCMD.EXE set config "Default
Web Site" -section:system.webServer/security/authentication/
clientCertificateMappingAuthentication /enabled:"True" /commit:apphost
```

New terms and **important words** are shown in bold. Words that you see on the screen, in menus or dialog boxes for example, appear in the text like this: "We'll open the Windows Server 2008 R2 Server Manager and right-click on **Roles**".

Warnings or important notes appear in a box like this.

Tips and tricks appear like this.

Reader feedback

Feedback from our readers is always welcome. Let us know what you think about this book — what you liked or may have disliked. Reader feedback is important for us to develop titles that you really get the most out of.

To send us general feedback, simply send an e-mail to feedback@packtpub.com, and mention the book title through the subject of your message.

If there is a topic that you have expertise in and you are interested in either writing or contributing to a book, see our author guide on www.packtpub.com/authors.

Customer support

Now that you are the proud owner of a Packt book, we have a number of things to help you to get the most from your purchase.

Errata

Although we have taken every care to ensure the accuracy of our content, mistakes do happen. If you find a mistake in one of our books — maybe a mistake in the text or the code — we would be grateful if you would report this to us. By doing so, you can save other readers from frustration and help us improve subsequent versions of this book. If you find any errata, please report them by visiting `http://www.packtpub.com/support`, selecting your book, clicking on the **errata submission form** link, and entering the details of your errata. Once your errata are verified, your submission will be accepted and the errata will be uploaded to our website, or added to any list of existing errata, under the Errata section of that title.

Piracy

Piracy of copyright material on the Internet is an ongoing problem across all media. At Packt, we take the protection of our copyright and licenses very seriously. If you come across any illegal copies of our works, in any form, on the Internet, please provide us with the location address or website name immediately so that we can pursue a remedy.

Please contact us at `copyright@packtpub.com` with a link to the suspected pirated material.

We appreciate your help in protecting our authors, and our ability to bring you valuable content.

Questions

You can contact us at `questions@packtpub.com` if you are having a problem with any aspect of the book, and we will do our best to address it.

1
Introduction to iPhone with Exchange Server 2010

The consumerization of technology over the last decade has blurred the lines between enterprise IT and the type of devices end users wish to use to connect to business resources, and there is no better example to show this than the Apple iPhone. As an intuitive, easy to use device, the iPhone is unparalleled, and since its original release in 2007, Apple's success in the smartphone marketplace has changed the mobile phone industry forever.

Not only is the iPhone a great consumer device, but due to its consistent feature-set across carriers and enterprise management features, it makes a great choice as a standard business device for connecting to Microsoft Exchange 2010 and Microsoft's cloud-based offering — Office 365.

The aim of this book is to provide you all the information you need to understand the iPhone and iOS range of devices, and to gain a basic understanding of how Exchange 2010 or Office 365's Exchange Online complement these devices. The book also aims to guide you through the process to plan, configure, and manage the relevant aspects of your environment. We will also cover some advanced topics such as device security, certificate management, and provisioning along the way.

In this chapter, we will:

- Gain an understanding of the range of iPhone and iOS devices available from Apple (including the iPhone) and what features they offer
- Provide an overview of Microsoft Exchange Server 2010, including a basic overview of the Exchange product and the innovations in the latest version
- Provide an overview of Office 365's Exchange Online service

- Provide an overview of Exchange ActiveSync, the technology used to connect iPhone and iOS devices to Microsoft Exchange

- Get a basic understanding of iPhone and iOS device security features

- Learn the basics about device provisioning in the context of providing an automated setup of iOS devices

Overview of Apple iOS device range and features

Apple's basic platform for mobile computing devices is collectively known as **iOS**. It is the common operating system that the iPhone and other devices like the iPad use to provide the user interface and underlying features across Apple's mobile computing device range.

In June 2007, Apple released the first generation of iOS devices, the iPhone 2G and its Wi-Fi only companion, the iPod touch. Inspite of it being Apple's first foray into the world of mobile phones it took the mobile industry by storm and was an instant hit with consumers. The original iPhone provided a competent mobile web browser, e-mail client, camera, media playback, and Wi-Fi along with GPRS mobile data capabilities.

A runaway success, the first iPhone was succeeded by the iPhone 3G, released the following year in July 2008. The second generation iPhone was complemented by the second release of the underlying operating system, iOS, and brought Exchange Server connectivity along with the ability to install mobile applications from the Apple App Store.

With the second generation's release, the iPhone became more than just another smartphone and with wide consumer adoption combined with the release of its first enterprise connectivity features, companies began to adopt the iPhone 3G as a business device to provide staff access to e-mail, calendaring, and contacts.

In June 2009, Apple released the third generation of its mobile phone, the iPhone 3GS, which as an incremental release improved the device battery life and processor speed, and brought the third major version of the underlying iOS operating system, adding features such as copy and paste and iCalendar subscription support.

April 2010 saw the release of the iPad, Apple's first touchscreen tablet computer, based upon the same underlying iOS underpinnings as the iPhone and iPod touch. Later that year, in June 2010, a major release of iOS was made available, version 4, along with a major refresh of the iPhone, the iPhone 4, and a new version of the iPod touch.

There were also software improvements, such as multi-tasking and the support for multiple ActiveSync accounts. The new version of the iPhone significantly improved the screen resolution and the case was changed to a durable glass front and back, a departure from the previous iPhone's curved plastic back.

In March 2011, the second version of the iPad was released, with a smaller footprint and faster processor. In October 2011, the current release of the iPhone, the iPhone 4S, was released, bringing new features such as an improved processor and camera. At the same time, a major release of iOS was unveiled, iOS 5, which improved upon the multi-tasking features of iOS 4, including much improved notifications, and for iPhone 4S devices added the voice-based assistant Siri, an advanced voice recognition system. From an ActiveSync perspective, iOS 5 added the ability to synchronize tasks with Exchange Server. Finally, in March 2012, Apple released the new iPad, which brought notable features such as an improved screen resolution, faster processor and fourth generation (4G) mobile connectivity.

A major benefit of the iOS device range is the common underlying operating system and its backward compatibility across multiple generations of devices, meaning that major improvements to core features are often made available to most, if not all, devices you are likely to deploy across your environment.

In the following image, you will see an example of the current Mail App interface on the iPhone:

The following table shows a summary of the current product range:

iOS device name	3G mobile data support	Wireless LAN support
iPhone 4S 16GB	Yes	Yes
iPhone 4S 32GB	Yes	Yes
iPhone 4S 64GB	Yes	Yes
iPhone 4 8GB	Yes	Yes
iPhone 3GS 8GB	Yes	Yes
iPad 2 Wi-Fi 16GB	No	Yes
iPad Wi-Fi 16GB	No	Yes
iPad Wi-Fi 32GB	No	Yes
iPad Wi-Fi 64GB	No	Yes
iPad 2 Wi-Fi + 3G 16GB	Yes	Yes
iPad Wi-Fi + 4G 16GB	Yes	Yes
iPad Wi-Fi + 4G 32GB	Yes	Yes
iPad Wi-Fi + 4G 64GB	Yes	Yes
iPod Touch 8GB	No	Yes
iPod Touch 32GB	No	Yes
iPod Touch 64GB	No	Yes

Overview of Microsoft Exchange Server 2010

Microsoft's Exchange Server is the leading messaging software that enterprise and small businesses use to communicate via e-mail and manage calendars. Since the original version 4.0 replaced MSMail more than 15 years ago, Exchange Server has steadily gained ground against competing products and has become the de-facto standard for business communication.

Earlier versions of Exchange Server up to version 5.5 utilized their own directory system to manage users, but since Exchange Server 2000, the messaging platform has relied upon Active Directory for its user directory. Exchange Server 2000 and earlier versions of Exchange Server 2003 didn't have any connectivity to mobile devices and relied on external software such as Microsoft Mobile Information Server or Blackberry Enterprise Server to provide real-time messaging and alerts; Exchange Server 2003 Service Pack 2 introduced push-e-mail, opening the metaphorical floodgates for communication from many devices including Windows Mobile, and of course, the iPhone.

Beginning with Exchange Server 2007, the product went through a major overhaul, dramatically reducing the costs associated with providing high-availability, large user mailboxes, and increasing the reliability and scalability of the product by separating the different components of Exchange Server into different roles.

Continuing this trend, the release of Exchange Server 2010 in September 2009 once again brought a number of architectural changes, further improving the options available for scalability, high availability, and the ability to provide users with even larger mailboxes at low cost by making use of low-cost storage. In addition to these underlying system improvements, Exchange Server 2010 also introduced features to make e-mail more productive through features, such as Conversation View (threaded message display), MailTips, Cross-Browser support for Outlook Web App, and Personal Archives.

With the release of Exchange Server 2010 Service Pack 1 in July 2010, Microsoft's new version of Exchange Server became mature enough for widespread adoption. With a further re-vamp of Outlook Web App, additional features such as the ability to easily share calendars using open standards such as iCalendar, confirmed Exchange Server 2010's place as the market leader for messaging.

The following image shows Outlook Web App in Exchange Server 2010:

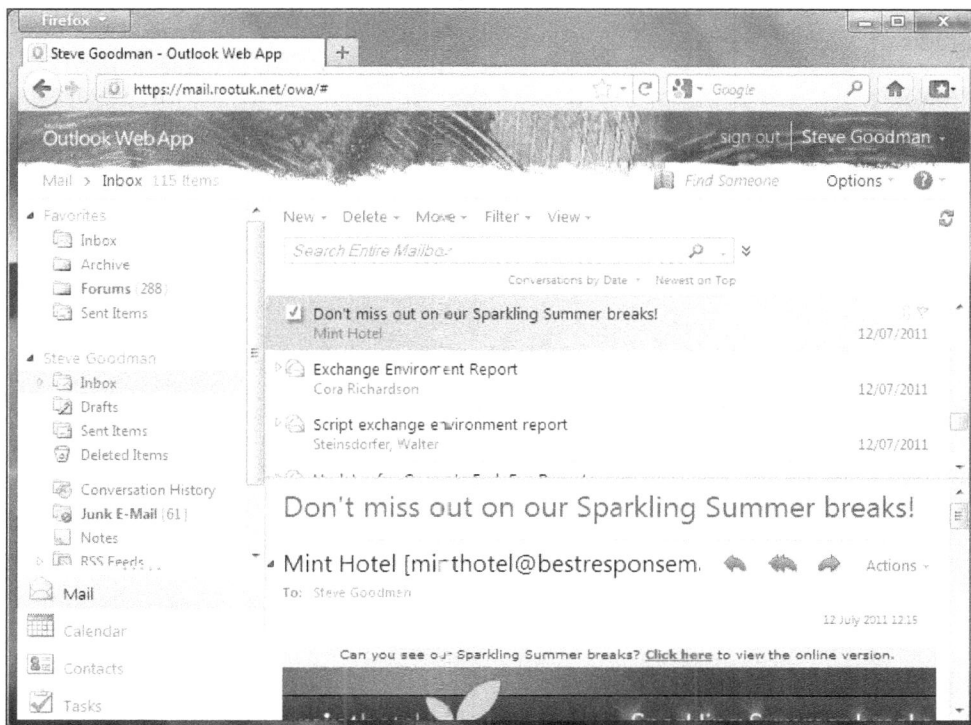

Competing products

Microsoft is not alone in the marketplace for messaging and groupware solutions. Before selecting Microsoft Exchange Server, it's worth being aware of some of the competitors, which include:

- Zimbra
- Lotus Notes
- Novell GroupWise
- Google Apps for Enterprise

Some competing products, including Zimbra and Google Apps, license Microsoft's own Exchange ActiveSync protocol for their own products and as such, iPhone devices can utilize the push-mail facilities available.

Compared to the competition, Exchange Server 2010 is particularly strong; it is no secret that Lotus Notes and Novell GroupWise users have been migrating en-mass to Exchange over the last few years; however, Google Apps for Enterprise has been slowly growing as a competitor, particularly against Office 365.

Zimbra, recently purchased by VMware, has remained static in the marketplace for a number of years, but due to the advanced technology it is based upon, it should not be ruled out.

Compared to the competition, Microsoft is the only messaging solution provider in the marketplace that provides a deeply-integrated on-premises cloud solution that allows you to pick and choose where your e-mail is hosted. From an end-user point of view the familiarity of the Microsoft Office suite is particularly compelling as business users are comfortable with the workflow that the Office suite provides, particularly when it comes to managing their e-mail.

Core features of Exchange Server 2010

Exchange Server 2010 provides many core features, including:

- Mail, contacts, tasks, and calendar management.
- Access from Microsoft Outlook along with any IMAP/POP3 or EWS-compatible desktop client.
- Distribution groups, to easily allow management of mailing groups at an organization level with delegated group management and creation to end users.

- Shared mailboxes and user-managed delegate access to other users' mailboxes that allow end users to manage e-mail more effectively.

- Voicemail/Unified Messaging facilities allow integration with many phone systems, allowing access to voicemails from any device along with dial-in access to e-mail.

- Application/API access using Exchange Web Services allows bespoke applications integrating custom business logic to be developed and used against Exchange.

- Full, premium, Outlook Web App experience allows web-based access to Exchange from browsers including Internet Explorer, Firefox, Safari, and Chrome.

- Productivity features, such as Conversation View, MailTips, and Ignore Conversation, allow the users to reduce the number of e-mails they see in their inbox, and help prevent sending of unnecessary mails by providing pro-active information. For example, while sending mail to a large number of users, if the person they are composing a message to has **Out of Office** enabled or a custom message has been set by the Administrator.

- Major cost reductions for backend Mailbox Server hardware by reducing the performance required to support many users with large mailboxes through the use of Direct-Attached SATA or Midline-SAS disks and support for larger mailbox databases.

- High availability across all Exchange components, including the ability to cluster mailbox servers across multiple sites using Database Availability Groups, on Exchange Servers hosting all roles.

- Personal Archives, which allow administrators to separate historical mail from current mail and eliminate PSTs across the organization while allowing archives to be stored separately in Exchange Server from the primary mailbox.

- Role-based access control to delegate management of Exchange at a granular level to IT staff and, to a certain degree, to the end users.

Mobility features

In addition to the core features of Exchange Server, a lot is offered for mobility, including:

- Push-e-mail using over-the-air synchronization
- Contacts synchronization
- Personal calendar synchronization

- Global Address List access
- Sharing calendars using iCalendar
- Tasks synchronization
- Outlook Voice Access for Unified Messaging-enabled environments
- Policies to control the features available on the device
- Security options for enforcing password policies and device encryption
- Remote wipe facilities to clear sensitive data from lost devices
- Support for S/MIME (if the mobile device supports it)

Combined together, these features provide a comprehensive solution for mobile access to Exchange Server.

For example, an end user device can have features such as camera disabled, strong password policies `enforcedm`, and the device wiped after a certain number of incorrect attempts to enter the password. Additionally, the user benefits from near-real time alerts to new mail, the ability to check out their calendar, get alerts to pending appointments on the device, and automatically synchronize the on-phone contacts with Exchange and Outlook.

Additionally, in a Unified Messaging environment, the user also benefits from voice access to Exchange Server from any mobile phone, including the iPhone, and using Outlook Voice Access. This enables the end user to call Exchange Server and not only listen to voicemail, but also verbally ask Outlook Voice Access to read mail, listen to their appointments for the day and even ask for appointments to be rescheduled if they are running late. Outlook Voice Access is a great addition for enabling hands-free access to Exchange from mobile devices, especially if your user community drives regularly during the course of the business day.

Exchange Server licensing and versions available

Microsoft Exchange Server is available through a number of different methods, each of which should be examined to ascertain which is most suitable for your organization.

Larger enterprises and educational establishments may already have access to either Volume Licensing agreements, such as Microsoft's Enterprise Agreement or Campus Agreement. These options allow the costs of software to be paid for as part of an organization-wide agreement and can provide the best value for money for larger organizations. Exchange Server is also available through retail channels as a boxed product, though this is typically the most expensive method of purchase.

Exchange Server itself is licensed in two ways: by the product itself, which requires a license for each individual server it is installed on, and then a Client Access License (CAL) is purchased for each user that connects to Exchange Server.

There are two different versions of Exchange Server available, Standard Edition and Enterprise Edition. The most significant difference between Standard Edition and Enterprise Edition is the number of Mailbox Databases that can be mounted on each server. Typically this means that Standard Edition is suitable for most server roles, with Enterprise Edition required for larger organizations with a high consolidation of user mailboxes onto a single server. It's typical for even large organizations to license Standard Edition for all Exchange Servers except larger Mailbox Servers.

In addition to Exchange Server product licenses, each server hosting Exchange Server requires Windows Server licensing. As a minimum, Windows Server Standard Edition is suitable for most Exchange Server features, with Windows Server Enterprise Edition or higher required to support any server that is a member of a Database Availability Group.

Client licensing for Exchange Server is typically on a per-user basis, and Client Access License (CAL) types can be mixed-and-matched with server editions. The core license required for connection to Exchange Server is a Standard Edition license, allowing the user to access the following Exchange Server features:

- Core messaging features, including e-mail, calendar, contacts, and tasks from clients such as Outlook, IMAP, POP3, Outlook Web Access, and Exchange ActiveSync
- Basic Exchange ActiveSync management policies, such as password requirements
- Journaling of mail on a per-database basis
- Use of default server-side policies for the retention of mail

With the addition of Enterprise CALs, each user with one assigned also gains the following features:

- All Exchange ActiveSync management policies
- Unified Messaging features
- Journaling of mail on a per-user basis
- Personal Archives
- Use of custom server-side policies for the retention and archiving of mail

- Discovery features such as multi-mailbox search and legal hold
- Features enabling information protection and control, such as transport protection rules and Outlook protection rules

Additionally, use of Microsoft Outlook requires separate licensing for Windows and Microsoft Office.

To simplify the options and combine the licensing into a single package, larger organizations typically take advantage of the options available in the aforementioned Enterprise and Campus Agreements to buy licensing in bundled form, reducing the complexity and typically reducing the cost too.

Small organizations can reduce the complexity of licensing by looking at product offerings that bundle a number of products together, such as Windows Small Business Server 2011. The Standard Edition combines the core functionality of Windows Server 2008 R2 with Exchange Server 2010 and SharePoint Foundation 2010, with the option of enabling SQL Server 2008 R2. Windows Small Business Server 2011 is available pre-installed on Server, through retail channels and through volume licensing.

Costs for licensing Exchange Server in retail form begin at 699 USD for Exchange Server Standard Edition, with an additional 67 USD per Client Access License.

> Licensing is a complex subject and the information here is only intended to give you a brief overview in the context of the product features available in Exchange Server 2010. You should always speak to Microsoft or a qualified reseller to ensure you choose the best licensing options. Further information about Microsoft's licensing options are available on the Microsoft website:
>
> http://www.microsoft.com/licensing/

Overview of Office 365 and Exchange Online

Office 365 is Microsoft's latest online services offering, often described as their answer to Google Apps. With Office 365, services are provided through a subscription-based model and hosted by Microsoft in the cloud-in datacentres managed by them in locations across the globe, providing high availability and allowing the administration and maintenance to be left to the experts.

The service is offered with a number of options, ranging from the small business offering suitable for small organizations ranging from 1 to 25 users, options for larger organizations allowing access to the full range of integration features, and for education with reduced pricing.

A big advantage of Office 365 above licensing Exchange Server 2010 is that the product can be bought with the desktop version of Microsoft Office 2010 included, combining the costs of the server and client software into a single monthly cost.

Before Office 365 was launched, Microsoft offered a number of different online service options; for business users, the primary option was BPOS (Business Productivity Online Suite), which combined hosted Exchange Server 2007, SharePoint 2007, Office Communications Server, and LiveMeeting. BPOS had a minimum requirement of a five user subscription and scaled to solutions for large enterprises. As a product, BPOS never received the acclaim Office 365 has been given, and the service suffered a number of widely publicized failures.

Education customers were catered for by Live@EDU, which started live as "Exchange Labs" and was effectively a beta version of the Exchange Online component of Office 365. The Exchange Online features of Office 365 were first offered through Live@EDU and as Exchange Server 2010 hit key stages in its development these features were brought to this platform before Exchange Server 2010's general release. With over 92 million mailboxes, the service provided an environment for proving the reliability of the Exchange Online component of Office 365 to a demanding group of customers.

The Exchange Online service provided by Office 365 is based upon Exchange Server 2010 and both products share many features. An administrator of Office 365 doesn't retain the fine level of control and management associated with an Exchange Server 2010 on-premises environment; all management of the underlying service is performed by Microsoft, including high availability management, patching, maintenance, upgrades, configuration, and maintenance of the underlying Windows environment.

However, on an organization and user level, most features and control are retained. Administrators have access to configure Exchange policies such as those related to Exchange ActiveSync and on a per-user basis Administrators can manage the settings and features for each mailbox.

For the enterprisers among us, full PowerShell access is provided to Exchange Online allowing experienced Exchange Server Administrators the ability to capitalize on existing Exchange Server 2007 and 2010 skills to manage users, and write and execute scripts in almost the same way as they would with Exchange Server 2010.

Finally, Exchange Online utilizes the same role-based access control model provided with Exchange Server 2010, allowing larger organizations to delegate administration to different IT groups and change the ability of users to perform actions such as changing personal information or creating and managing distribution groups.

Complementary features

As a comprehensive product, Office 365 includes a number of products. Managed through a central administrative portal, a subscription includes the following:

- Exchange Online
- Lync 2010
- SharePoint 2010

In combination, these products work well together to provide a complete communications and collaboration suite.

The following image shows the Office 365 central management portal, and illustrates how Microsoft attempts to present the products together as one offering:

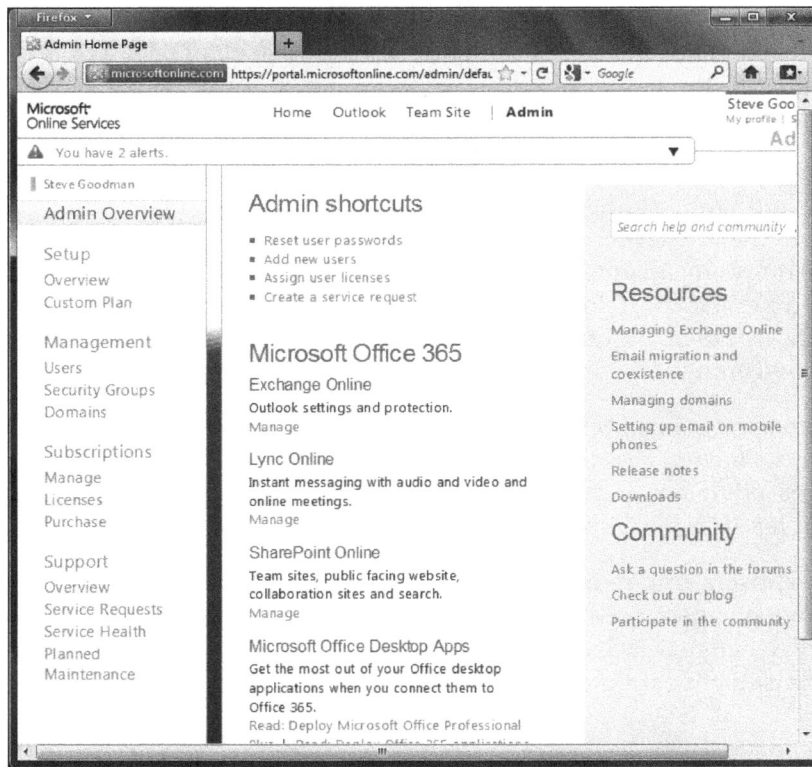

So, let's have a look at the other products included, apart from Exchange.

The second product included is Microsoft Lync Online, which is the successor to Office Communications Server and LiveMeeting. Lync is a real-time communications tool which contains instant messaging, voice and video call, group chat, screen sharing, and conference call facilities. The version of Lync included in Office 365 is similar to the version that can be deployed on-premises; however, it has a number of limitations. For example, Lync Online doesn't support full PBX facilities, such as connecting to the PSTN phone network or support for IP phones, or PSTN dial-in conferencing facilities without the use of a third-party provider.

Lync Online integrates well with Exchange and SharePoint, allowing end users to schedule conference calls directly from Outlook and start calls and conversations directly from Outlook Web App, SharePoint, and the desktop versions of Office.

The following image shows the desktop Lync client. You'll notice it looks very similar to a typical IM client:

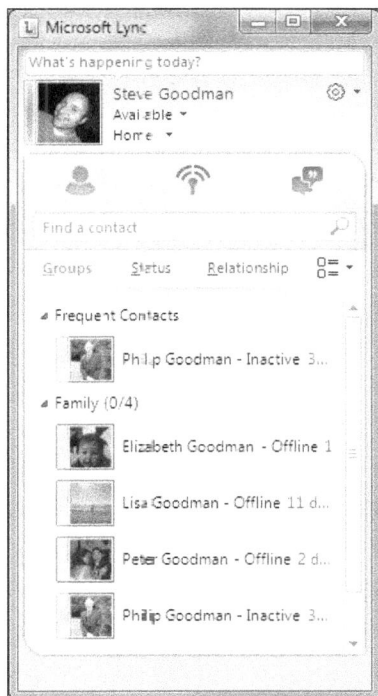

iPhone and iOS users, along with their Windows Phone, Android, and Nokia counterparts, also benefit from access to the Lync Mobile client. This complements the mobility features of Exchange Server to provide access to availability, instant messaging, and conferences directly from the iOS device.

The final product included in Office 365 is SharePoint Online. SharePoint is a web-based document management system providing the ability to manage web pages and office documents, and can even be used for project management, blogs, and wikis. Office 365's version of SharePoint allows Administrators to set up a staff intranet, share documents with external partners, or even use the system as a content management system for a company's external web presence.

SharePoint Online's complement to Exchange's Outlook Web App is the suite of Office Web Apps, including Word Web App, Excel Web App, PowerPoint Web App, and OneNote Web App. These provide a similar feature set to the desktop versions of the product along with the ability for multi-user-collaborative editing.

From a mobility point of view, Office 365's SharePoint facilities allow iPhone access including mobile site views and access to Office documents through the Office Web Apps suite.

The following image shows access to a Microsoft Word document using Word Web App on Office 365:

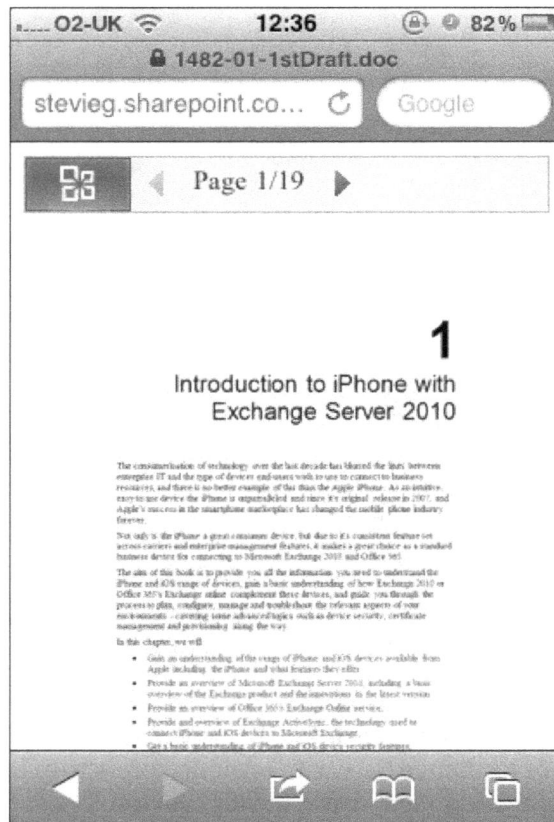

Integration with on-premises systems

If you're already running your own Windows Servers and Active Directory, it's logical that you may wish to use the existing usernames and passwords in use when deploying Office 365. With the exception of the basic version of Office 365, it is possible to synchronize the local Active Directory information up to Microsoft's data centers using Microsoft's DirSync tool, and by utilizing a server running ADFS 2.0 (Active Directory Federation Services) your users can log in to Office 365 using their normal Active Directory username and password.

The integration becomes more interesting if you're already running Exchange Server on-premises, or wish to run a mixture. With the addition of atleast on Exchange 2010 server in your perimeter network, Calendars can be shared between On-Premises Exchange and Exchange Online along with Free/Busy information. It's also fairly straightforward to move mailboxes to and from Exchange Online using the same techniques you would use to move mailboxes between On-Premises Exchange Servers.

If you are looking to migrate an existing system to Office 365, there are other options available. Staged Exchange Migration allows setup and management of migrations from Exchange 2003 and later, and any IMAP mail system. These can be managed either through the web interface or through PowerShell.

Versions available

Just like Exchange Server 2010 there are a number of options when it comes to licensing Office 365. Thankfully, it's a lot simpler as there are just three main products:

- **Office 365 for professionals and small businesses**: The most basic plan is for 1 to 25 users. It includes Exchange, SharePoint, and Lync but doesn't include desktop Office or allow integration with on-premises systems.

- **Office 365 for midsize businesses and enterprises**: Ranging from very cheap to quite expensive, the "full" version of Office 365 has access to all the integration and advanced management features, with add-ons to allow larger mailboxes, licensing for desktop Office, on-premises servers, and integration with your existing PBX for voicemail facilities.

- **Office 365 for Education**: Live@EDU's successor is very similar to the midsize business and enterprise version, except for the pricing. Starting at free for students and basic staff facilities, the 'paid for' versions add in similar enterprise features.

Before purchasing, all versions are available as a 30-day trial.

If you've not currently got access to an Exchange Server and want to try out most of the techniques demonstrated in this book without additional expense, the Office 365 trial may be of interest.

Overview of Exchange ActiveSync

Smartphone synchronization software has been released by Microsoft under the name ActiveSync since 1996, including the forerunner to today's Exchange ActiveSync, released as part of the Mobile Information Server 2002 product. However, it wasn't until the release of Exchange Server 2003 SP2, back in 2005, that it bore a resemblance to its current form today. Version 2.5 was the first version to support the modern features, such as push-e-mail and mail, calendar, contact, and task synchronization, along with a basic set of security features.

With the release of Exchange Server 2007, and later Exchange Server 2007 Service Pack 1, a large number of device management and security policies were incrementally added, and in the current release of Exchange Server 2010 the full complement of features are available, including those related to conversation view (message threading).

Exchange ActiveSync works by using features built into **HTTP (Hypertext Transport Protocol**, as used by web sites) to allow the mobile device to ask the server, over a secure connection, to let it know when there is an update. It works by issuing a request to the Exchange Server and when there is a change, such as a new e-mail, the server replies to that request with an update. This allows push-email over a normal mobile data connection such as 2G/3G without excessive data and battery usage.

The following diagram shows this process:

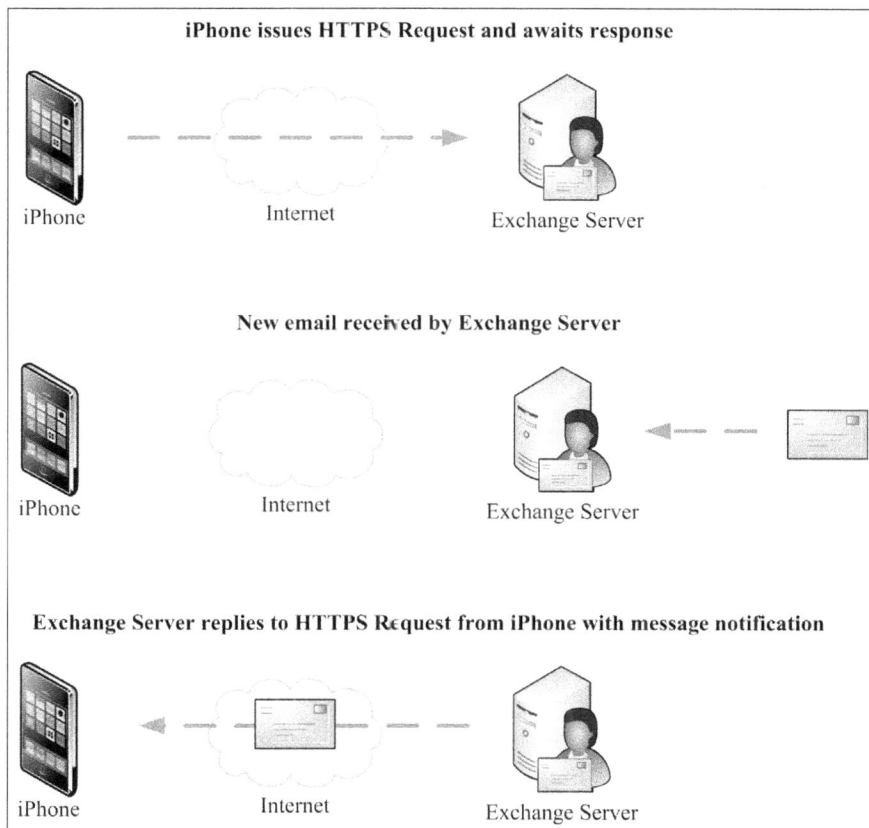

Exchange ActiveSync, although a proprietary protocol has been licensed by a number of other server products and helped by support from smartphones like the Apple iPhone, is becoming one of the most common ways to support push mail. Exchange ActiveSync has been licensed by other mail server products in addition to Exchange Server and Office 365. The following are just a few examples:

- Google Mail
- Windows Live Hotmail
- Zimbra
- Kerio
- MDaemon
- ATMail

Nonetheless, there are other options for synchronizing and delivering push e-mails to Smartphones. Most people have heard of the Blackberry, which was one of the first providers to allow push e-mail to their mobile devices using their proprietary Blackberry Enterprise Server, and it's clear that the rising popularity of the product inspired Microsoft to develop the Exchange ActiveSync protocol further.

Another well-known option is Good Technologies' cross-platform mobile synchronization product, which includes support for the iPhone. Often used in some of the most secure environments it offers a full end-to-end solution, including a custom Mail application for the iPhone and server-side software.

For most purposes though, Exchange ActiveSync is more than capable and with broad device support, including great support from Apple for the iOS range of devices, it is often an easy choice to make, thanks to the out-of-the-box support it provides.

Overview of provisioning

Provisioning iOS devices to end users encompasses the activation and deployment of the settings that make up the basic device configuration. The basic settings deployed within an iOS Device Configuration Profile might include the Exchange Server settings, any prerequisite VPN connection settings, device options that aren't covered in Exchange Server security policies, or certificates required for secure connection.

Although iOS devices can make use of Microsoft Exchange's Autodiscover service to automatically detect the correct Exchange Server settings, utilizing the provisioning options from Apple enables you to ensure that these settings are applied consistently across your organization, can be updated centrally when required, and cannot be easily removed by your end users.

In addition to Exchange Server settings, provisioning devices using iOS Device Configuration Profiles also allows the following:

- VPN (Virtual Private Network) Connection Settings
- Wireless LAN Connection Settings
- Addition of Root Certificates to devices
- Addition of Identity Certificates used in place of password authentication
- Subscriptions to CalDAV and iCalendar format calendars
- LDAP, POP3, IMAP, and SMTP Configuration settings for non-Exchange ActiveSync environments
- Deployment of custom applications

As illustrated above, there are a lot more options available than just getting Exchange Server connected and depending on your environment—for example if your security policy does not allow access to Exchange Server unless connected via a VPN connection—it may be necessary to ensure these settings are deployed to users before they are able to synchronize with Exchange Server.

iOS Device Configuration profiles can be distributed to users in a variety of ways, and it really comes down to the policies you have in place or infrastructure available to deploy the configuration profiles. If you are buying devices centrally and performing activation and setup before issuing them to users, your method for provisioning may be different from if you allow users to order devices themselves or buy and bring their own. Options include:

- Deployment via iTunes on an Apple Mac or Windows PC
- Deployment via the iPhone Configuration Utility
- E-mail the configuration profile to end users, typically for deploying updated profiles
- Deployment from a website using a static configuration profile
- Deployment from a website using a custom, dynamically generated configuration profile
- By using over-the-air certificate enrolment and configuration using **SCEP (Simple Certificate Enrolment Protocol)**

During the course of this book, we will cover how to use the various deployment methods outlined above so you can understand which will be the most applicable method for the environment you manage.

Summary

In this chapter we've covered the basics of the products available, from the iOS devices such as the iPhone, iPad, and iPod touch, and the Exchange Server 2010 options available including on-premises deployment of Exchange Server 2010 and Office 365.

The iOS range is a well-developed line of products and has a suitable mobile device to suit most needs. Exchange Server 2010 provides a stable, reliable environment for a messaging platform and is the market leader. Office 365 makes deployment options even easier and like the on-premises version of Exchange it is also compatible with iOS devices, as it utilizes the same Exchange ActiveSync technologies.

Additionally, Office 365 provides some great features, such as the bundling of other Microsoft collaboration products, Lync Online, and SharePoint Online, both of which support the iPhone.

We've learnt through the course of this chapter about the basic protocol that connects iOS devices and Exchange together—Exchange ActiveSync. This protocol uses standard mobile data connections and the same protocol that websites use to synchronize data and provide push mail to phones, whilst using a relatively small amount of data and saving on battery life.

Finally, we've learnt the basics of why we should use provisioning techniques to deploy configuration to iOS devices and introduced the basic techniques used.

In the next chapter, we'll learn about putting the core infrastructure in place to support Exchange and iOS devices as pre-requisites for a successful implementation.

2
Architecture and Implementation Planning

Before you install Exchange Server 2010 and start connecting your mobile devices, it's critical to make sure the fundamentals are correct and you understand how Exchange Server 2010 fits together. Although you can certainly just buy a server and install Exchange Server with its defaults instead of configuring it by trial and error, spending some time learning the core roles and carefully understanding what your organization needs will help ensure that you've got a solid foundation to build upon, and give you some confidence that what you build will perform as you expect.

This chapter introduces the roles Exchange Server provides and explains what each role does when compared with other roles. The first thing you should understand though, is that a role does not equal an individual server. Roles in Exchange Server separate the functions from one another and can be combined or separated as you need. You could run all the core functions of Exchange on a single server if you wish, or you could split the functions of Exchange into different servers dedicated to servicing different functions. Not only can you combine roles, but as your needs grow you can add more servers as you need them, and split roles. And, with careful initial planning you can grow your Exchange infrastructure without even impacting your end users.

Later in this chapter, after we've gained an understanding of each role and its function, we will look at how to perform basic capacity planning for an example organization using Microsoft's best practices and tools they provide. This chapter isn't intended to cover every aspect of Exchange Server capacity planning but it will certainly help you understand the critical aspects you need to consider before you introduce Exchange Server 2010 to your environment. If you've already got your environment up and running, then you also might find the information useful to help validate that what underpins your environment is suitable to introduce mobile devices onto.

Finally we'll cover some of the basics around namespaces — the server names clients use to connect to Exchange and the networking required to allow external access to the environment.

Overview of Exchange Server 2010 roles

Exchange Server 2010 has five main roles: Client Access, Mailbox, Hub Transport, Edge Transport, and Unified Messaging. These five roles represent how end users interact with Exchange, how messages are stored, how messages are routed within and outside the organization, and how we can integrate telephony in Exchange. In addition to these five roles, there is also a critical component in any Exchange deployment — Active Directory, which stores the user directory information and Exchange configuration for the organization.

The following diagram shows a general overview of how the roles interact with each other and external systems:

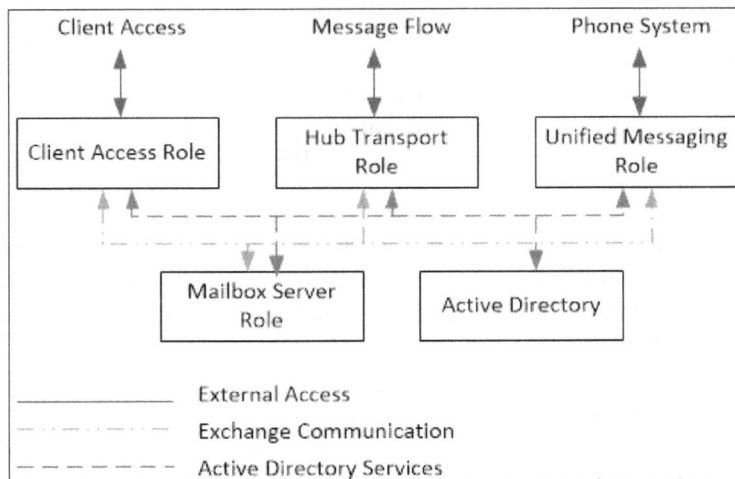

First we'll take a look at each of the Exchange roles and then look at how Active Directory is used.

Client Access Role

The Client Access Role in Exchange Server 2010 functions as the interface between most of Exchange Server's other roles and end user client devices. When a client connects to Exchange Server from an Outlook Client, Web Services Client, POP3, IMAP, or ActiveSync device, they connect to the Client Access Role, which either services the request, redirects the request, or proxies the request to other roles.

In particular, the Client Access Role fulfils the following functions:

- Provides Autodiscover functionality to help auto-configure some clients and devices, and assist clients in discovering which Exchange Servers to connect to

- Serves Outlook Web App to end users, providing a web-based interface to Exchange Server

- Serves web-distributed Free/Busy information through the availability service

- Provides the end-point for downloading Offline Address Book information

- Provides the NSPI endpoint and proxies Active Directory lookups and searches, for facilities such as the Global Address List (GAL)

- Services Exchange Web Services (EWS) requests for custom applications, backend Outlook functions, and dedicated EWS-based clients, such as Mac Mail, Entourage 2008 Web Services Edition, and Outlook 2011

- Acts as the connection point for Outlook Anywhere using the HTTPS-based RPC Proxy services

- Provides the RPC Client Access Service which MAPI-based clients connect to mailboxes through, rather than directly to mailbox servers themselves

- Participates in Client Access Arrays, which allow a pool of servers with the Client Access Role to use a common name for MAPI client access and make use of load-balancing technologies for scalability and high availability of the RPC Client Access Service

- Acts as the interface for services such as federation, remote mailbox moves, and access to cloud-hosted personal archives

- Manages and processes requests for mailbox management, such as mailbox moves and exports

In comparison to earlier versions of Exchange, there is a big difference that cannot be underestimated, and that's the move of the RPC Client Access layer to the Client Access Role as a "middleware" platform. This is often referred to as **MAPI on the Middle Tier (MoMT)** as a normal Outlook client; using MAPI to connect to the mailbox now connects to this middle tier rather than the backend mailbox database itself.

For smaller environments, especially single-server environments, this makes very little difference. For larger organizations with more than a single server, it's a big benefit, particularly for high-availability — which we'll cover shortly.

In an environment that is providing external access for mobile devices, it is typical to have an external-facing entry point into your Exchange infrastructure. When planning this, you need to bear in mind that Microsoft does not support the Client Access Role within the **perimeter network** where a firewall exists between the perimeter network and the internal network.

This means for many scenarios you need to implement a solution within the perimeter network that acts as a reverse-proxy back to the Client Access servers located on the internal network. There are a number of options, particularly when considering a highly available solution, but the key point of note is that provision for this should be planned from the outset.

When investigating what you need from a reverse proxy, bear in mind that you don't necessarily need a reverse proxy that can handle the RPC Client Access part of the Client Access Role. Your main consideration for a basic reverse proxy is to handle web-based traffic using the HTTPS protocol, as this is what external clients will use to communicate with Exchange. For a basic Exchange Server deployment this simplifies the requirements and allows the opportunity to use basic reverse proxies ranging from open source solutions, such as Apache Web Server and Squid Proxy Server to solutions from Microsoft, like ISA 2006, Forefront TMG and Forefront UAG Servers.

The traffic flow through a simple Client Access Server is shown in this simplified diagram:

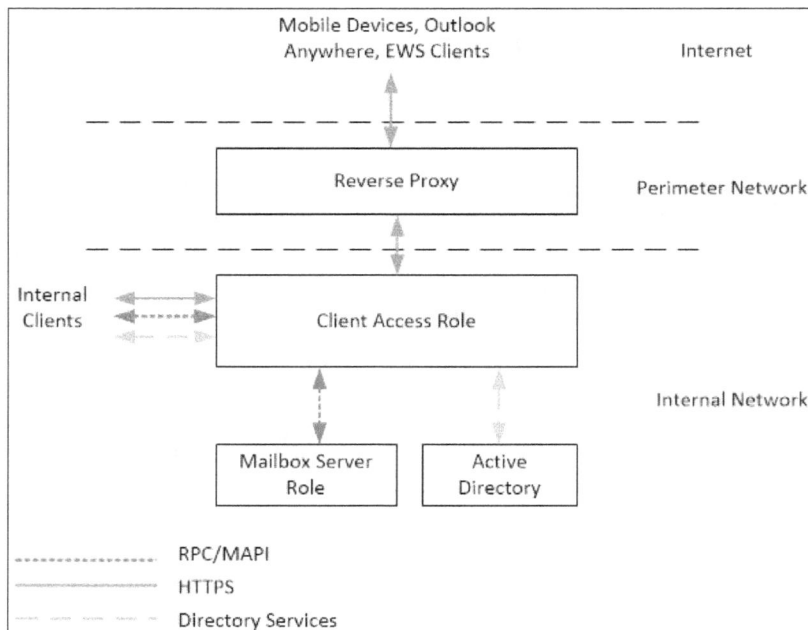

Providing high availability for the Client Access Role

Even with a reverse proxy solution, your mobile device will ultimately connect to the Client Access Role on your Exchange Server, so if you can, it's important to make sure that a server failure, or even routine maintenance will not impact end user access to your Exchange Server 2010 environment.

Client Access Arrays

When designing high availability and load-balancing for your Exchange environment, it's important to understand that you will be providing high availability for two distinct services: the web-based services provided by IIS, and the RPC Client Access service.

This is where the Client Access Array comes into play. A client access array is a logical construct that is defined on a per-Active Directory site basis and is simply a single name that can be used to refer to a number of Client Access Servers. When you create a client access array in Exchange Server 2010, you don't add servers to it through the Exchange interface. The name you define is created as additional DNS record pointing at a single server, or it points to your highly-available, load-balanced environment. It doesn't need to match the name used for your highly-available web services either. From an Outlook client perspective it is the name that once correctly configured, clients will see as their Exchange Server mailbox server name.

Hardware or Virtual Load Balancers

The best way to provide high availability for the Client Access Role (both web services and the RPC-based Client Access Array) is to use a dedicated **Hardware Load Balancer** or a **Virtual Load Balancer**. These devices from suppliers such as Cisco, F5, Citrix, Barracuda, KEMP technologies and Open Source alternatives, available as a physical black-box or in the case of a Virtual Load Balancer virtual appliance, provide intelligent load balancing and failover capabilities.

Although you can use **Windows Network Load Balancing** (WNLB) to perform this function in combination with a reverse proxy in the perimeter network, Load Balancers designed for Exchange are application-intelligent and can detect issues with parts of your Client Access infrastructure that WNLB would not. For example, an issue that prevents OWA from working on one of the servers running the Client Access Role wouldn't be detected by WNLB out of the box. Another reason to opt for a Load Balancer is that when you combine the Client Access Role with the Mailbox Role on a server participating in a Database Availability Group, WNLB cannot be used due to conflicts with the failover clustering feature that underpins Database Availability Groups.

In addition, a Load Balancer can sometimes replace the need for a reverse proxy as it can also perform this function, and as you will typically use it for all communication with the Client Access infrastructure you can also consider using SSL offload facilities to take some of the load off the Client Access servers. Finally, remember that Load Balancers can fail too, so consider purchasing a solution that has some resilience built-in.

Finally, if you are combining the Client Access and Mailbox Server Roles in a **Database Base Availability Group (DAG)** environment, then you are not able to make use of WNLB, and to obtain high availability, a Load Balancer will be a necessity.

The following diagram shows a typical highly-available Client Access infrastructure utilizing a load balancer:

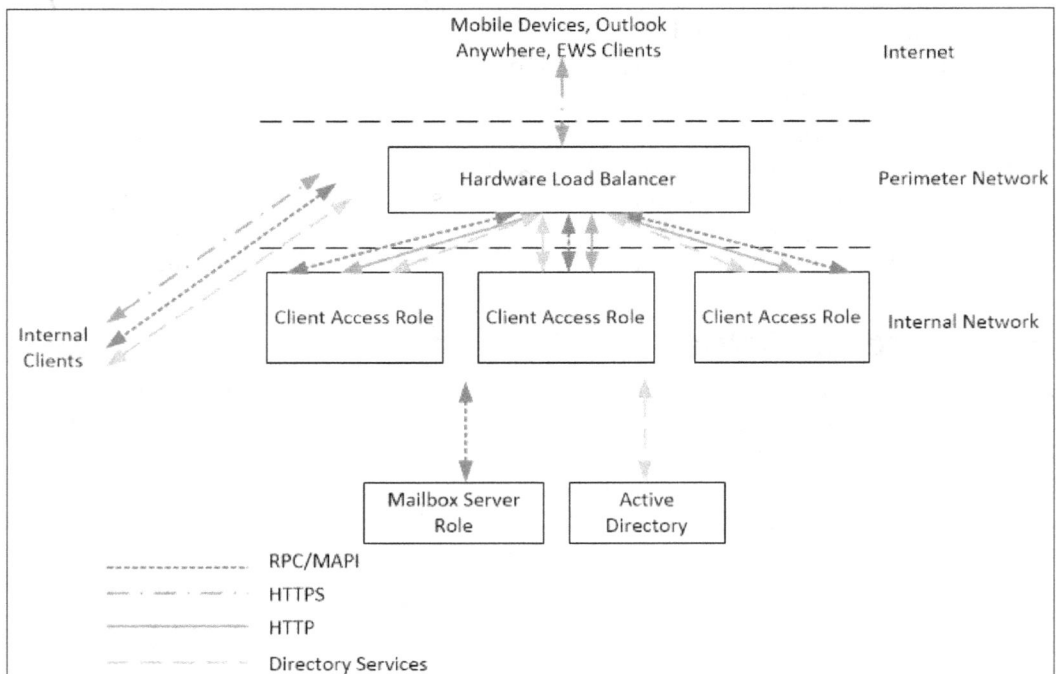

Mailbox Role

The Mailbox Role is the component of Exchange Server that, in particular, hosts Mailbox and Public Folder databases. When comparing the functionality to previous versions of Exchange Server, it is very similar to the Mailbox Role in Exchange Server 2007 or a backend server in Exchange Server 2003, with the major exception being that MAPI-based clients such as Outlook connect to Client Access Servers for Mailbox database access.

In particular, the Mailbox Role fulfils the following functions:

- Hosts Mailbox Databases, which store user mailbox data.

- Hosts and provides client access to Public Folder databases. Although Public Folders are a de-emphasized feature of Exchange Server 2010, they are still present and one-off cases where clients connect directly to the Mailbox Server Role itself.

- Generates Offline Address Books distributing them based on policies to Client Access Servers and where required, to Public Folder Databases.

- Manages and participates in Database Availability Groups, Exchange Server 2010's primary high-availability, and clustering feature.

- Provides indexing and searching facilities to content stored in Exchange Server databases.

- Manages and processes policies for managing mailboxes and mailbox database, such as policies to remove or archive mailbox data and maintain databases through processes such as online defragmentation.

If you're not familiar with the concept of a Mailbox or Public Folder Database, the best way to describe it is as a single, large file on disk optimized for storing lots of structured data in a way that allows for very fast access.

When a message is received by the Mailbox role, its contents are examined and all the relevant fields, such as who the message is from, who the message is addressed to, the message's ID, and of course the content, are added into database tables, similar to an Access or SQL database. This allows for better indexing and retrieval of the data, and just like an SQL database, before any data is written to the database file itself, data is written to a binary transaction log.

The database format that Exchange Server uses is called the Extensible Storage Engine (ESE) and in Exchange Server 2010 it has been optimized for storing large mailboxes on slower disks, such as SATA. To help with performance, the Exchange Server hosting the Mailbox Role utilizes the available RAM in the server to cache a large amount of data, helping significantly with performance.

In previous versions of Exchange Server, Mailbox and Public Folder Databases were logically owned by individual Exchange Servers, and contained within Storage Groups, which themselves could contain multiple Databases with a single set of Transaction Logs. The concept of Storage Groups is no longer used in Exchange Server 2010, and Databases are now logically separate from Exchange Servers, instead using an attribute to define the current server that "owns" the database.

Providing high availability for the Mailbox role using Database Availability Groups

Exchange Server 2010 uses a technology new to this version of the product for clustering and replication of Mailbox Databases, known as Database Availability Groups (DAGs). Exchange Servers that are a member of a DAG use network-based replication to keep copies of Mailbox Databases up-to-date.

Previously, in Exchange Server 2007, the clustering technologies available were bound by Mailbox Database being logically owned by a single server, and therefore even servers utilizing the pre-cursor to DAGs, Cluster Continuous Replication (CCR), had limits on the scalability as only one Exchange Server per CCR Cluster could be active at one time. This limitation also affected the now removed technology also used in Exchange Server 2003, Single Copy Clusters (SCC), where shared storage was used to store a single copy of the Mailbox Databases owned by the server.

In Exchange Server 2010, each Mailbox Database can only be active on a single server at one time. However, the major change is that the clustering is performed on a per-database level rather than a server level. This allows all members of a Database Availability Group to have active databases, and due to the placement of the RPC Client Access Service on the Client Access Server Role, clients do not get disconnected when a database is switched between Exchange Servers hosting Mailbox Databases.

All DAG member servers participate in the cluster itself. However, the underlying cluster configuration is managed by Exchange Server rather than the Administrator themselves. As a majority node set cluster, a DAG requires a majority (over 50 percent) of the DAG member servers to be online for the cluster to be operational. To ensure resilience in the case where there is an even number of DAG member servers, a Windows file share is used to provide an extra cluster "vote". This is known as the **File Share Witness**, and is typically configured on another Exchange Server, typically a Hub Transport Server.

Additionally, the previous limitation on the number of Mailbox Database copies has been increased; each Mailbox Database can have up to 16 copies in a DAG. This improvement in the number of copies that can be achieved has allowed the Exchange Team to suggest new options for providing cheaper Mailboxes, such as supporting the use of direct-attached storage that doesn't use RAID, known as **JBOD**, or **Just a Bunch Of Disks**. JBOD is supported in scenarios where at least three Database copies exist in a DAG.

The following diagram illustrates an example of a scenario where four Exchange Servers hosting the Mailbox Role are participating in a DAG, using four copies per database:

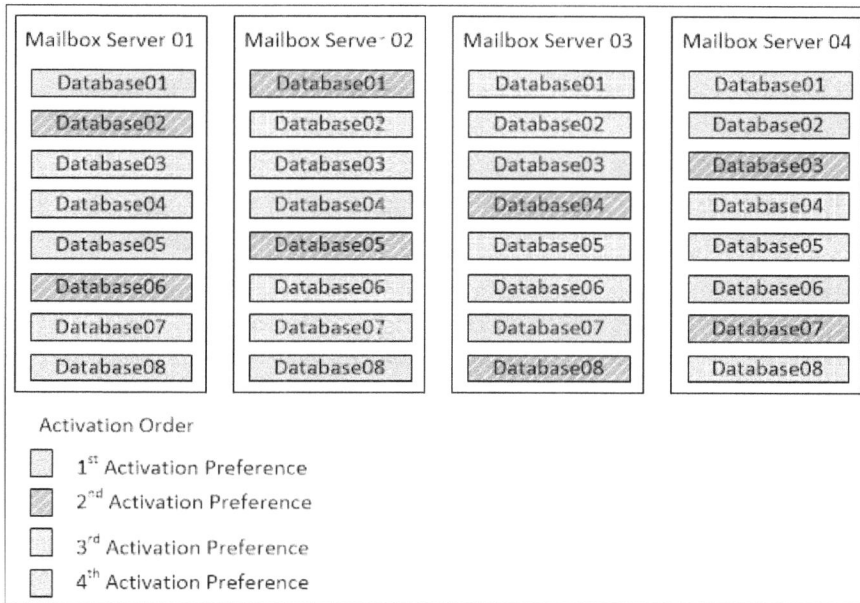

In the diagram above, you will see that each copy of a database has an activation preference. The activation preference is taken into account when a server fails to determine the next server that should make a database active. Typically, the database will be active on the server that has the first database activation preference set, except during a failover or when a server is down for maintenance.

Replication technology

Exchange Server 2010 replicates mailbox databases using a technology that ships the transaction log files to other DAG member nodes that host a copy of the database, known as **Continuous Replication**. The transaction logs are replayed to the other database copies, which means each copy of each database is independent and not subject to replication of general block-level corruption of the underlying database caused by file system errors. Logs are shipped over the TCP/IP protocol and either shipped as entire log files, or as each transaction has occurred (known as **Block Mode**). Exchange Server 2010 automatically determines which mode to use and generally when copies are up-to-date, block mode is used. Public Folder Databases are not replicated using the same Continuous Replication technology used by Mailbox Databases.

Instead replication between servers is performed using the same technology Public Folder Databases have used in earlier versions of Exchange, where each Public Folder Database is effectively standalone and replication is performed on a schedule via Hub Transport servers. Therefore, to achieve Public Folder Database resiliency, Databases should be created on a number of Exchange Servers hosting the Mailbox Role, and the Public Folders within should have replicas added to each. In general though, unless you need Public Folders, they are best avoided altogether.

Site resilience

Database Availability Groups can span multiple datacenters to provide resilience and disaster recovery abilities in the case of a total or temporary loss of a data center.

Failover between datacenters is not an automatic process and involves going through a process to "shrink" the cluster before bringing it online at the secondary datacenter, and associated reconfiguration of other services, such as DNS names for Client Access Servers.

When the original primary datacenter is brought back online, it's important to avoid a situation where the original servers attempt to activate their Database copies — the last thing they knew was that they owned the Databases before the failover occurred. This would result in a situation where the Database copies become inconsistent and require a full copy from the active secondary datacenter.

Such a situation, known as **split brain**, can be avoided through the use of a technology called **Datacenter Activation Co-ordination Protocol (DACP)**. This technology prevents the DAG member nodes in the original datacenter from activating databases and attempting to take ownership of the cluster though the use of an in-memory flag, the DAC memory bit. When the original servers come back online, they will attempt to contact other Mailbox Servers to check for servers with the DAC memory bit set to 1. If they cannot contact another server, they won't attempt to mount Databases. When they can contact the secondary datacenter with the currently active Databases, they will be able to continue startup with knowledge of the cluster state, mounting Databases without the risk of a "split brain".

Although the Database Availability Group site resilience facilities in Exchange Server 2010 initially sound complicated, with careful planning and understanding of how a switchover and switchback is managed, it is actually fairly straightforward and a worthwhile consideration for building a resilient Exchange Server infrastructure that can withstand a major disaster with little to no data loss and minimal downtime.

Hub Transport Role

The Hub Transport Role deals with the transfer of mail between sender and recipient in Exchange Server 2010. Without the Hub Transport Role, mail goes nowhere. When a message is submitted to Exchange, the Hub Transport deals with determining where the message needs to go and takes responsibility for ensuring as best as it can that the message was delivered successfully.

In particular, the Hub Transport Role fulfils the following functions:

- Mail transfer (using SMTP) between user mailboxes and public folders (even on the same server or mailbox database)

- Mail routing and transfer in and out of the organization, up to the Edge Transport Role or other SMTP gateway

- Routing of mail within the Exchange organization

- Managing mail queues

- Where appropriate, storing copies of mail until it is successfully delivered to its destination using technologies, such as the Transport Dumpster and Shadow Redundancy

- Acts as the mail submission server for clients using SMTP to send mail (such as POP3/IMAP clients)

- Performs business logic on SMTP mail using Hub Transport Rules

Looking deeper into the Hub Transport role, the first thing you will notice is there is configuration at two levels. The first is at the Organization level and this covers the address spaces (or internet domains) that the Hub Transport server is responsible for accepting or relaying mail for, and connectors to manage sending mail outside of the Exchange Organization, known as Send Connectors.

Send Connectors are typically used for sending mail to the Internet and can use the standard DNS-lookup-based method (MX records) for finding the correct mail server to deliver to, or can be configured to use a smart-host to pass the mail on to for eventual delivery.

The second set of configuration takes place on a per-server basis and in particular it's important to understand what Receive Connectors are. The Receive Connector is the configuration for each "listener" that a Hub Transport server uses to accept incoming mail. Like Internet mail servers, this uses the SMTP protocol and has configuration options to determine what TCP/IP port and IP address each Receive Connector listens on for new connections, and settings to determine who or what can connect and what authentication methods should be accepted. By default, Receive Connectors are created to listen on the standard TCP/IP port, 25, for server-to-server communication (such as Mailbox Servers submitting mail for delivery) and a client-focused Receive Connector listening on port 587, a secondary standard TCP/IP port allocated for client SMTP submission. By default, no unauthenticated connections are allowed and mail can only be relayed by authenticated senders.

Mail Routing in Exchange Server 2010

Beginning with Exchange Server 2007, Active Directory sites are used for routing mail within an Exchange environment. In previous versions of Exchange, mail routing was managed separately to the Active Directory site infrastructure through the use of routing groups and bridgehead servers. Exchange Server 2007 simplifies the management of mail routing by respecting the configured Active Directory site information, but it does mean that the design of Active Directory is important to the Exchange environment.

The following diagram illustrates the mail routing in Exchange 2010:

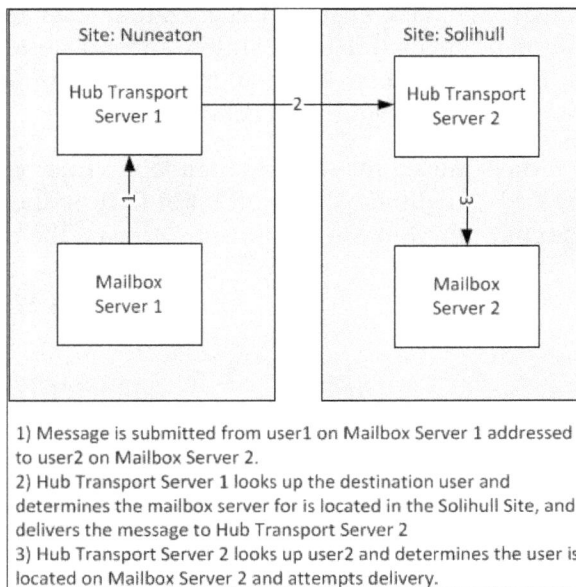

Site: Nuneaton

Hub Transport
Server 1

Site: Solihull

Hub Transport
Server 2

Mailbox
Server 1

Mailbox
Server 2

1) Message is submitted from user1 on Mailbox Server 1 addressed to user2 on Mailbox Server 2.
2) Hub Transport Server 1 looks up the destination user and determines the mailbox server for is located in the Solihull Site, and delivers the message to Hub Transport Server 2
3) Hub Transport Server 2 looks up user2 and determines the user is located on Mailbox Server 2 and attempts delivery.

Providing high availability for the Hub Transport Role

The Hub Transport Role is one of the easiest roles in Exchange Server to provide high availability for. While the Client Access Role requires session information to be maintained, particularly for services, such as Outlook Web App, each session to the Hub Transport Role is distinct, and subsequent sessions do not require either the client or server to know about previous sessions; quite simply when an SMTP client logs in and sends a message — once it's been accepted at the end of that session, the transaction is complete.

Internally, Exchange Servers are capable of dealing with a failed Hub Transport server with no impact on the end-user experience. And no load balancing for Hub Transport-to-Hub Transport communication is necessary or indeed supported. DNS round-robin can be used for rudimentary balancing of end-user client connections that use SMTP, as can a load balancer; however, compared to the configuration required for a Client Access Server, load balancer configuration is straightforward.

One traditional weakness of the Hub Transport server in a highly available environment is the mail queue database. If a Hub Transport server fails before delivering messages, typically messages can be lost. Exchange Server 2010 improves upon this with a feature called Shadow Redundancy. Within Exchange Server 2010, this feature delays deletion of the submitted message until all the message hops with the Exchange environment have completed. If they fail, the message is re-submitted, meaning no messages are lost if a Hub Transport server fails.

The following diagrams illustrate how this functions, firstly, in normal operation without a failure:

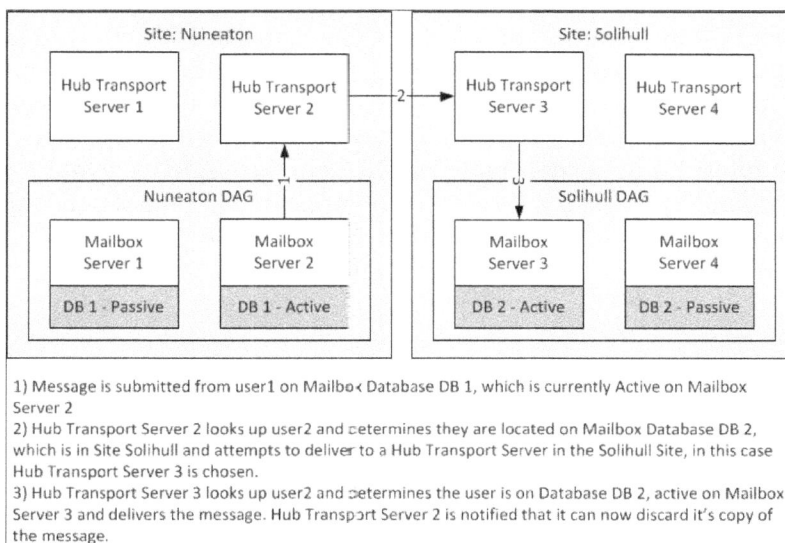

1) Message is submitted from user1 on Mailbox Database DB 1, which is currently Active on Mailbox Server 2
2) Hub Transport Server 2 looks up user2 and determines they are located on Mailbox Database DB 2, which is in Site Solihull and attempts to deliver to a Hub Transport Server in the Solihull Site, in this case Hub Transport Server 3 is chosen.
3) Hub Transport Server 3 looks up user2 and determines the user is on Database DB 2, active on Mailbox Server 3 and delivers the message. Hub Transport Server 2 is notified that it can now discard it's copy of the message.

Next, let's look at how shadow redundancy functions when there is a server failure:

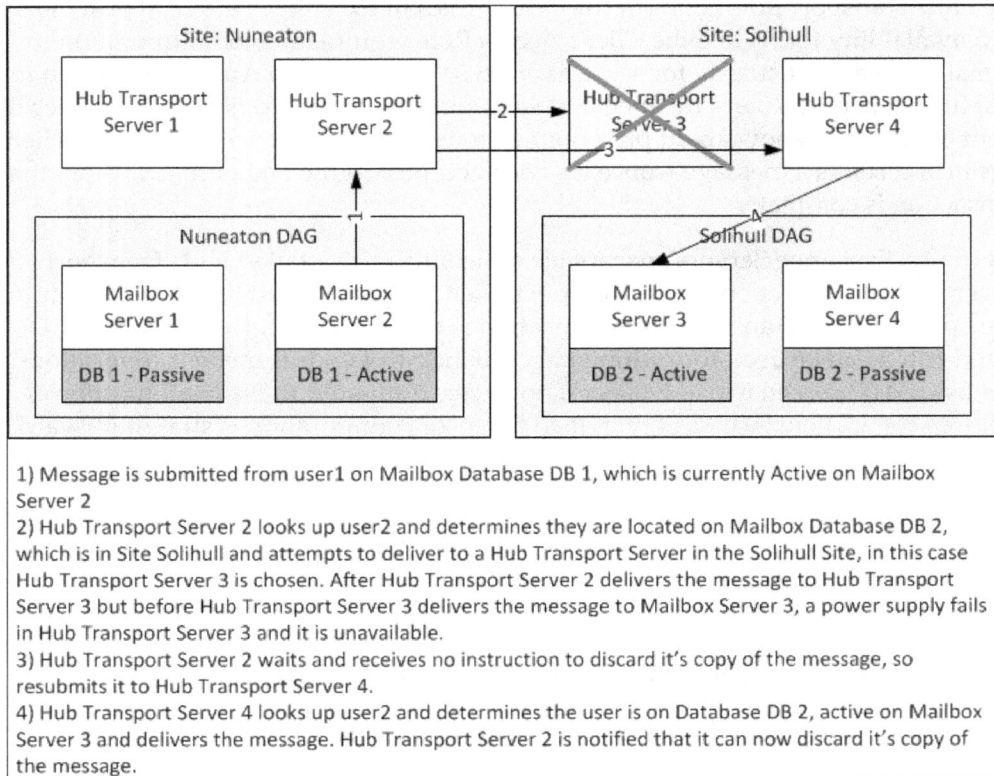

1) Message is submitted from user1 on Mailbox Database DB 1, which is currently Active on Mailbox Server 2

2) Hub Transport Server 2 looks up user2 and determines they are located on Mailbox Database DB 2, which is in Site Solihull and attempts to deliver to a Hub Transport Server in the Solihull Site, in this case Hub Transport Server 3 is chosen. After Hub Transport Server 2 delivers the message to Hub Transport Server 3 but before Hub Transport Server 3 delivers the message to Mailbox Server 3, a power supply fails in Hub Transport Server 3 and it is unavailable.

3) Hub Transport Server 2 waits and receives no instruction to discard it's copy of the message, so resubmits it to Hub Transport Server 4.

4) Hub Transport Server 4 looks up user2 and determines the user is on Database DB 2, active on Mailbox Server 3 and delivers the message. Hub Transport Server 2 is notified that it can now discard it's copy of the message.

Finally, the Hub Transport role contributes to the high availability features of the Mailbox Role, using the feature known as the **Transport Dumpster**. When a message is delivered to a Mailbox Server, the message will not be deleted permanently from the Hub Transport server until it has been notified that the message has been replicated to all copies of the destination mailbox database. In the event of a "lossy" database failover, any messages that were not replicated in time will be re-submitted to the Mailbox Server hosting the currently active database.

The following diagram illustrates how this re-submission process functions:

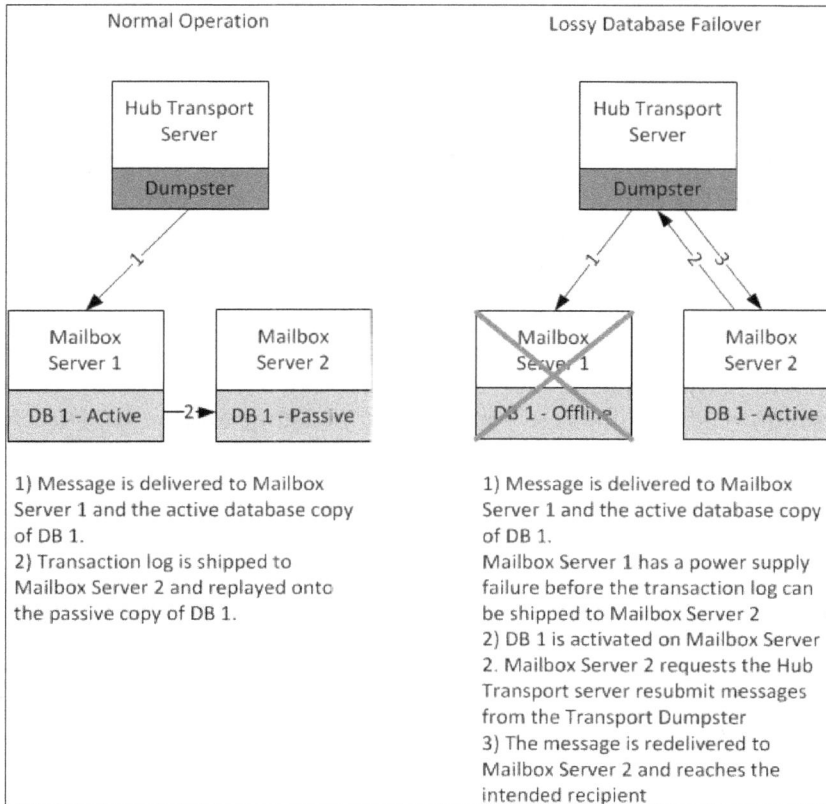

Normal Operation	Lossy Database Failover
1) Message is delivered to Mailbox Server 1 and the active database copy of DB 1. 2) Transaction log is shipped to Mailbox Server 2 and replayed onto the passive copy of DB 1.	1) Message is delivered to Mailbox Server 1 and the active database copy of DB 1. Mailbox Server 1 has a power supply failure before the transaction log can be shipped to Mailbox Server 2 2) DB 1 is activated on Mailbox Server 2. Mailbox Server 2 requests the Hub Transport server resubmit messages from the Transport Dumpster 3) The message is redelivered to Mailbox Server 2 and reaches the intended recipient

Edge Transport Role

The Edge Transport Role in Exchange Server 2010 is the first of the two optional components in an Exchange Server deployment. The Edge Transport Role can only be installed separately from other Exchange Server roles on a server that is not a domain member. The Edge Transport Role is very similar to the Hub Transport role, in that it deals with transport of mail. The major difference is that is it focused on communicating with external clients and is typically situated in your Edge network (also known as a DMZ).

The main functions of the Edge Transport Role are:

- External SMTP facilities for incoming and outgoing messages from the organization
- Message hygiene facilities to junk e-mail through the use of real-time block and by allowing lists and content scanning
- To host a local copy of relevant directory information using Active Directory Lightweight Directory Services (previously known as Active Directory Application Mode, or ADAM), used to store information about known users and user-managed junk e-mail lists

Conceptually, the Edge Transport role is very similar to the Hub Transport Role. The technology used for transporting messages is the same; the key difference is that it's not directly attached to the Active Directory domain. Instead, an Edge synchronization relationship is created to allow Exchange and Active Directory data to be published regularly to the Edge Transport Role.

The Edge Transport Role is the ideal place to use as your first line of defense against spam, malware, and other threats. Basic techniques to cut down spam include the use of Real-time Block Lists (RBLs) from providers such as SpamHaus. Using a combination of the right RBLs can cut down on most common spam. The Edge Role also has the ability to perform content-based scanning to further help with reducing Spam, and by installing Malware scanning tools like Forefront Protection for Exchange you can add on inbound scanning for Malware and Spyware and provide enhanced Spam-filtering before any mail reaches the core Exchange organization.

Providing high availability for the Edge Transport Role

The techniques for providing high availability for the Edge Transport role are very similar to those used to provide high availability for the Hub Transport Role. Multiple Edge Transport servers can be placed within the organization, ideally at strategic points, such as multiple paths to and from the Internet.

Incoming mail resilience and high availability is built into the SMTP protocol through the use of Mail Exchanger, or MX records. These DNS records are created for each domain and are used to direct inbound mail to the correct mail server. Each entry would typically be the external hostname of each Edge Transport server and a weighted number is specified to determine which one other SMTP server on the Internet should attempt to try first; the lower the number the higher the priority. If you're simply providing resilience and want to provide a degree of load balancing between the two, it's common to give all the Edge Transport servers the same priority.

The following diagram illustrates a highly-available Edge infrastructure across two sites:

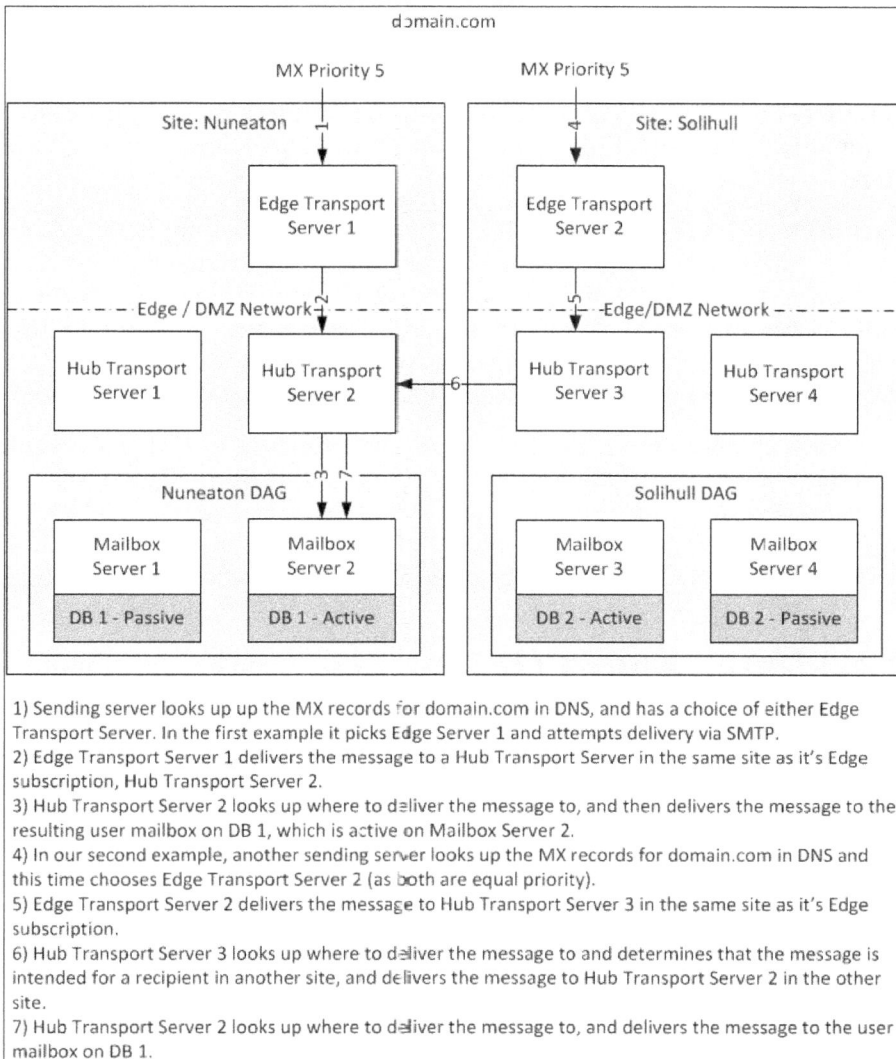

1) Sending server looks up up the MX records for domain.com in DNS, and has a choice of either Edge Transport Server. In the first example it picks Edge Server 1 and attempts delivery via SMTP.

2) Edge Transport Server 1 delivers the message to a Hub Transport Server in the same site as it's Edge subscription, Hub Transport Server 2.

3) Hub Transport Server 2 looks up where to deliver the message to, and then delivers the message to the resulting user mailbox on DB 1, which is active on Mailbox Server 2.

4) In our second example, another sending server looks up the MX records for domain.com in DNS and this time chooses Edge Transport Server 2 (as both are equal priority).

5) Edge Transport Server 2 delivers the message to Hub Transport Server 3 in the same site as it's Edge subscription.

6) Hub Transport Server 3 looks up where to deliver the message to and determines that the message is intended for a recipient in another site, and delivers the message to Hub Transport Server 2 in the other site.

7) Hub Transport Server 2 looks up where to deliver the message to, and delivers the message to the user mailbox on DB 1.

Alternatives to using the Edge Transport Role

The Edge Transport Role isn't your only option when looking to manage your inbound and outbound messaging requirements.

For small environments, especially those with a single server, Administrators can configure the Hub Transport server to accept messages directly from the Internet, enable the Anti-Spam facilities typically provided by the Edge role, and install and configure anti-malware protection. While not an ideal solution, for those on a limited budget, it can be a simple solution.

However, there are many other solutions in the marketplace that will provide the functionality of the Edge Role either as a hosted service, dedicated software, or appliance.

Hosted services such as Forefront Online Protection for Exchange (FOPE), Google Postini, and Symantec Message Labs act as your inbound Mail Exchangers to the outside world and accept and deliver inbound and outbound mail on your Exchange organization's behalf. Messages from these services are typically delivered directly to your Hub Transport servers, which use firewall rules to only allow SMTP connections from your hosted provider's Internet address space.

Dedicated software or appliances are conceptually similar to the Edge Transport servers, in that they run within your datacenter, located in your Edge/DMZ network. Examples of solutions include BarricadeMX, Barracuda, and GFI MailEssentials. However, there are many on the market, including free, open source solutions like MailScanner which can be downloaded and installed at no charge.

Unified Messaging Role

The Unified Messaging Role is the second optional component of Exchange Server 2010. This role provides voice-based access to the Exchange organization—accepting voice mail and delivering it to user mailboxes or allowing voice-based access to Exchange 2010. First introduced in Exchange Server 2007, the Unified Messaging Role is in its second incarnation and integrates smoothly with many third-party IP phone systems.

In particular the Unified Messaging Role provides the following features:

- Voicemail services including transcription of voice messages into text with supported languages
- Voice access to end user mailboxes allowing messages to be read out loud to the end user
- Configurable voicemail routing and call transfer based on user-configured rules, such as the options to provide a different message if the user is out of office or in a meeting
- Directory access for external callers using the Auto Attendant services
- Uses the MP3 codec making playback of voicemail straightforward on iOS devices

As a component of Exchange, the Unified Messaging Role is fairly straightforward to manage and on a per-server level there is little configuration, apart from determining the protocols it will use to listen for IP PBX connections on and installation of language packs for your region.

At an organization level, configuration is a little more complicated and requires understanding of IP telephony technologies to configure correctly. For a successful implementation mapping between users' telephone extensions and mailboxes needs to be performed and a Dial Plan configured to define the relationship between Exchange and the IP PBX, along with rules for number translation, a **Session Initiation Protocol (SIP)** trunk to carry voice traffic between Exchange and the IP PBX or PSTN gateway.

Providing high availability for the Unified Messaging Role

A highly available Unified Messaging service relies somewhat on the capabilities of your IP PBX or PSTN gateway - by providing multiple Exchange Servers hosting the Unified Messaging Role, you provide the infrastructure that can receive incoming and make outgoing SIP sessions with the associated IP PBX or PSTN gateway.

As each Unified Messaging server is effectively stateless, once it has processed each inbound call or voicemail the balancing of calls is handled by the IP PBX or PSTN gateway and its capabilities to associate multiple servers with a SIP Trunk.

Active Directory

Although not an Exchange role, Active Directory plays one of the most critical roles in Exchange Server. Without Active Directory, your Exchange Server can't do very much at all. In particular, Active Directory provides the following to Exchange:

- User, Contact, and Distribution Group information, including end user directory information, e-mail addressing, and mailbox configuration information, such as what mailbox database a user mailbox is located on.

- Directory information used to generate Offline Address Books and used by clients, through the Client Access Server to look up Global Address List information.

- Nearly all configuration for Exchange Server including information about Mailbox and Public Folder databases, database availability groups, policies, and organization-wide settings such as accepted mailboxes, and basics such as the Exchange Server computer accounts.

- User authorization and authentication services for end-users. Much like all clients log-ons are passed by Exchange Server to Active Directory.
- Administrative permissions, including Active Directory-based permissions and configuration information for Exchange Server's role-based access control.

As you can see, if your Active Directory infrastructure has a problem, Exchange Server has a problem. Therefore if you are building high-availability into Exchange Server, you also need to consider building high-availability into your Active Directory infrastructure.

Before installation of Exchange Server 2010 there are some basic pre-requisites for the Exchange environment; the forest functional level must be at least Windows Server 2003 or higher, and the domain controllers should be Windows Server 2003 SP1 or higher. Naturally, later functional levels and Windows Server operating systems are supported, especially for larger environments. 64-bit domain controllers are recommended due to their ability to cache more information in server memory.

Active Directory is a multi-master directory service, so by installing extra domain controllers in each site and designating appropriate ones as Global Catalog servers, you provide resilience to your environment, including your Exchange Server infrastructure.

In smaller environments it is tempting to install Exchange Server and Active Directory Domain Controller Role onto the same server, and although this is the configuration for a specialized product like Small Business Server 2011, in a generic Exchange Server environment it is not considered best practice. If you install Exchange Server onto an Active Directory domain controller, you cannot choose later on to demote the Domain Controller — to do so you would need to uninstall Exchange Server first.

Capacity planning for Exchange ActiveSync clients

So far in this chapter we've covered, at a conceptual level, the major components in Exchange Server 2010, how they interlink and depend on one another, and ways to provide resilience. Now that we understand more about Exchange Server, it's time to move onto getting practical, but before that we need to plan our installation.

Capacity planning is important for any environment as it gives you a chance to investigate what the load requirements are for your infrastructure before you let end users use the system. The last thing you want to do is purchase new server hardware, spend a great deal of time configuring your environment, and then find that it cannot be used by your end users because you didn't plan and test what you were going to do.

Because capacity planning is a vast subject, even just for Exchange, this book can't cover all the bases, such as if you are utilizing Virtualization and SAN storage, and we won't focus on capacity planning in the context of a multi-site environment. We also won't look at the migration from an earlier version of Exchange Server, either. These topics are covered in great detail elsewhere, both in other books and on the Internet, and aren't really the focus of this book.

What we will focus on is the basic tasks you need to perform when planning capacity in general for Exchange, a task that if performed correctly will ensure that iPhone ActiveSync clients will perform well when connected to Exchange.

Our example organization

Throughout the book we'll be using a fictional company to represent the iPhone and Exchange Server 2010 deployment we're working on, "Lisa Jane Designs".

Lisa Jane Designs is a creative company that designs and manufactures colorful and inspiring creations, such as mugs and T-shirts. With a staff of 100 employees, out of which, the majority are working from home and 20 work from the head office, Lisa Jane Designs is looking for a solution to connect its workforce so they can communicate better.

As a small start-up, they currently utilize a shared e-mail account from their web hosting company for sales-related mail and communicate with staff using their personal e-mail accounts. They have no facilities to share e-mail, organize meetings using calendars, and we have been tasked to implement Exchange Server 2010 into their head office and provision iPhones for all staff to ensure that the staff can communicate regardless of whether they are in front of a PC or not.

The company currently has a recently installed Active Directory domain, based on servers running Windows Server 2008 R2. Two Domain Controllers are in use along with a Windows 2008 R2-based NAS server. The Active Directory domain name is the same as the company's external domain name, `lisajanedesigns.co.uk`.

Internet access is currently provided by a 100Mb/s leased line that currently has less than 10% usage, and the network infrastructure includes firewall technology and managed switches with the capability to create a secure Edge network.

Server backups are currently provided by a hosted backup provider, which also provides support for Exchange Server 2010 backups.

The following diagram illustrates Lisa Jane Design's current infrastructure:

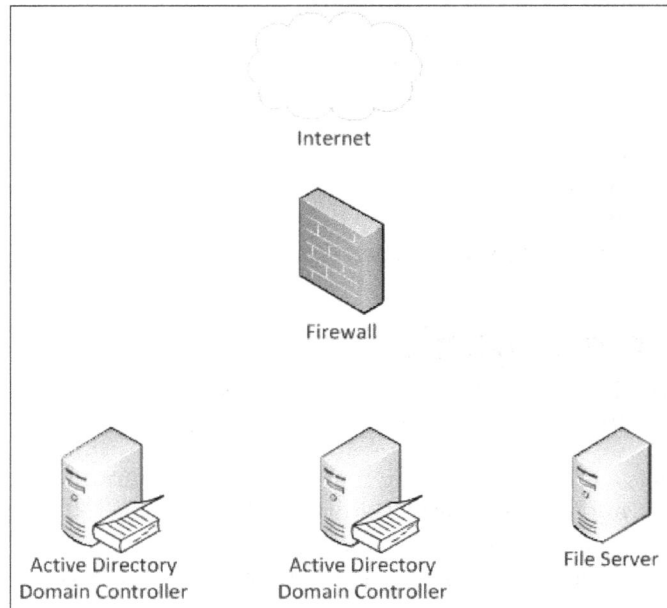

Based on discussions with the company about their requirements and a process to examine the number of e-mails the staff currently sends and receives per day, using both the company account and personal accounts, we have agreed to base our specification on the following parameters:

- Provide a resilient messaging environment that can withstand a single server failure
- Provide 5GB mailboxes for each member of the staff with a profile of 100 sent/received per day of approximately 75KB per message
- Provide remote access for staff using up to 100 iPhone devices connecting via the Internet
- Provide internal and external access for Outlook and Outlook Web App clients

- Perform traditional weekly, full, and nightly incremental backups using the existing hosted backup solution to ensure off-site backups are in place
- Minimise costs where possible

Based on those parameters, the next step is to turn those requirements into a basic design:

- Use two Exchange Servers participating in a Database Availability Group with each server hosting the Client Access and Hub Transport Roles in addition to the Mailbox Role
- Provide two copies per database
- Utilize 1TB, 7,200RPM SAS drives with RAID for additional resilience
- Use a Load Balancer to provide high availability, load balancing, and Edge/ DMZ Network facilities for the Client Access role
- Use an external SMTP protection service, Forefront Online Protection for Exchange instead of the Edge Transport Role to reduce the number of physical servers required while providing the required resilience
- Utilize 2 x 6-core 2.93Ghz Intel Xeon X5670 processors per Client Access/ Hub Transport/Mailbox Server
- Use Windows Server 2008 R2 Enterprise Edition for each combined Client Access/Hub Transport/Mailbox Server with Exchange Server 2010, Standard Edition

Now that we've decided on our base platform, we'll utilize tools Microsoft provides to determine the storage requirements.

Combined Client Access/Hub Transport/ Mailbox Server Role requirements

Microsoft provides an Excel-based tool to assist with calculating the requirements for your environment. We'll make use of this tool to rapidly assist us with turning the requirements and our base design into a specification that has been calculated against Microsoft's own recommendation for sizing storage, memory, and CPU.

The Mailbox Server Role Requirements Calculator for Exchange Server 2010 can be downloaded from the following URL:

```
http://blogs.technet.com/b/exchange/archive/2009/11/09/3408737.aspx
```

The next step before we begin entering our design parameters into the calculator is to get some additional data, the SPECint 2006 rating for the processor which is used by the calculator to determine whether the processer meets the eventual requirements. The easiest way to determine this value is to download the Exchange Processor Query Tool:

```
http://blogs.technet.com/b/exchange/archive/2010/10/27/3411397.aspx
```

After downloading the Processor Query Tool, launch it in Excel, enabling Macros when prompted, and enter the Processor model—in our case "X5670":

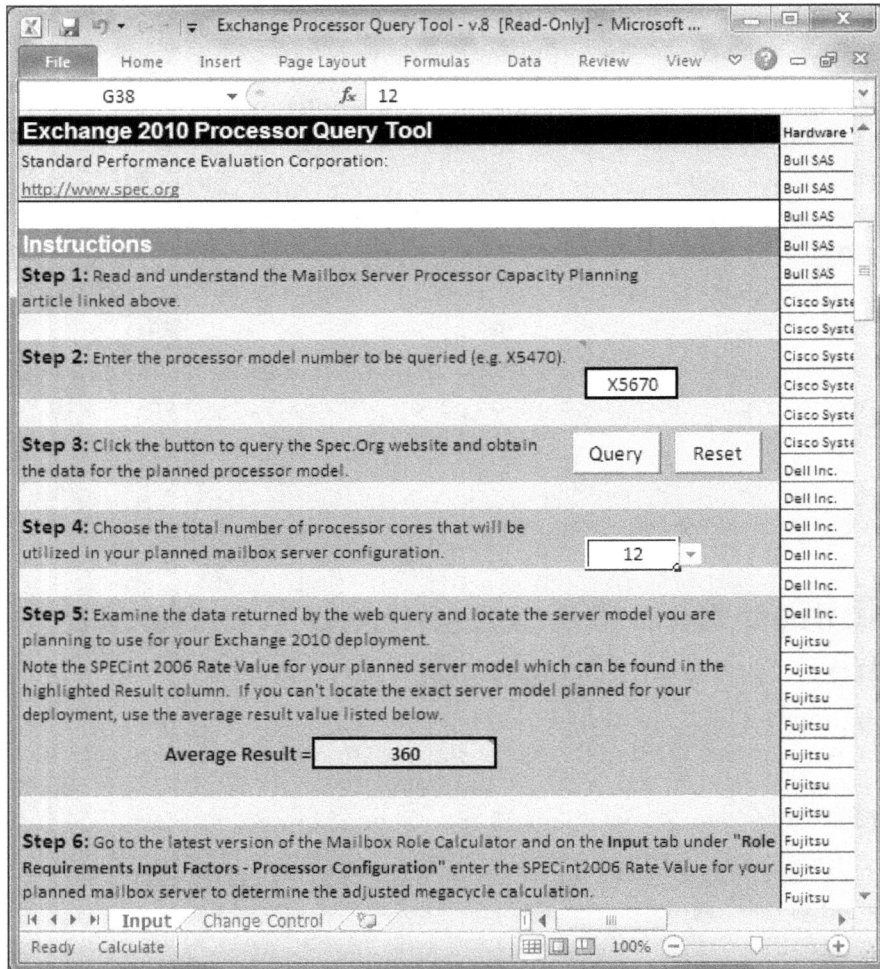

You'll need to record the SPECint rate value, which in our case is 360.

Next, we'll enter this along with other parameters into the Exchange 2010 Mailbox Server Role Requirements Calculator:

Role Requirements Input Factors – Environment Configuration

Step 1 - Please enter in the appropriate information for cells that are blue and choose the appropriate drop-downs for database copies you have selected for the number of mailbox servers.

Exchange Environment Configuration	Value
Global Catalog Server Architecture	64-bit
Server Multi-Role Configuration (MBX+CAS+HT)	Yes
Server Role Virtualization	No
High Availability Deployment	Yes
Number of Mailbox Servers Hosting Active Mailboxes / DAG	2
Number of Database Availability Groups	1

Mailbox Database Copy Configuration	Value
Total Number of HA Database Copy Instances (Includes Active Copy) within DAG	2
Total Number of Lagged Database Copy Instances within DAG	0
	0
	0

Exchange Data Configuration	Value
Data Overhead Factor	20%
Mailbox Moves / Week Percentage	1%
Dedicated Maintenance / Restore LUN?	Yes
LUN Free Space Percentage	20%
	Enabled
	30%

Exchange I/O Configuration	Value
I/O Overhead Factor	20%
Additional I/O Requirement / Server	0.00

In Step 1, we enter information about the environment, specifying the following in particular:

- We have 64-bit Domain Controllers
- We are planning for a multi-role configuration
- We are planning a high-availability deployment that is not site-resilient
- We are planning to use two Exchange Servers for our multi-role servers
- We want to ensure we have dedicated maintenance/restore LUN

- • The DAG should have a symmetrical database distribution—due to us only having 100 users and two servers, it will most likely only specify a single database, otherwise meaning we won't share any mailbox load between the servers

Role Requirements Input Factors – Mailbox Configuration

Step 2 - Please enter in the appropriate information for cells that are blue and choose the appropriate drop-downs for information in the Tier-2 and Tier-3 User Mailbox tables. Otherwise, only use the Tier-1 User Mailbox table.

Tier-1 User Mailbox Configuration	Value
Total Number of Tier-1 User Mailboxes / Environment	100
Projected Mailbox Number Growth Percentage	0%
Total Send/Receive Capability / Mailbox / Day	100 messages
Average Message Size (KB)	75
Mailbox Size Limit (MB)	5120
Personal Archive Mailbox Size Limit (MB)	0
Deleted Item Retention Window (Days)	14
Single Item Recovery	Enabled
Calendar Version Storage	Enabled
IOPS Multiplication Factor	1.00
Megacycles Multiplication Factor	1.00
Desktop Search Engines Enabled (for Online Mode Clients)	No
Predict IOPS Value?	Yes
Tier-1 User IOPS / mailbox	0.00

Next, in Step 2, we enter information about our requirements and findings for the mailboxes themselves. These are used by the calculator to determine the underlying processor, memory, disk size, and disk IO requirements:

- • 100 mailboxes
- • 100 sent and received per day
- • 75KB average mailbox size
- • 5GB Mailbox limit

We also keep some defaults checked as well, as they will be useful to end users, such as the Deleted Item Retention, Single Item Recovery, and Calendar Version storage. Combined, these features will assist in avoiding recovery from backups.

Role Requirements Input Factors – Backup Configuration

Step 3 - Please enter in the appropriate information for cells that are blue and choose the appropriate drop-downs for database from the transaction logs.

Backup Configuration	Value
Backup Methodology	Software VSS Backup/Restore
Backup Frequency	Weekly Full / Daily Incremental
Database and Log Isolation Configured	Yes
Backup/Truncation Failure Tolerance	7
Network Failure Tolerance (Days)	0

In Step 3, we enter information about the backup requirements based on the hosted service we are using and the frequency of backups in the requirements. Note that we've changed the default so we are isolating the Database and Transaction Logs. While in JBOD environments without backup it's common to combine the Database and Logs together. It's commonly considered best practice to isolate the Database and Logs when performing backups via a traditional method.

In particular this means that should we be unlucky enough to lose both copies of the database disks, but still have the latest copy of the Transaction Logs, we can restore the Database from traditional backups and then replay the Transaction Logs and avoid a period of data loss during that day.

Role Requirements Input Factors – Storage Configuration

Step 4 - Please select the appropriate disk capacities and disk types that you will be using for your database, transaction logs, and restore LUNs whether to require RAID, or allow the calculator to determine whether the solution can designed with JBOD storage.

Storage Options	Value	

Primary Datacenter Server Disk Configuration	Disk Capacity	Disk Type
Database	1000 GB	7.2K RPM SAS 3.5"
Log	1000 GB	7.2K RPM SAS 3.5"
Restore LUN	1000 GB	7.2K RPM SAS 3.5"

In Step 4, shown in the preceding screenshot, we enter information about the physical disks we will use for the Database, Log, and Restore LUNs. In our base design, we've chosen 1000GB 7.2K RPM SAS drives, therefore we've selected them in the calculator.

Role Requirements Input Factors – Processor Configuration

Step 5 (Optional) - Please enter in the appropriate information for cells that are blue and choose the appropriate drop-downs for cells that are SPECint2006 Rate Value, please see http://www.spec.org.

Server Configuration	Processor Cores / Server	SPECint2006 Rate
Mailbox Servers	12	360

Finally, as shown in the preceding screenshot, in Step 5 we enter the number of cores, 12 (2 x 6 core CPUs) and the SPECInt2006 rate we determined earlier, 360.

After entering the information we can examine the results and determine the recommendations for the Exchange Servers. First, we'll look at the Role Requirements tab:

Role Requirements Calculations Pane	
Role Requirements Results Pane - Environment Configuration	
Processor Core Ratio Requirements	**/ Primary Datacenter**
Number of Mailbox Cores Required to Support Activated Databases	1
Recommended Minimum Number of Hub Transport Cores	--
Recommended Minimum Number of Client Access Cores	--
Recommended Minimum Number of Global Catalog Cores	1
Environment Configuration	**/ Primary Datacenter**
Number of DAGs	--
Number of Active Mailboxes (Normal Run Time)	100
Number of Mailbox Servers / DAG	2
Number of Lagged Copy Servers / DAG	0
Total Number of Servers / DAG	**2**
User Mailbox Configuration	**Tier-1**
Number of User Mailboxes / Environment	100
Number of Mailboxes / Database	50
User Mailbox Size within Database	5445 MB
Transaction Logs Generated / Mailbox / Day	20
IOPS Profile / Mailbox	0.10
Read:Write Ratio / Mailbox	3:2
Database Copy Instance Configuration	**/ Primary Datacenter**
Number of HA Database Copy Instances / DAG	2
Number of Lagged Database Copy Instances / DAG	0
Total Number of Database Copy Instances	**2**
Database Configuration	
Number of Databases / DAG	2
Recommended Number of Mailboxes / Database	50
Available Database Cache / Mailbox	20.48 MB
Database Copy Configuration	**/ Server**
Number of Database Copies	2

In the output from our example requirement, we see that the CPU requirements are easily met by our design of using 2 x 6 core processors, as we only require one core to run the Mailbox Role.

Exchange Server recommendations for multiple role servers are as follows:

- For every four Mailbox Role cores required, three Client Access Role cores are required.
- For every seven Mailbox Role cores required, one Hub Transport Role core is required. (Or a 5:1 ratio if malware protection is installed on the server.)

Therefore, with 11 cores free per server, we have more than enough capacity to host the Client Access and Hub Transport Roles on the server configuration we are planning.

Particular attention should be paid to the ratios, especially for the Client Access Role. By following these ratios correctly we are ensuring that we will have sufficient capacity in our environment to meet the CPU requirements for our iPhone ActiveSync clients.

Specific up-to-date guidelines for ratios of different configurations can be found at the following URL:

`http://technet.microsoft.com/en-us/library/dd351197.aspx`

We also see other information including the total size of the mailbox data on-disk, the amount of transaction logging that is expected to occur, and the IOPs profile per user.

The IOPs (Input/output Operations Per Second) profile per user is important, as this is a major factor in determining the storage that can be used for Exchange. The calculator has used this to determine what we should do, but this figure will be referred to when validating our storage before Exchange is deployed.

Finally we see that two databases per server are recommended — this is likely to be based on our selection to balance the number of databases between the two Exchange Servers.

Further down this tab, we look at the Server-specific requirements:

Role Requirements Results Pane - Server Configuration			
Server Configuration	/ Primary Datacenter Server (Single Failure)	/ Secondary Datacenter DR Server	/ Lagged Copy Server
Recommended RAM Configuration	8 GB	--	--
Server Total Available Adjusted Megacycles	63994	--	--
Mailbox Role CPU Megacycle Requirements	220	--	--
Mailbox Role CPU Utilization	0%	--	--
Possible Storage Architecture	RAID	--	--

Role Requirements Results Pane - Log, Disk Space, and IO Requirements			
Transaction Log Requirements	/ Database	/ Server	/ DAG
User Transaction Logs Generated / Day	1200	1200	2400
Average Move Mailbox Transaction Logs Generated / Day	467	467	933
Average Transaction Logs Generated / Day	1667	1667	3333
Disk Space Requirements	/ Database	/ Server	/ DAG
Database Space Required	319 GB	638 GB	1276 GB
Log Space Required	11 GB	23 GB	46 GB
Database LUN Space Required	--	877 GB	1755 GB
Log LUN Space Required	--	28 GB	57 GB
Restore LUN Space Required	--	413 GB	826 GB
Host IO and Throughput Requirements	/ Database	/ Server	/ DAG
Total Database Required IOPS	6	12	24
Total Log Required IOPS	1	3	5
Database Read I/O Percentage	60%	--	--
Background Database Maintenance Throughput Requirements	5 MB/s	10 MB/s	20 MB/s

The Server-specific configuration gives us information about each individual server; we can see that the minimum for a multi-role server, 8GB of RAM is recommended. This makes sense as Microsoft state that the requirements should be based on 4GB RAM plus 3-30MB per user depending on Database Cache requirements. In the preceding section it was calculated that 20.48MB per user was required, which for 100 users brings us to 6GB, under the minimum, hence 8GB is stated.

We also see that 319GB is required per Database and 11 GB per Log volume.

On the next tab, we can delve into more detail about the configuration that is recommended and how the configuration should work.

Much of this information is re-iterating our requirements, though the LUN Requirements and Storage Design should be examined as these will help us determine the storage hardware required and how it should be configured.

In the LUN Requirements, we can see how the storage should be presented to the Exchange Server:

Restore LUN Design	
Restore LUN Size	413 GB

Note: The DB and Log LUN Design Table identifies databases by a unique number. However, databases copies are distributed across the servers, and thus, these numbers hold no significance and are used solely as an example to show a server's LUN layout.

DB and Log LUN Design / Server		
Database Copy	DB LUN Size Required	Log LUN Size Required
DB1	439 GB	14 GB
DB2	439 GB	14 GB
--	0 GB	0 GB
	0 GB	0 GB

We see that we'll need five Exchange related LUNs per server—two Database, two Log, and one for the Restore LUN.

On the Storage Design tab in particular, we are interested in the number of disks recommended:

Storage Design Results Pane - RAID Storage Architecture			
RAID Storage Architecture	Primary Datacenter Servers	Secondary Datacenter Servers	Lagged Copy Servers
RAID Storage Architecture Required?	Yes	--	--
RAID Storage Architecture / PDC Server	Database	Log	Restore LUN
Disk Capacity / Type	1000 GB / 7.2K RPM SAS 3.5"	1000 GB / 7.2K RPM SAS 3.5"	1000 GB / 7.2K RPM SAS 3.5"
Optimal RAID Configuration	RAID-1/0	RAID-1/0	RAID-1/0
Optimal Number of Disks	2	2	2

For our example deployment, we have a fairly straightforward set of recommendations—six disks dedicated to Exchange Server as three separate RAID sets, comprising two disks each.

Combining that together, we now know we can consider two servers with the following specification:

- 2 x Xeon X5670 6-core processors
- 8 GB RAM

- 8 x 1 TB 7200 RPM SAS disks, configured as four RAID 1 groups:
  - ° System/boot as a single LUN
  - ° Databases, presented by the storage as two LUNs of at least 439 GB
  - ° Logs, presented by the storage as two LUNs of at least 11 GB—in reality these LUNs will be the same size as the Database LUNs
  - ° Restore and Maintenance LUN

Our next consideration for our Exchange Database Availability Group is what server we will use for the File Share Witness. The default recommendation is to use a Hub Transport server; however, as we are combining roles, a separate Hub Transport server is not available. The recommendation for a Hub Transport Server for a File Share Witness is based upon the logic that the server should be managed by the same group of Administrators as the Database Availability Group. In our example deployment, the Windows-based File Server is managed by the same IT team, and policies in place allow changes to security groups on the File Server, therefore this will be a suitable candidate for a File Share Witness.

Load Balancer

Since we selected a two-node Database Availability Group to host the Client Access Role, we cannot take advantage of Windows Network Load Balancing (WNLB) for load balancing and high availability for the Client Access Role. Therefore, instead, we will use the Load Balancer technology.

Choosing a Load Balancer depends on a number of factors, such as existing suppliers and skills, cost, and what other services the device may need to integrate with.

Microsoft provides a list of Load Balancers tested by vendors with Exchange 2010 at the following URL:

```
http://technet.microsoft.com/en-us/exchange/gg176682.aspx
```

For our example organization and deployment in the next chapter, we could choose any of the models listed on the Microsoft website, but for the purposes of our example, we'll use the free HAProxy-based Load Balancer available from my website:

```
http://www.stevieg.org/e2010haproxy
```

Active Directory considerations

We have established that Lisa Jane Designs already has a resilient Active Directory infrastructure based on Windows Server 2008 R2, a 64-bit operating system.

For each Exchange Server, our Mailbox Role requires one core, therefore based on the ratio recommended by Microsoft of one Active Directory domain controller core for every eight Mailbox Role cores we require in total, one quarter of a core to achieve the required performance level.

By monitoring the CPU usage of the Active Directory domain controllers and further investigating the configuration of these servers, we find that the servers are based on single six core Xeon X5670 processors with an average of 5% utilization; therefore, it is safe to deduce for our example deployment that the Active Directory infrastructure is capable of supporting our Exchange Server implementation.

Planning for namespaces and certificates

Now that we've determined the hardware configuration we will use for Exchange Server 2010, we need to decide on the namespace to be used for access to the Exchange Organization.

Our example organization is based around one site with remote clients, and our DNS domain name for external clients matches our Active Directory domain name. We will use a single namespace based on the company domain name, lisajanedesigns.co.uk.

For each namespace, a number of DNS names are recommended for ease of client access, encompassing the HTTPS DNS name used to access services such as Outlook Web App, Exchange Web Services and ActiveSync, the AutoDiscover DNS name and the DNS name used for the Client Access Array, the name that RPC-based MAPI clients use to connect to the Client Access Servers:

- **HTTPS**: mail.lisajanedesigns.co.uk
- **AutoDiscover**: autodiscover.lisajanedesigns.co.uk
- **Client Access Array**: outlook.lisajanedesigns.co.uk

Because we intend on using these names both inside and outside the organization, we need to consider the DNS setup in place. Some organizations use a single DNS infrastructure servicing both internal and external clients; while others — particularly those that use the same DNS name for Active Directory internally as used for external facing services — typically use a split-DNS setup where external clients use a different set of DNS servers to resolve DNS records for the domain. This is particularly sensible when the organization does not want to expose internal DNS records, such as those specific to internal clients or Active Directory service records to the outside world.

In our example organization, Lisa Jane Designs, a split DNS setup is used where external DNS records are managed by the hosting provider with only the minimum DNS records in place to support external services such as the website. Internally, Active Directory DNS is used through the domain controllers and records relevant to external services are added to the internal DNS manually.

Therefore when configuring DNS we will add the external facing DNS names, `mail.lisajanedesigns.co.uk` and `autodiscover.lisajanedesigns.co.uk` to the externally facing DNS; internally we will also add the `outlook.lisajanedesigns.co.uk` record and specific server names for each individual Exchange Server.

Subject Alternative Name certificates

Microsoft recommends the use of Subject Alternative Name (SAN) certificates for providing SSL services Exchange Server 2010 client access. Third-party SAN certificates are available from a range of vendors such as VeriSign, GoDaddy, GlobalSign, and Comodo. By running an internal Certificate Authority, it is also possible to issue certificates internally. However, to ensure ease of initial access to Exchange Server from iPhone devices it is helpful to use a trusted Third Party certificate.

The list of trusted certificate providers for iOS devices is listed on the Apple support website at the following URL:

`http://support.apple.com/kb/HT4415`

For Lisa Jane Designs, we will use a certificate from *GoDaddy*. Based on our namespace planning, we will need SSL certificates for the following DNS names:

- `mail.lisajanedesigns.co.uk` (Subject Name, or primary name on the certificate)
- `autodiscover.lisajanedesigns.co.uk`

Note that we don't need the `outlook.lisajanedesigns.co.uk` DNS name on the certificate, as it is used by the Client Access Array for RPC Client Access only. RPC Client Access can be encrypted, but it does not use SSL, and therefore does not require an SSL certificate.

Network configuration

To provide a secure configuration, we will create an Edge/DMZ section of the Lisa Jane Designs network, and place the Hardware Load Balancers within this zone.

Exchange Servers will be placed within the internal network.

Internally, we will allow LAN clients to connect to Exchange through the Load Balancer and present no restrictions on the TCP/IP ports they can use to initiate connections.

Externally, we will only require the following ports open for incoming traffic:

- TCP/IP Port 80 and 443 for HTTP/HTTPS traffic to the Load Balancer virtual IP address
- TCP/IP Port 25 for SMTP traffic, restricted to the IP range of the FOPE service with access allowed to the Load Balancer virtual IP address

Internally to initiate connections outbound, we will need to initiate connections from the Exchange Servers to the IP range of the FOPE service, on port 25.

The Load Balancer will have interfaces in both the Edge/DMZ network and Internal Network but in particular will need to communicate with the Exchange Servers on the following ports:

- TCP/IP Port 80 and 443 for HTTP/HTTPS traffic to the Client Access Role
- TCP/IP Port 25 to deliver incoming mail to the Hub Transport Role
- TCP/IP Port 135 and in our deployment, statically assigned ports for RPC communications, 60000 and 60001

By only requiring the Load Balancer infrastructure to be placed in the Edge/DMZ you can see we have simplified the firewall configuration necessary to allow access to the Exchange Server for external clients; this is the reason why Microsoft does not support the Client Access Role in the Edge/DMZ, since, if it does so, a lot of internal communication must be allowed between different services, such as Active Directory, causing issues for troubleshooting and ongoing maintenance.

Summary

In this chapter, you've received a crash-course in Exchange Server 2010's architecture, covering all the roles that make up Exchange:

- Client Access
- Mailbox
- Hub Transport
- Edge Transport
- Unified Messaging

We've looked at what facilities each of these Exchange roles provides and how they interact with other components of Exchange Server; additionally we've looked at how these roles can be built as highly available components of Exchange and what other technologies such as Load Balancers can be used to build a secure and reliable Exchange environment suitable for a mobile workforce that need to depend on messaging services.

In the second part of this chapter we've covered the basics of planning an Exchange Server deployment, using an example organization that we'll focus on throughout the practical examples next chapter onward.

In our planning for the Exchange Server deployment we've made use of the architecture knowledge gained in the first part of the chapter and then used freely-available tools from Microsoft to help validate the proposed design and understand what hardware is required for the implementation.

We've looked at the Exchange namespaces that need to be used for our example organization and determined what names will be needed on the certificates used for Client Access, then finally covered the TCP/IP ports required to provide external and access to services.

In the next chapter we'll be taking a more practical approach and will set up Exchange Server 2010 for our example organization, Lisa Jane Designs, based on the design we've just covered.

3
Exchange Server Configuration for iOS Connectivity

In this chapter, we're going to walk through the full implementation of Exchange Server 2010 in our example organisation, Lisa Jane Designs, using the design and planning done in the previous chapter. Just to recap, we'll be configuring two Exchange Servers configured into a Database Availability Group with each server hosting the three typical Exchange Server roles, namely, Client Access, Hub Transport, and the Mailbox Role.

As part of the implementation we'll start with the basics — configuring the disk layout to match the specifications recommended by Microsoft's planning tool, and going through the step by step installation using the GUI where possible. There are a couple of times we dip into the command line and Exchange Management Shell, but only briefly. The process is organized as follows:

- Installation of Microsoft Exchange Server
    - ° Basic server configuration, such as disks and networking
    - ° Active Directory preparation
    - ° Installation of pre-requisites and Exchange Server
- Configuration of Microsoft Exchange Server
    - ° Configuring databases
    - ° Configuring the Database Availability Group
    - ° Configuring the Client Access Array
    - ° Configuring DNS names
    - ° Configuring certificates

- ° Configuring Outlook Anywhere
- ° Configuring the Send Connector
- ° Configuring the Receive Connector

- Testing client connectivity
  - ° Creating a test mailbox
  - ° Testing basic client connectivity
  - ° Testing AutoDiscover and ActiveSync functions
  - ° Testing iPhone connectivity

Before we begin with the installation though, let's quickly review the example environment and where the servers fit in.

More about our example environment

In the last chapter we reviewed the current environment at Lisa Jane Designs and found they already had infrastructure in place that we can use. This includes a good quality network, two suitable Active Directory Domain Controllers, and a File Server that would be ideal for use as a File Share Witness.

Network diagram

The following diagram shows the planned configuration of the servers and associated network subnets:

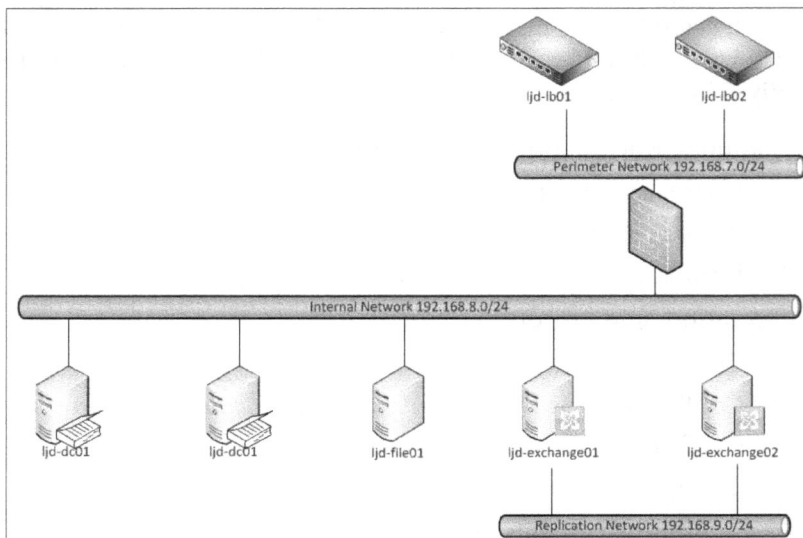

As shown in the diagram, you will see we will be using the following three subnets:

- **192.168.7.0/24**: as the perimeter network, with a firewall protecting internal clients from unauthorized access
- **192.168.8.0/24**: as the internal network, that is used by internal servers and workstations and will include our Exchange Servers
- **192.168.9.0/24**: as the Database Availability Group (DAG) replication network, allowing us to segregate replication traffic within the DAG from the client networks

In the diagram, we also see the following current and new servers:

- **ljd-dc01** and **ljd-dc02**: act as Active Directory Domain Controllers and Global Catalog Servers for the lisajanedesigns.co.uk domain, within the single site "Nuneaton".
- **ljd-file01**: acts as the central file server for Lisa Jane Designs. As all servers are managed by a single administration group, this server will act as our File Share Witness.
- **ljd-exchange01** and **ljd-exchange02**: the two new Exchange Servers.
- **ljd-lb01**: the new Load Balancer appliance.

IP addressing

Before we begin the installation, we'll quickly list the current IP addressing given to both the existing servers, and the servers that we're going to install Exchange Server 2010 on:

Name	Type	Interface	IP address	Gateway
ljd-dc01	Server	Internal Network	192.168.8.90	192.168.8.2
ljd-dc02	Server	Internal Network	192.168.8.91	192.168.8.2
ljd-file01	Server	Internal Network	192.168.8.92	192.168.8.2
ljd-exchange01	Server	Internal Network	192.168.8.101	192.168.8.2
		Replication Network	192.168.9.101	N/A
ljd-exchange02	Server	Internal Network	192.168.8.102	192.168.8.2
		Replication Network	192.168.9.102	N/A
ljd-exch-dag-01	Virtual IP	Internal Network	192.168.8.100	N/A

Name	Type	Interface	IP address	Gateway
ljd-lb01	Load Balancer	Perimeter Network	192.168.9.250	192.168.9.2
mail/ autodiscover/ outlook	Virtual IP	Perimeter Network	192.168.9.249	192.168.9.2

As shown in the table, we have a fairly small number of server IP addresses to consider, with the addition of a virtual IP address for the Database Availability Group's Cluster IP, and a virtual IP address to be used by the active load balancer.

Installation of Microsoft Exchange Server 2010

With all the servers ready and in place, we're now in a position to install Microsoft Exchange Server 2010 on our new Windows servers.

For the installation at Lisa Jane Designs, due to the small IT domain and single domain we're able to use the Administrator account, which is a member of the pre-requisite groups, including Enterprise Admins, Domain Admins, and Schema Admins.

Before we proceed with the installation of Exchange Server itself though, we've got a little bit of server configuration and pre-requisite installation to perform.

Basic server configuration

Overall, the basic configuration of the server is like any other Windows 2008 R2 server. We need to configure the Exchange Servers to use internal network addresses as listed earlier, along with appropriate DNS server settings against Active Directory domain controllers to ensure name resolution works as expected. Then, we join the servers into the lisajanedesigns.co.uk domain.

After this is complete, we move onto configuring the disk layout and configuring the interface used for the Database Availability Group replication network.

Disk configuration

Our two Exchange Servers have been set up utilizing RAID storage, with disks configured according to the design in the previous chapter. We'll now be creating the disk partitions and presenting them to the operating system.

For our implementation, we will be using disk mount points, rather than logical drive letters. This allows us to clearly see the purpose of the disks and in larger installation can avoid the limitations of running out of available drive letters.

Therefore, before we partition and format the disks, we'll need to create folders in the root of the c: drive to use as mount points for each partition.

In this installation, we'll create a folder named according to its intended use by Exchange:

- c:\DB1: To be used by the first Mailbox database
- c:\DB1_Log: To be used by the first Mailbox database's log files
- c:\DB2: To be used by the second Mailbox database
- c:\DB2_Log: To be used by the second Mailbox database's log files
- c:\DB_Recovery: Our recovery LUN, used for performing restores from a backup

After creating the folders, we open up **Server Manager** and examine the disks presented by the RAID array to the operating system:

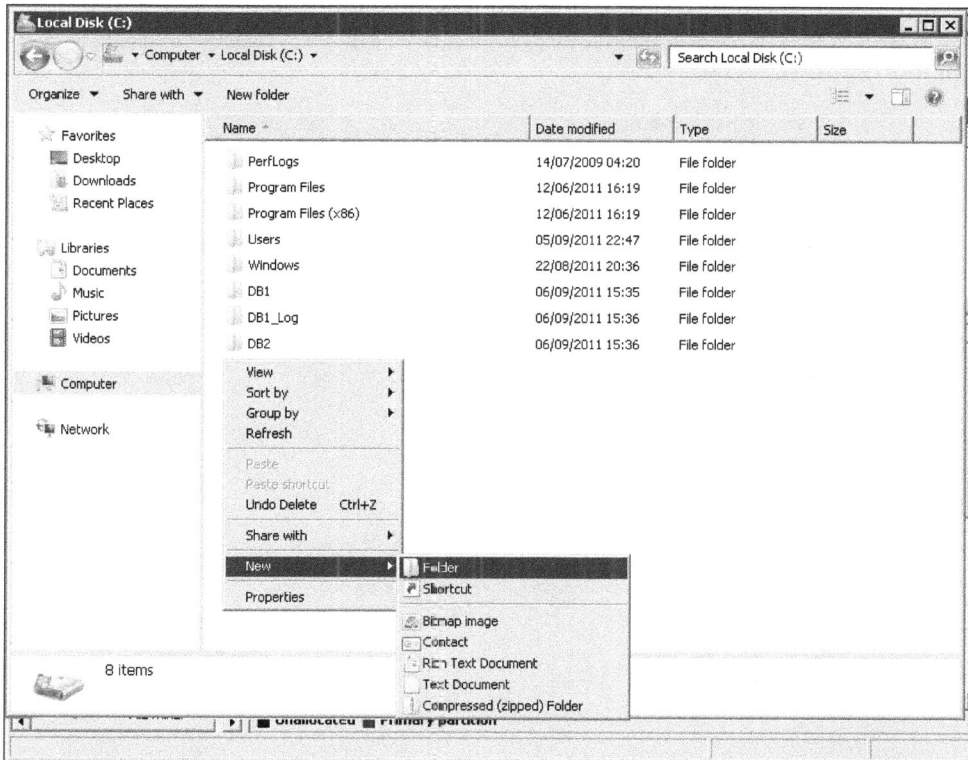

At this point, you'll see the disks are uninitialized; therefore the first step is to right-click on the first uninitialized disk and choose to initialize it, choosing **GUID Partition Table (GPT)**, which is the recommended partition style by Microsoft due to its support for larger partitions:

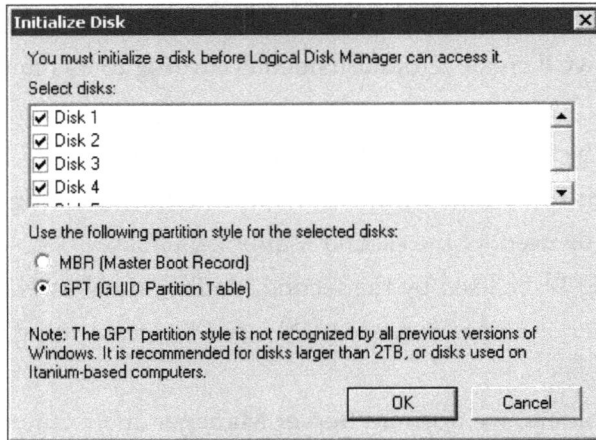

After initializing the disks, the next step is to create a partition. We right-click on the first unpartitioned disk, and choose to create a new simple volume. The **New Simple Volume Wizard** should appear:

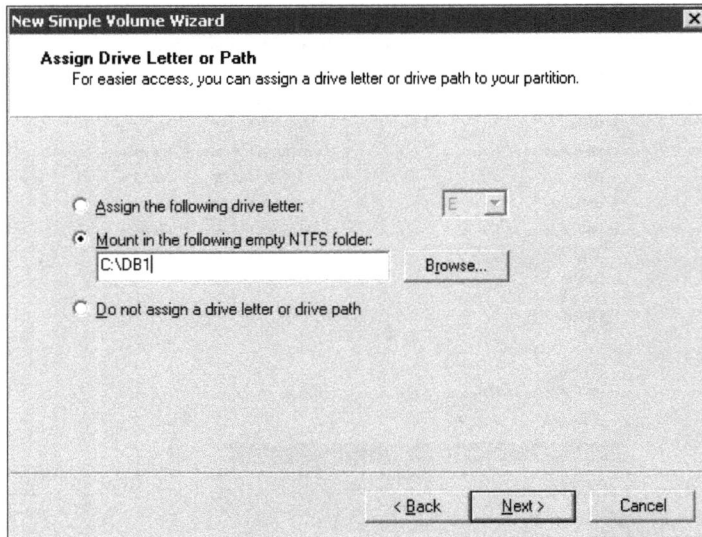

Rather than assign a drive letter, we choose the option to mount the partition in the corresponding folder mount point we created earlier.

The next step is to format the partition. Microsoft recommends an NTFS allocation unit size of 64KB for partitions that contain database or log files, and that the partitions are correctly aligned, which combined give optimum performance. Windows 2008 Server and above correctly align partitions, so we just need to change the allocation unit size; choose 64K from the drop-down list. To aid with identifying the partition in the **Disk Management** section of **Server Manager**, we'll also set each volume label to match the folder mount point name:

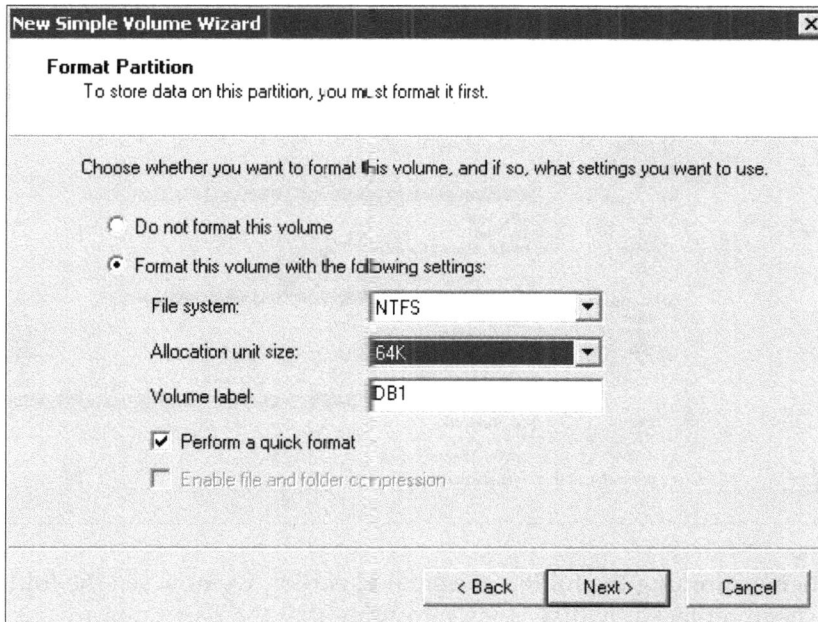

After repeating this process for each disk, we should now see all partitions formatted and correctly showing labels signifying each partition's purpose:

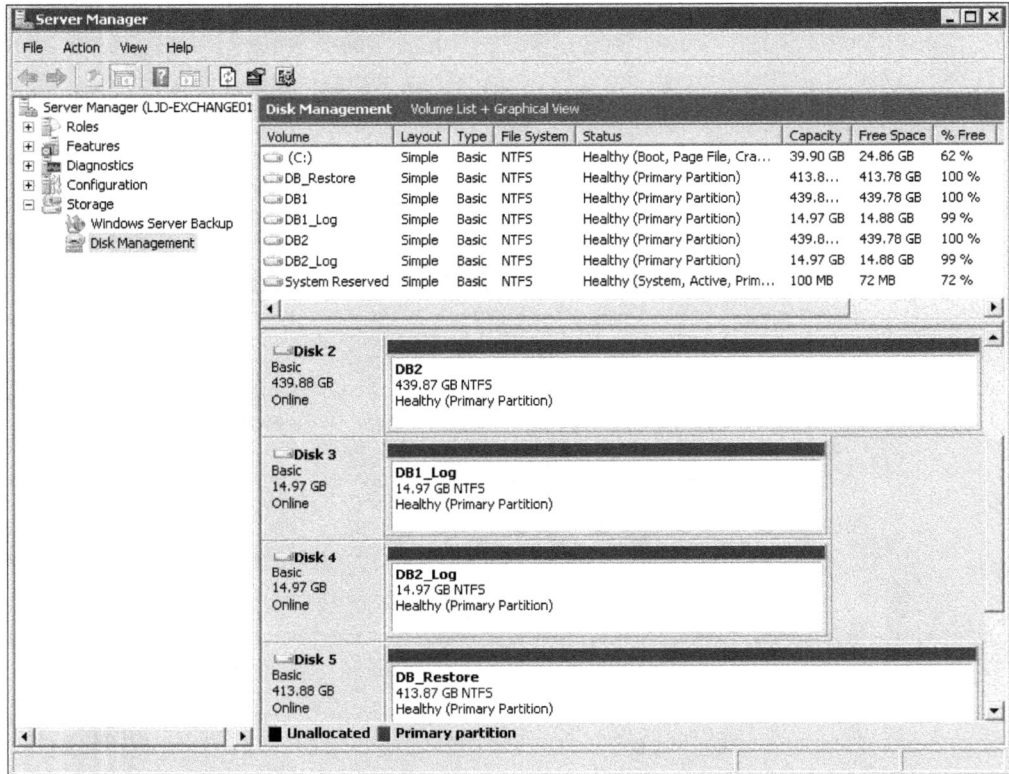

Finally, when examining the folders we created earlier, we now see the folder icons have been replaced by disk icons signifying that the partitions are correctly configured with the mount points:

The process is repeated on the second Exchange Server, providing an identical disk configuration.

> **Validating your storage performance**
>
> Before installing Exchange Server, it's advisable to validate that the performance of your underlying storage system meets the design. Issues with faulty hardware, firmware, or drivers are best identified and corrected before placing a server into production. Microsoft recommend, as a minimum, using Jetstress to perform these tests.
>
> A full guide on performing Jetstress testing is available in the form of the *Jetstress Field Guide*, by Neil Johnson (Microsoft Consulting Services), available on the Exchange Team Blog at the following URL:
>
> ```
> http://blogs.technet.com/b/exchange/
> archive/2010/11/15/3411534.aspx
> ```

Network configuration

After configuring the basic IP addressing for both server interfaces (in accordance with the information presented earlier in the *IP Addressing* section of this chapter) and ensuring communication between both services using utilities such as ping, we need to ensure that advanced settings are configured on the Replication interfaces to ensure that Windows File and Print Sharing services do not use the interface.

To access the advanced settings, we navigate to **Network Connections**, and after holding down the *Alt* key to ring up the menu, we choose **Advanced | Advanced Settings**:

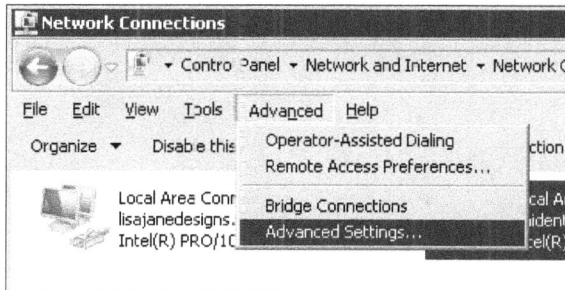

After highlighting the adapter used for Replication, we change its order so it is used second after the primary interface. Then un-tick any bindings configured against **File and Printer Sharing for Microsoft Networks** and **Client for Microsoft Networks**:

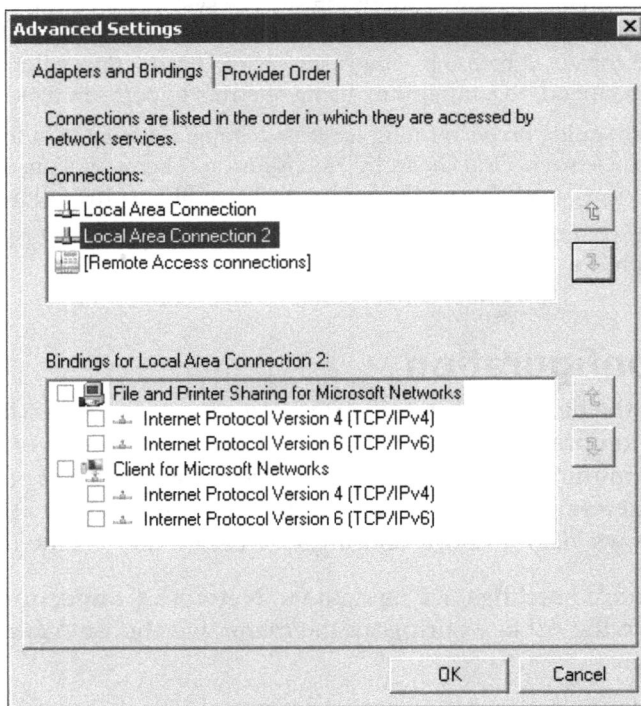

This process is repeated on both Exchange Servers.

Obtaining installation media

When purchasing Exchange Server 2010, you may be provided with the installation files on DVD or as an ISO image from the Microsoft Volume Licencing Website. Typically, this installation media will not have the current service pack for Exchange Server integrated into it.

To avoid the requirement for installation of the current service pack on top of the older version of Exchange Server 2010, you can instead simply download the current service pack and after extraction, use it as installation media. The Service Pack download is not only suitable for upgrades but contains the full installation files for the full version of Exchange Server 2010, whether you use it as a trial or a licensed installation of Exchange Server Standard or Enterprise edition.

Active Directory preparation

Exchange Server relies heavily on Active Directory to store user attributes and server configuration. Therefore, Exchange requires modifications to the schema of Active Directory. These changes can be performed during installation, automatically if the user account performing the installation is a member of the Schema Admins group, or separately at the command line from any 64-bit Windows computer in the same site as the Schema Master.

The schema changes place quite a heavy load on Active Directory, so it's recommended to perform these changes when user activity is at a minimum to ensure it doesn't impact users.

To perform the schema changes, we launch an Elevated Command prompt and change directory to the Exchange Server 2010 installation media, then run the following command:

```
setup.com /PrepareSchema
```

The process to upgrade the schema typically can take upwards of five minutes and after completing successfully we see output at the command line as shown:

```
Administrator: Command Prompt                                    _ □ ×
installation. By continuing the installation process, you agree to the license
terms of Microsoft Exchange Server 2010.
If you don't accept these license terms, please cancel the installation. To
review the license terms, please go to
http://go.microsoft.com/fwlink/?LinkId=150127&clcid=0x409/

Press any key to cancel setup...............
No key presses were detected. Setup will continue.
Preparing Exchange Setup

    Copying Setup Files                              COMPLETED

No server roles will be installed

Performing Microsoft Exchange Server Prerequisite Check

    Organization Checks                             COMPLETED

Configuring Microsoft Exchange Server

    Extending Active Directory schema               COMPLETED

The Microsoft Exchange Server setup operation completed successfully.

C:\Exchange2010>
```

After performing the schema updates, we must wait until the changes have been replicated within Active Directory before commencing with the installation of Exchange Server.

Installation of pre-requisites

Prior to the release of Service Pack 1 for Windows Server 2008 R2, a large number of Microsoft Windows updates (979744, 983440, 979099, 982867, and 977020) needed to be downloaded separately. Therefore, ensure Service Pack 1 or higher is applied before attempting installation of Exchange Server 2010.

One recommended external pre-requisite however, is the Microsoft Office 2010 Filter Packs, which enable Exchange Server to index and allow search within Microsoft Office documents. The 64-bit version can be downloaded from the following URL:

```
http://www.microsoft.com/download/en/details.
aspx?displaylang=en&id=26604
```

After download, simply run the `filterpack2010sp1-kb2460041-x64-fullfile-en-us.exe` executable on each Exchange Server and complete the simple installation.

Installation of Exchange Server 2010

Exchange Server installation can be performed in a number of ways, firstly by using the graphical setup program, `setup.exe` or via the command line `setup.com` (which we used above to prepare the schema). Using the command line can save a lot of time, especially when installing a large number of Exchange Servers, but to help illustrate the process more visually, we'll be installing Exchange using the graphical setup program.

To launch the graphical Exchange Server setup, execute `setup.exe` from the installation media. Choose the option to **Install Microsoft Exchange**, then after choosing whether to accept the License Agreement and enable Error Reporting, we will be presented with the **Installation Type** dialog.

As both Exchange Servers for our installation will host the Client Access, Hub Transport, and Mailbox Roles, we choose a **Typical Exchange Server Installation**. To automatically install Windows components for features such as IIS, we ensure the **Automatically install Windows Server roles and requires required for Exchange Server** checkbox is ticked:

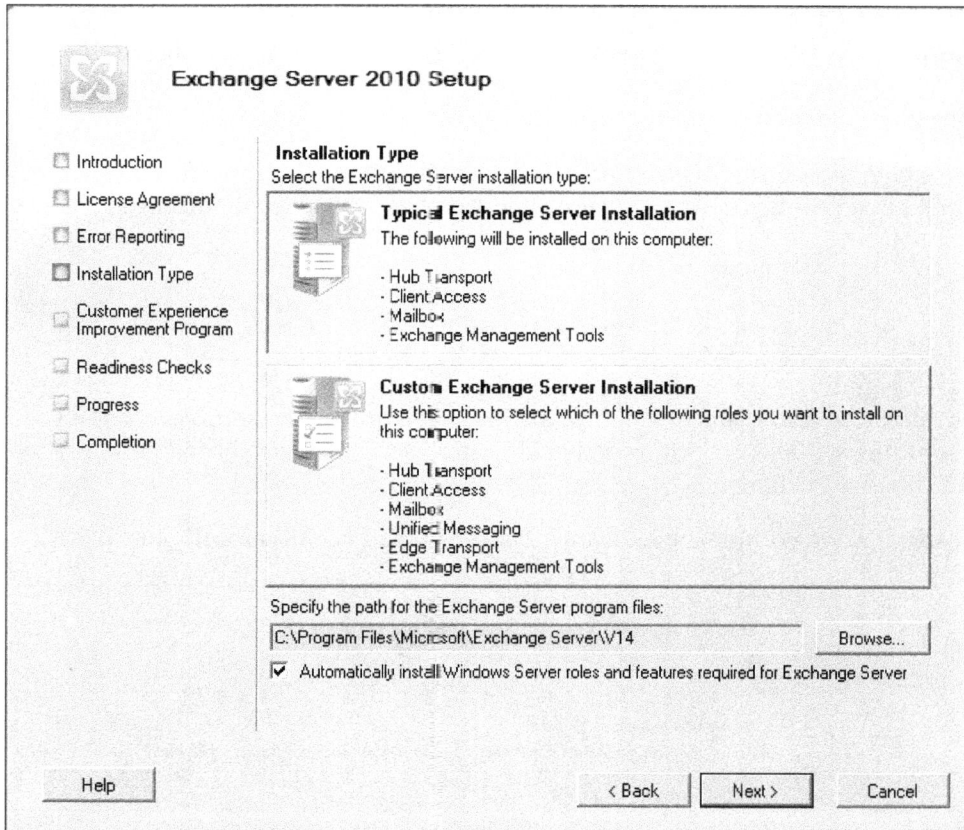

Next, as this is the first Exchange Server installed into the Active Directory forest, we're prompted for the Exchange Organization name; enter the company name, Lisa Jane Designs.

We're also given the option to apply a split permissions model to Active Directory, suitable when different IT groups manage Exchange and Active Directory. Lisa Jane Designs only has one IT group that will manage both Active Directory and Exchange, therefore we don't need to use the split permissions model.

We will be asked about Client versions connecting to Exchange. Outlook 2003 requires a legacy feature of Exchange, known as Public Folders, to operate. As we won't have any clients running Outlook 2003 at Lisa Jane Designs, we can choose **No** and avoid creation of Public Folder databases.

Finally, we'll also be asked about the external name to use for the Client Access Namespace. As per our namespace planning, it's important we configure this as `mail.lisajanedesigns.co.uk`. Configuring this as part of setup avoids the need to configure these settings after installation.

At this stage the pre-requisite checks and installation of Windows features will begin. At this point, you may be requested to reboot the system and restart setup.

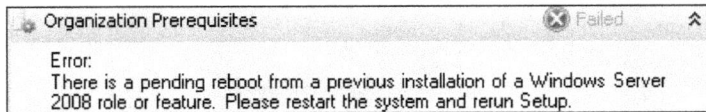

After rebooting and restarting setup, it should remember the settings chosen so far and continue with setup. After re-checking pre-requisites, we should be ready to install the first Exchange Server.

After installation completes, Exchange Server should be successfully installed.

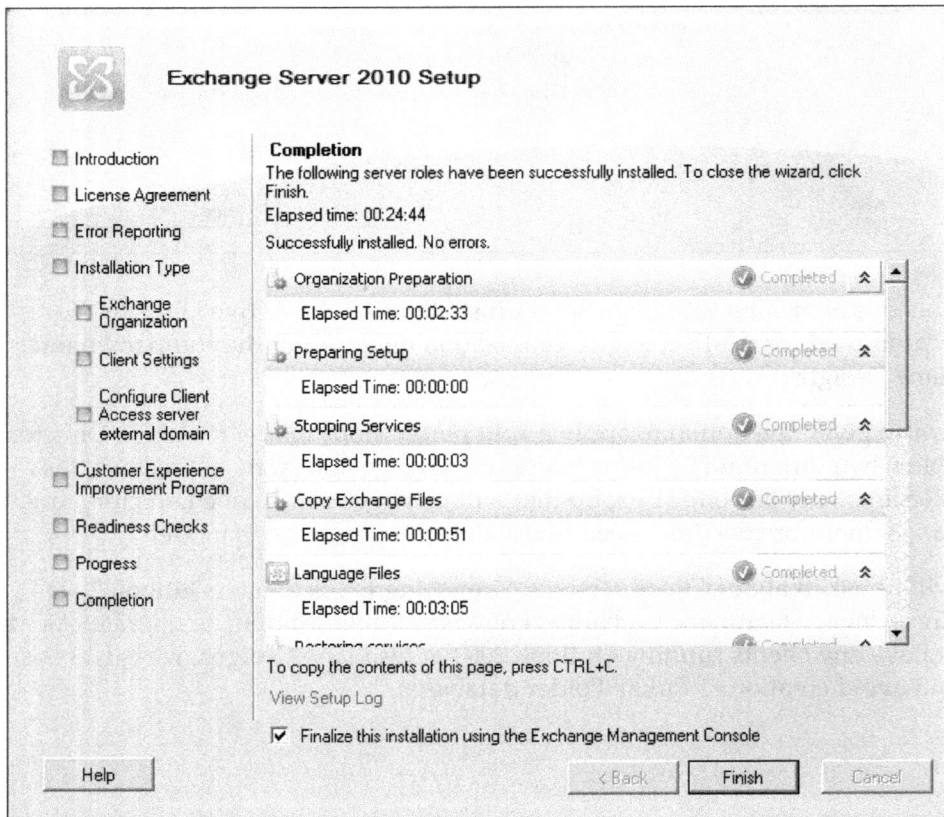

The process is repeated on the second Exchange Server after using Windows Update to ensure that the server is running the latest Update Rollup of Exchange Server 2010, although as the Exchange organization has been set up in Active Directory during the first Exchange Server configuration, we won't need to specify the Organization Name the second time around.

Configuring Microsoft Exchange Server 2010

After successful installation of both servers, we can now begin configuring the Exchange Management Console.

Before we begin, we'll take a brief look at the Exchange Management console to gain an understanding of how it's organized:

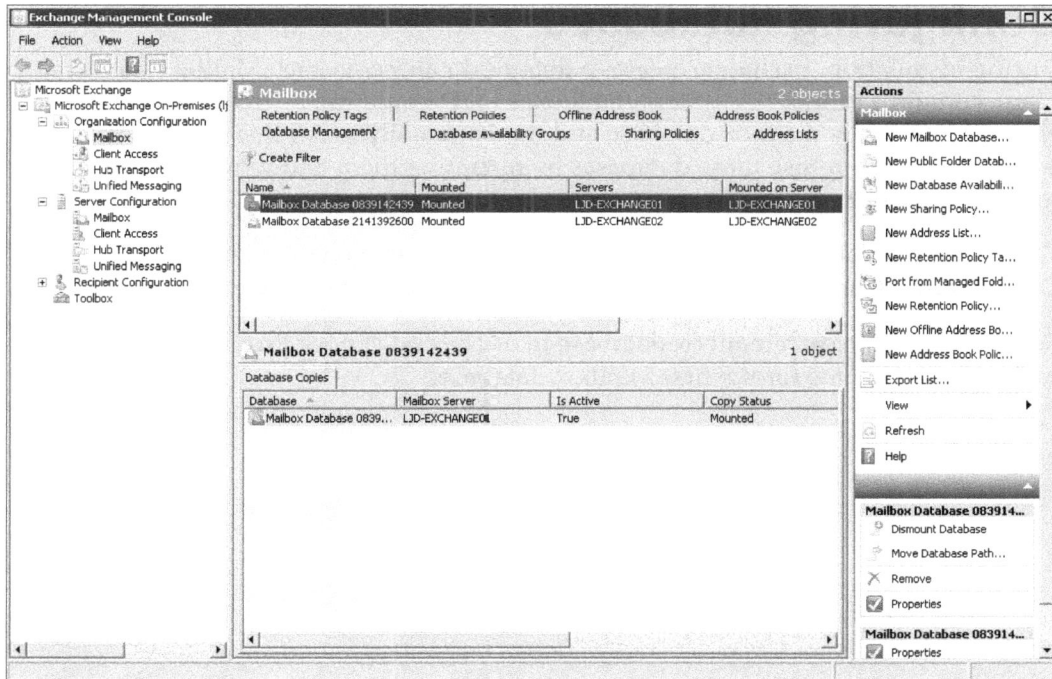

After launch, we see that the Exchange Management Console is split into four distinct sections:

- **Organization Configuration**: used to configure settings that affect all Exchange Servers
- **Server Configuration**: used to manage and configure specific Exchange Servers
- **Recipient Configuration**: used to create, remove and manage Mailboxes, Mail-Enabled Users/Contacts, and Distribution Groups
- **Toolbox**: provides utilities to monitor and troubleshoot Exchange Server

It's worth taking some time to become familiar with each section, drilling down into settings for all the different Exchange roles. To continue our installation, though, we need to begin by reconfiguring the default databases created at installation time.

Configuring databases

During installation, Exchange creates a default database on each Mailbox server. These contain a number of system mailboxes that should not be deleted. We can either create a new mailbox database and then manually move these mailboxes across, or we can re-use these databases by renaming them and moving them to the correct storage. The simplest option is the latter.

To rename the database, navigate in the Exchange Management Console to **Organization Configuration | Mailbox** then click on the **Database Management** tab.

Right-click on the each mailbox database in order, and choose **Properties**. Rename it to the planned name for the first Mailbox database.

At the same time, we'll click on the **Limits** tab and set the mailbox quotas to match the specifications defined in the previous chapter, and on the **Client Settings** tab set the **Offline Address Book** to the **Default Offline Address Book**.

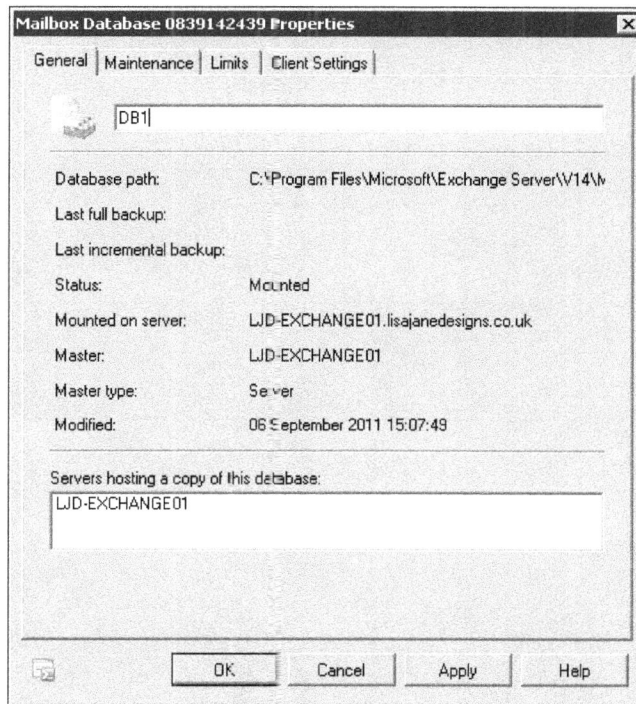

Next, on each server, right-click on the database it hosts and choose the **Move Database Path** option.

The **Move Database Path** wizard should appear, allowing us to enter new database and log folder paths for each database. We'll be entering the mount points for the storage we configured earlier in the chapter:

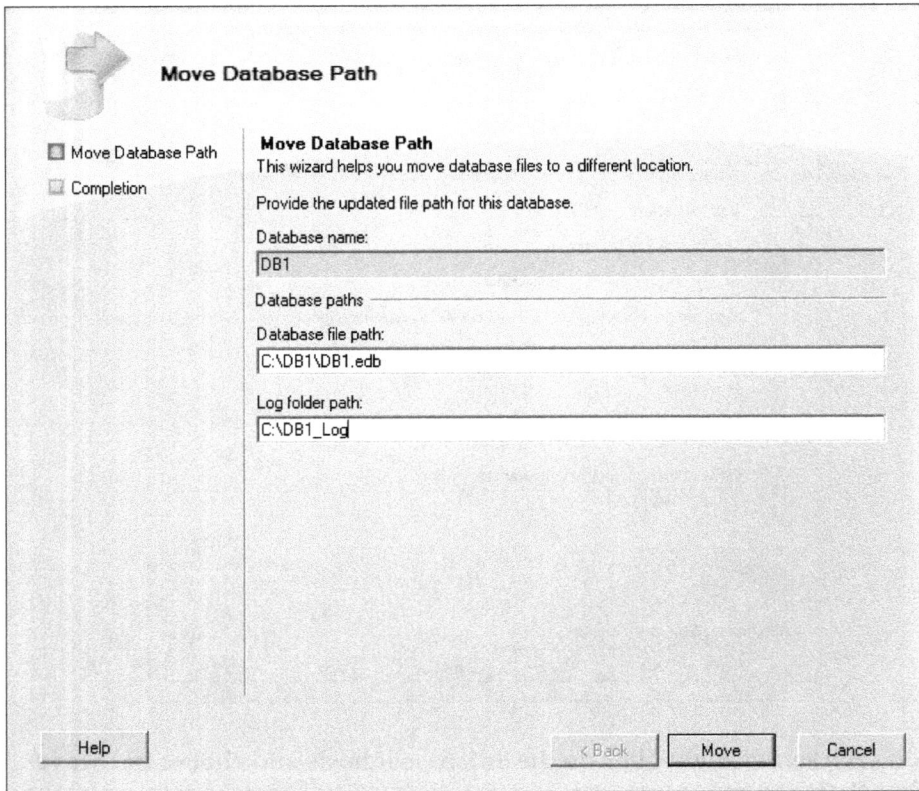

As part of the process, the **Move Database Path** wizard will dismount the Mailbox database, move the database and log files to the new location, then re-mount the Mailbox database in its planned location. We repeat the process for each Mailbox database.

After successfully moving each database to its correct location, we can begin the configuration of the Database Availability Group.

Configuring the Database Availability Group

For our small Exchange organization, the configuration of the Database Availability Group is fairly straightforward, we need to:

1. Ensure the correct permissions are in place on the File Witness Server.
2. Create the Database Availability Group.
3. Add each Exchange Server to the Database Availability Group.
4. Configure the MAPI (Client) and Replication networks.
5. Configure the Database Availability Group and set the Cluster IP address.
6. Add Database Copies to each of our two Mailbox Databases.

We've chosen to use our file server under our control, `ljd-file01` as our File Share Witness server, so we need to add the **Exchange Trusted Subsystem** to the **Administrators** group on the file server. This allows Exchange Server and associated clustering services to create, manage, and access the associated file share:

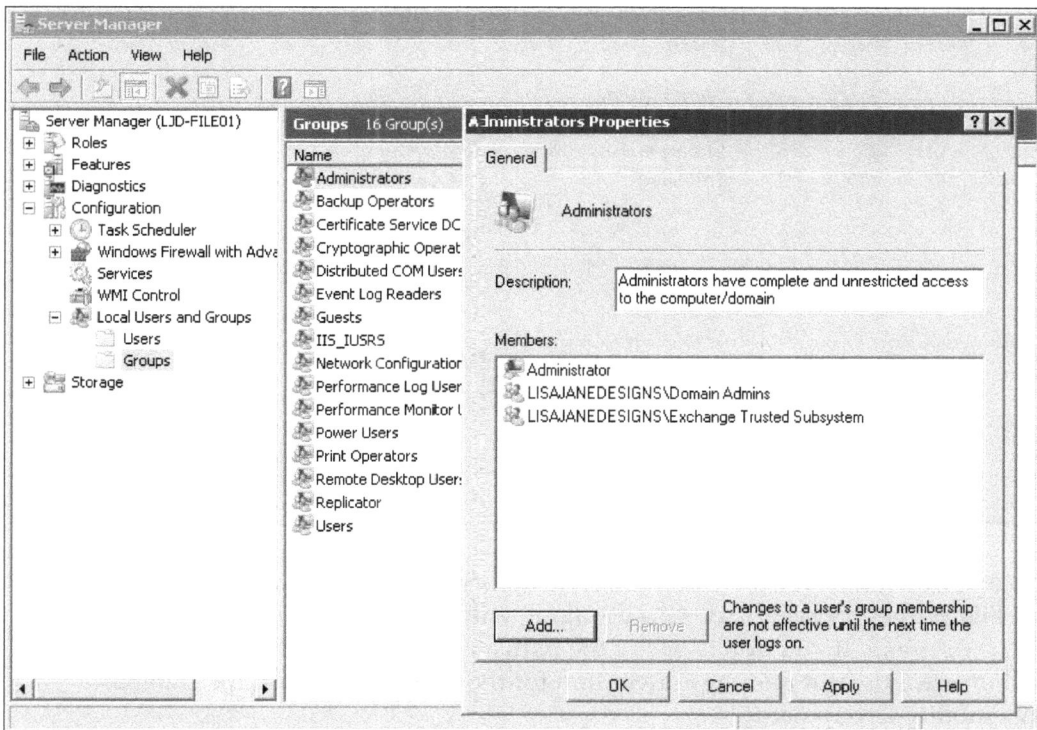

Next, we'll jump back to one of our Exchange Servers, and using the **Exchange Management Console** navigate to **Organization Configuration | Mailbox**.

Click on the **Database Availability Groups** tab, then right-click and choose **New Database Availability Group**. The **New Database Availability Group** wizard should appear:

We enter the name for the Database Availability Group `ljd-exch-dag01` and add the File Witness Server, `ljd-file01`, along with a local path on the server, such as `C:\Witness`. If you don't specify the path at this point, Exchange Server 2010 will utilize a default naming convention for the path based upon the Database Availability Group name.

After creating the Database Availability Group, we add both Exchange Servers
as members. Do this by right-clicking the Database Availability Group name and
choosing **Manage Database Availability Group Membership**, then adding each
Exchange Server using the wizard:

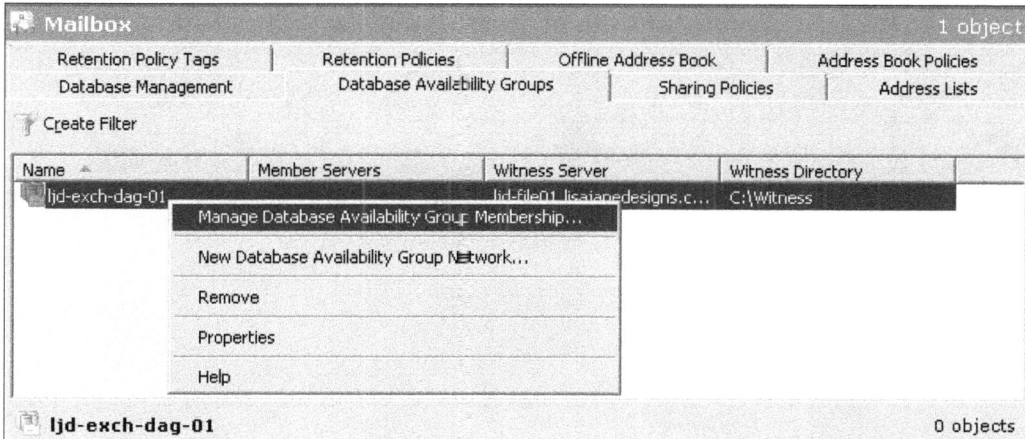

Next, we'll configure the Database Availability Group Networks to reflect our
design, by renaming the default networks to reflect their purpose and disabling
replication on the MAPI/Client network:

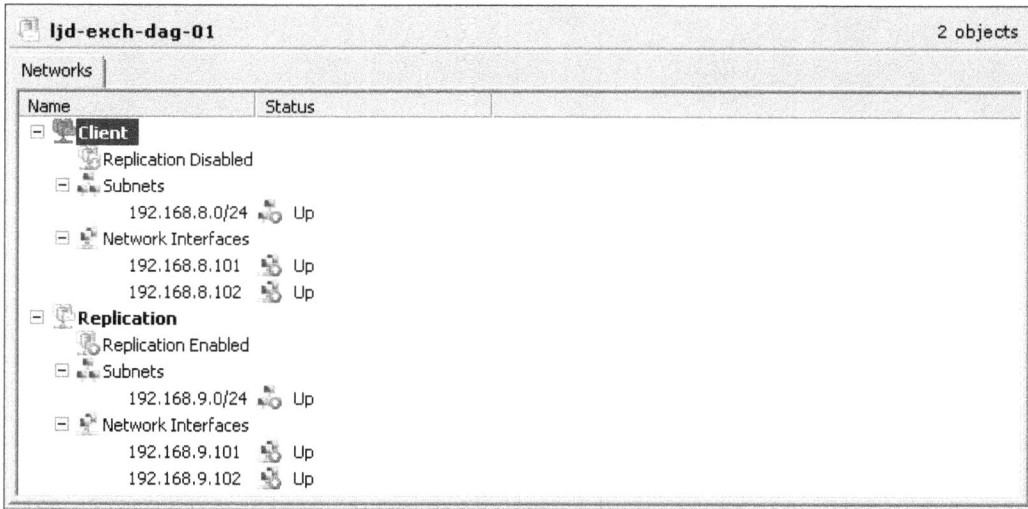

One of our final tasks is to set the Database Availability Group cluster IP address. To set the cluster IP address, we right-click on the Database Availability Group in the list, and choose **Properties**:

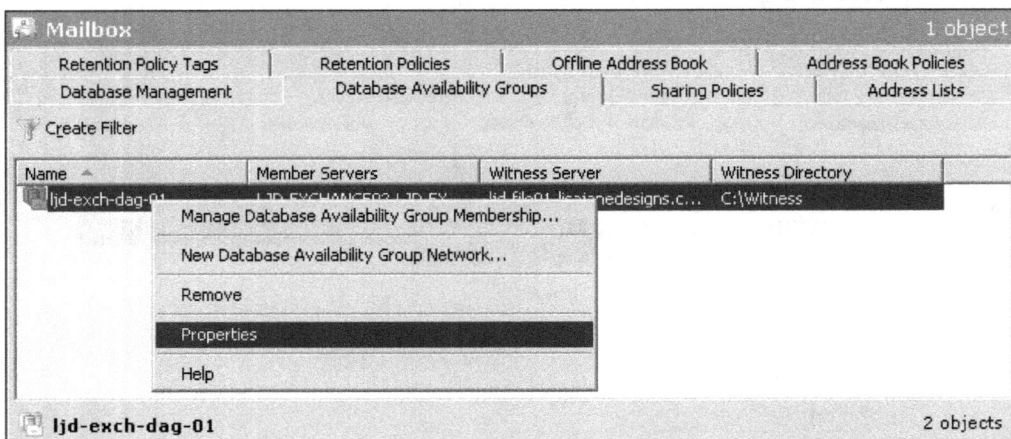

Navigate to the **IP Addresses** tab and add the IP address as defined earlier in the chapter, then press **OK**:

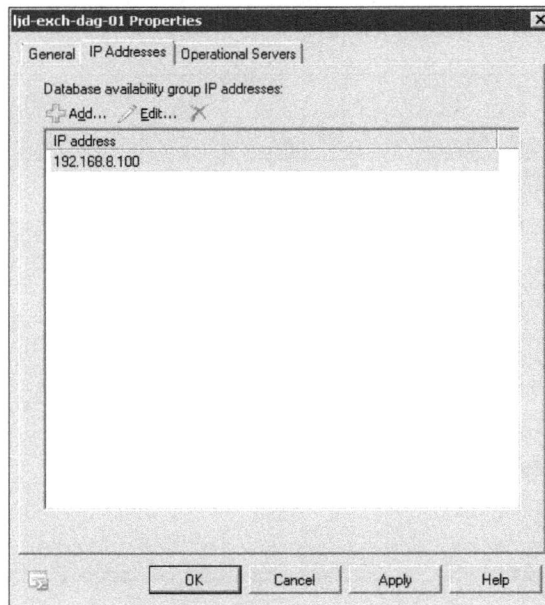

Our final task is to add Mailbox database copies to each server, to ensure that the databases area is protected from a single server failure as per the design.

To add a second database copy for each Mailbox database, right-click each database and choose **Add Mailbox Database Copy**. For the first database, we'll add the second server and perform the reverse for the second database:

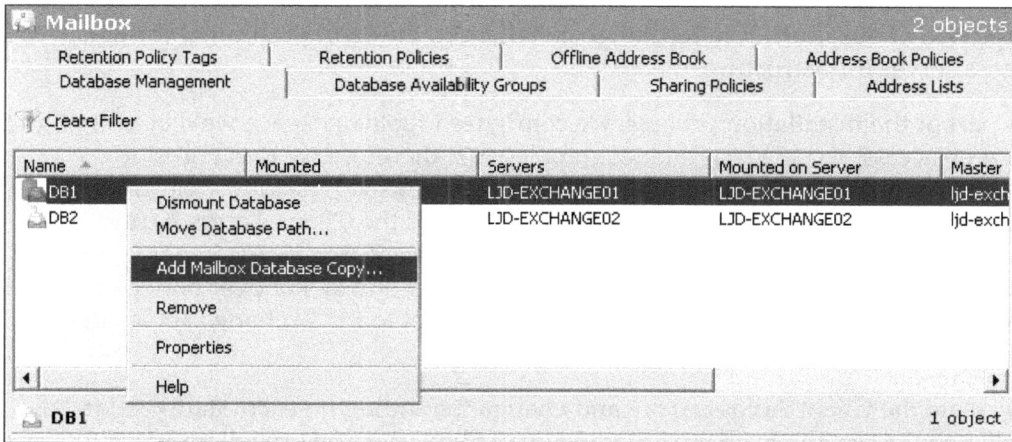

After configuring each database copy, we can check its status. For each database, we expect to see two copies, one with a **Copy Status** of **Mounted** and the second with a status of **Healthy**:

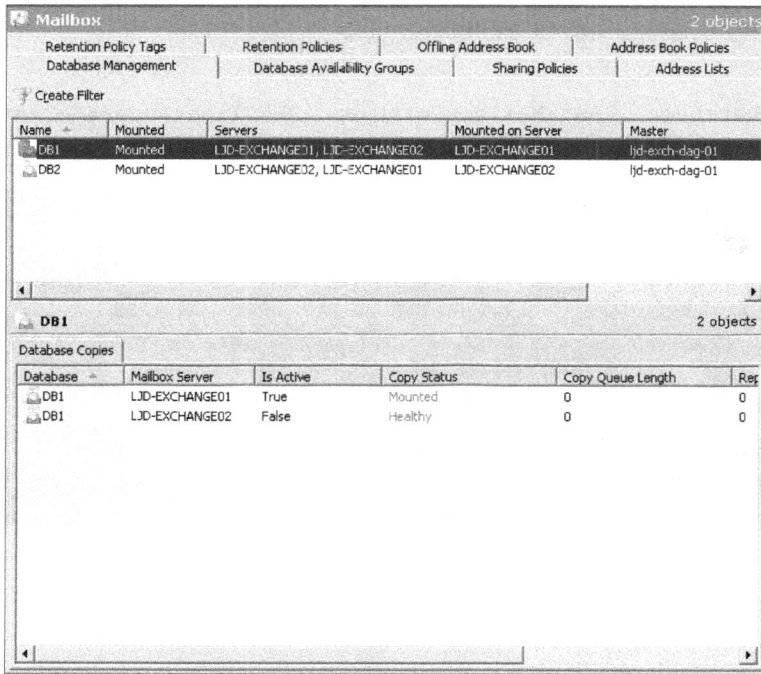

Configuring the Client Access Array and Load Balancing

After configuring the Database Availability Group, we're now ready to move onto stage two of our multi-role Exchange installation, the configuration of the client access server infrastructure.

As part of the installation process, we configured the namespace we'll be using for web access, `mail.lisajanedesigns.co.uk`; therefore we don't need to manually configure these settings again. We do, however, need to create our logical namespace, `outlook.lisajanedesigns.co.uk` for the Client Access Array, used for RPC Client Access. We'll also need to set the Client Access Array name on each Mailbox database to ensure that a database failover or a switchover between servers does not affect the end user. By default it will be set to the Exchange server that created its name.

To create the Client Access Array and change the setting on each Mailbox database, we'll need to use the Exchange Management Shell (the PowerShell interface to Exchange Server).

Launch the Exchange Management Shell from the **Start** menu on one of the Exchange Servers and run the following cmdlets:

```
New-ClientAccessArray -Name outlook.lisajanedesigns.co.uk -Fqdn outlook.
lisajanedesigns.co.uk -Site Nuneaton
```

```
Get-MailboxDatabase | Set-MailboxDatabase -RPCClientAccessServer outlook.
lisajanedesigns.co.uk
```

The New-ClientAccessArray cmdlet is used to create the logical entry for the Client Access Array itself. We specify an arbitrary name for the Client Access Array. In this case we've used the same as the namespace, the **Fully Qualified Domain Name (FQDN)** and we also specify the site that the Client Access Array belongs to.

After creation, it automatically assigns all servers with the Client Access role in the chosen site to the array. As it's a logical construct, it doesn't actually change any settings on the Client Access Servers themselves or create a DNS record; we'll use the Load Balancer to specify the Exchange Servers to send traffic to, and create the DNS records manually.

The second set of cmdlets, Get-MailboxDatabase and Set-MailboxDatabase, show how we can use a technique known as pipelining to retrieve information and then use that as input into a second cmdlet. We retrieve both Mailbox databases by using the Get-MailboxDatabase cmdlet, then using the pipe symbol, pass those two servers to the Set-MailboxDatabase cmdlet to perform the change of the RPC Client Access server name to the array name on both Mailbox databases.

Next, we need to configure the Load Balancer. As each Load Balancer configuration can be drastically different, we won't go through the process here, but in brief, we will specify the services, such as HTTP, HTTPS, SMTP, and RPC traffic that we will balance between Exchange Servers and add each Exchange Server as a target for the traffic.

The following screenshot shows the configuration screen of a free Load Balancer appliance aimed at Exchange 2010 installations:

Configuring DNS names

After configuring the Client Access Array and Load Balancer, the next step is to add DNS names to match our Exchange namespaces, ideally with each **Host (A)** record set to a **Time To Live (TTL)** value of 5 minutes to ensure that in the event of a total failure of the Load Balancer, clients can be redirected at an individual Client Access Server quickly.

In the implementation at Lisa Jane Designs, we'll be using a split DNS setup with entries for `mail.lisajanedesigns.co.uk` and `autodiscover.lisajanedesigns.co.uk` added to the external DNS and internal Active Directory DNS entries for `mail.lisajanedesigns.co.uk`, `outlook.lisajanedesigns.co.uk`, and `autodiscover.lisajanedesigns.co.uk` corresponding to the external IP address forwarded by the firewall, and the internal shared virtual IP address of the Load Balancer respectively:

mail	Host (A)
outlook	Host (A)
autodiscover	Host (A)

Configuring certificates

SSL Certificates allow HTTP communications to be encrypted, typically known as HTTPS. By default, Exchange installs a self-signed certificate onto each server after installation. Aalthough this is ideal to ensure the core functionality works, we'll need to replace the certificate with one signed by a trusted authority before we get ready for production use.

We have two options for certificates:

- We can install and configure our own certificate authority and publish our certificate authority's certificate to clients
- We can utilize a third-party certificate authority that is already trusted by the clients we're planning to use

The recommended certificate type for Exchange Server is a **Subject Alternative Name (SAN)** certificate. This type of certificate is ideal because it allows more than one DNS name to be associated with a single certificate—common with nearly all Exchange deployments. Wildcard certificates can also be used (where a certificate covers an entire domain); however, SAN certificates are typically the best option.

For Lisa Jane Designs we're initially going to use a third-party certificate authority, but the process within Exchange to generate a certificate using the Exchange Management Console is identical.

To begin, we'll click on the **Server Configuration** node and select the first Exchange Server to examine the current certificates, then right-click and choose **New Exchange Certificate**:

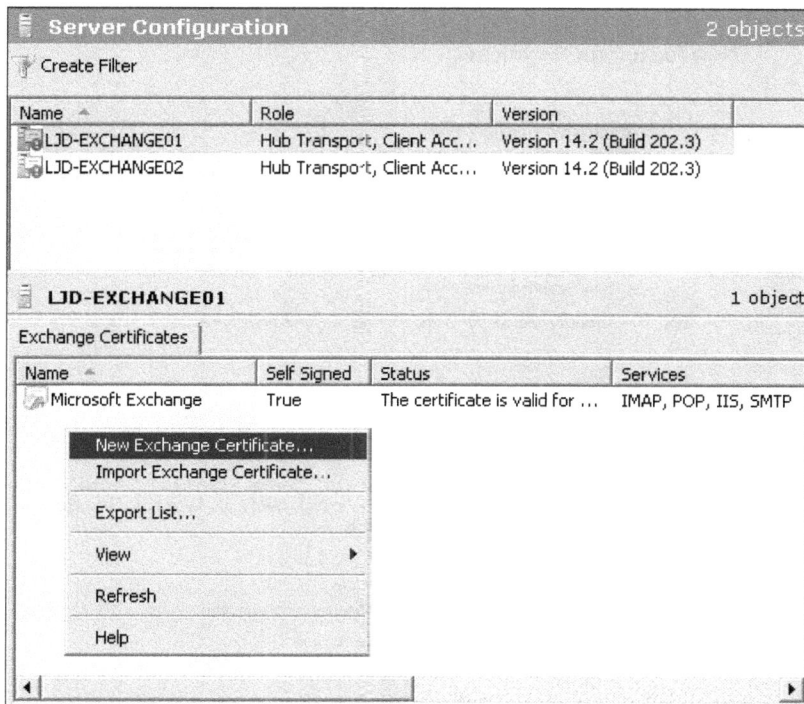

The **New Exchange Certificate** generation wizard provides an ideal chance to review the Exchange namespaces chosen. Note that we don't require the Client Access Array logical name `outlook.lisajanedesigns.co.uk` on the certificate, and identify any names that may also be required—typically it can be troublesome to add extra names to a certificate after it's been issued. We review the suggested names, correcting and removing them where required:

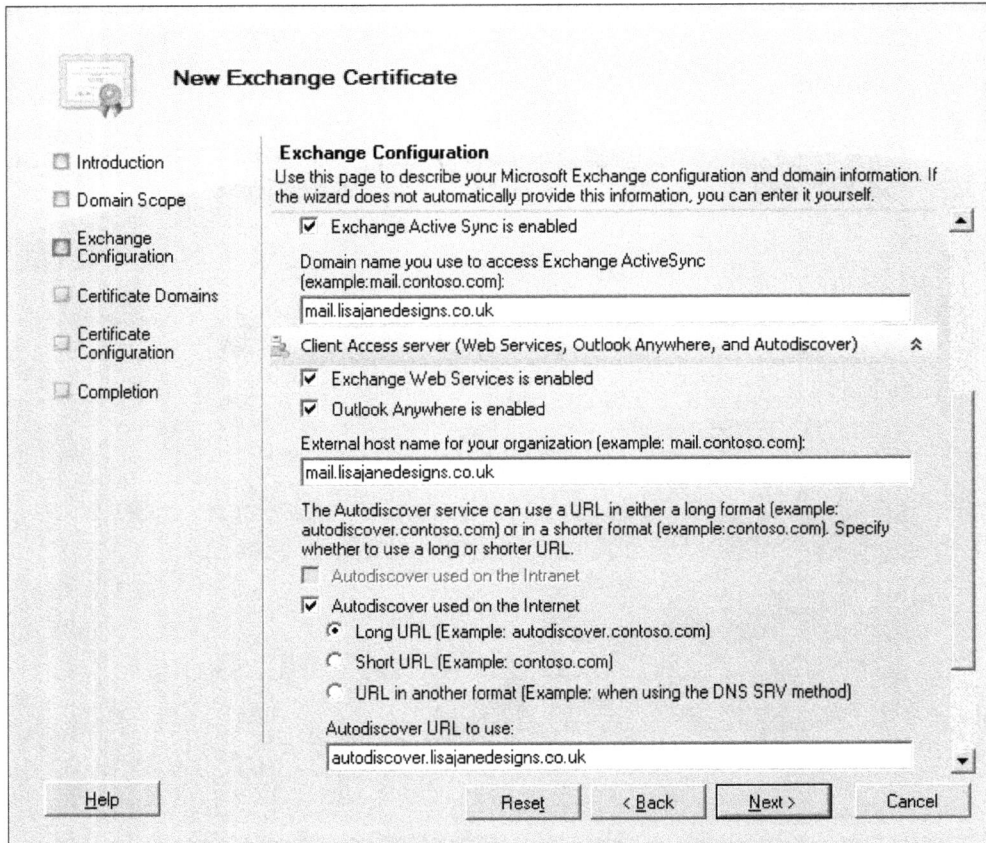

After completing the wizard, we will have generated a text based file known as a **Certificate Signing Request (CSR)**. We'll use the CSR in the process to request the certificate from the third-party certificate authority, then after certificate issuance, right click on the certificate request in the Exchange Management Console and choose **Complete Pending Request**, specifying the location to the certificate CRT or CER file:

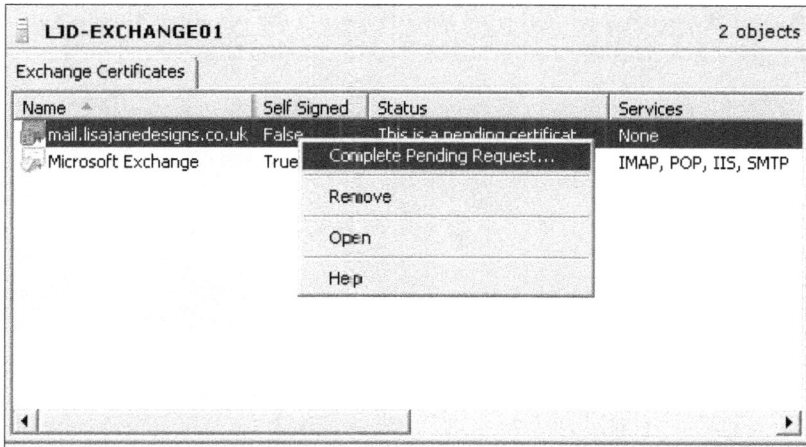

After completing the certificate request on the first server, we'll need to export the certificate and its private key to a file so that we can import it into the second Exchange Server.

To export the certificate, right-click on the certificate, and choose **Export Exchange Certificate**:

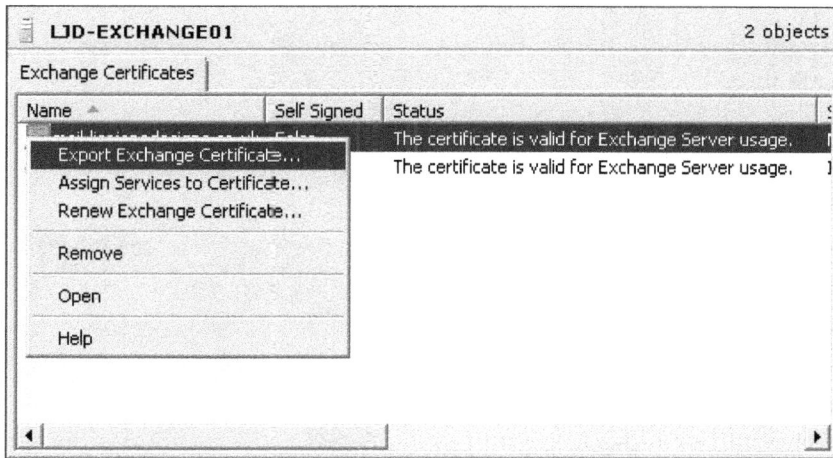

After exporting the certificate and private key to a file, we select the second Exchange Server, and right-click and choose **Import Exchange Certificate**:

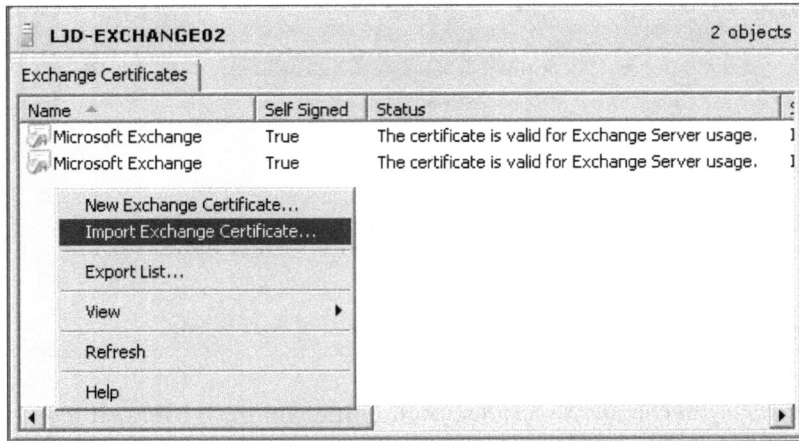

Finally, with both Exchange Servers holding a valid copy of the certificate, we can enable them for use by IIS, and therefore Exchange services like ActiveSync and Outlook Web App by right-clicking the certificate on either server and choosing **Assign Services to Certificate**.

We have options to choose both services and options to pick IIS as a service to assign the certificate to.

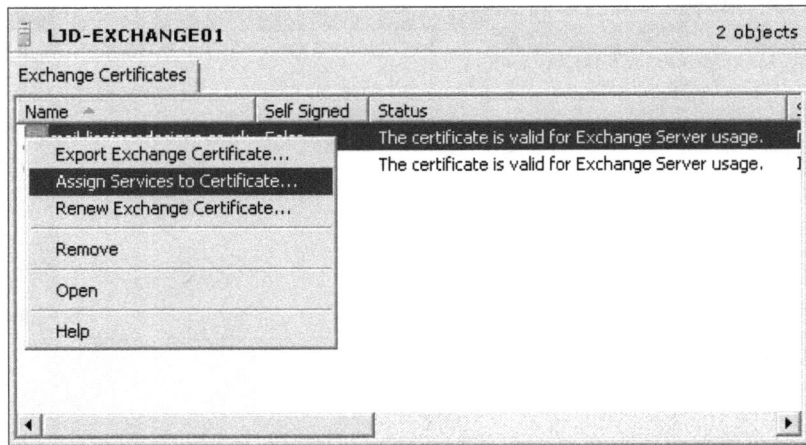

Configuring Outlook Anywhere

Our final Client Access related task is to enable **Outlook Anywhere**. Although not a requirement for iPhone connectivity, for the purposes of our example organization, we have a large number of remote users and Outlook Anywhere will allow access to Exchange Server from the Outlook client without any requirement for a VPN. Outlook Anywhere works by using RPC over HTTPS, encapsulating RPC traffic within a secure HTTPS session to provide MAPI access without exposing the RPC Client Access layer directly to the Internet.

To enable Outlook Anywhere, navigate to **Server Configuration | Client Access** and right-click on each Exchange Server and choose **Enable Outlook Anywhere**. When prompted, we'll enter our primary HTTP based namespace, `mail.lisajanedesigns.co.uk`:

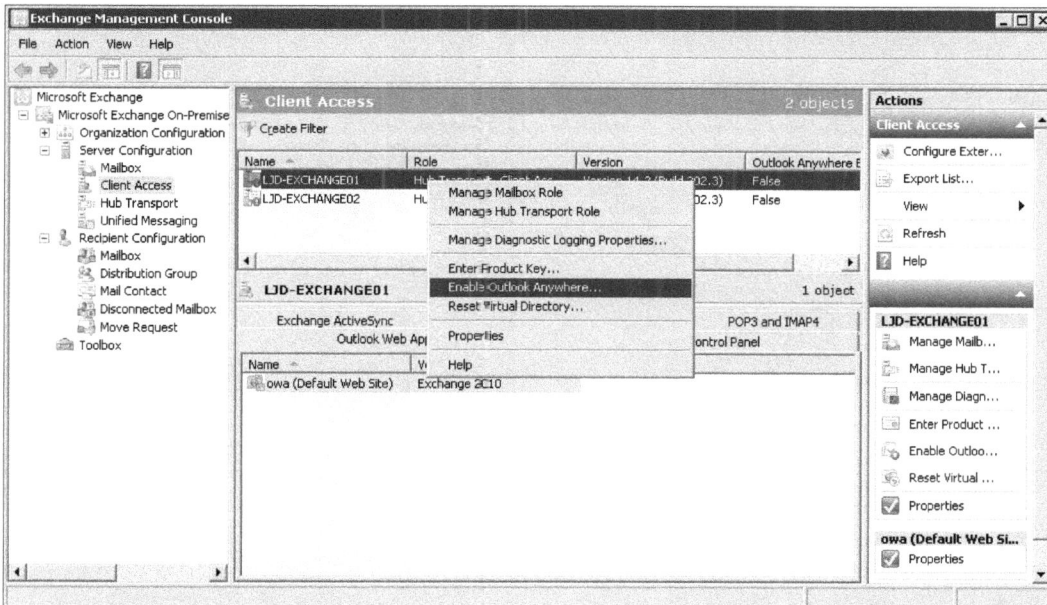

Configuring Send Connector

Before we complete our configuration, we'll need to set up the Exchange Servers so they can send and receive mail from the Internet.

First, we'll configure the Send Connector, which is responsible for delivering outbound mail to its destination. When choosing how to route mail, we've got a couple of options. We can either choose to allow the Exchange Server to look up the destination mail servers itself, and attempt to deliver mail directory, or we can use a smart host. A smart host is a mail server that we can deliver all outbound mail to and it will take the responsibility for routing mail to its final destination.

As part of our design, we'll be using Microsoft's **Forefront Online Protection for Exchange (FOPE)**. The FOPE service allows us to use their services as a smarthost. After registering our public IP addresses with their service, we'll configure our Send Connector to use their smarthost.

To begin, we navigate to **Organization Configuration | Hub Transport** and click on the **Send Connectors** tab. Right-click and choose **New Send Connector**:

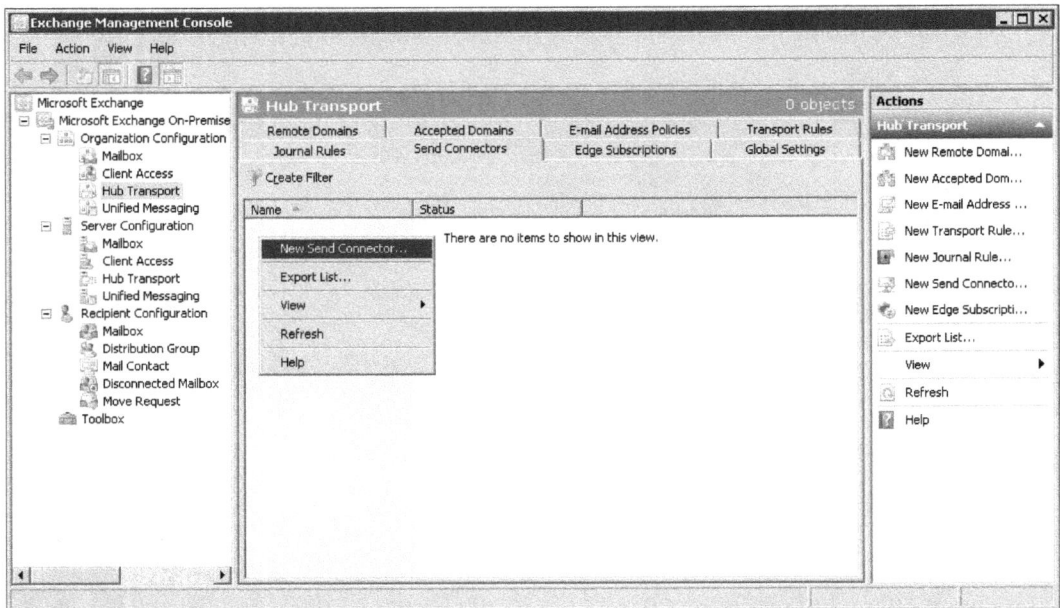

When creating the **Send Connector**, we'll use the following options:

- Custom Send Connector
- An address space of "*"
- Route mail through the smart host specific to FOPE, `mail.messaging.microsoft.com` with no authentication
- Use both Exchange Servers as source servers for the send connector

After configuration of the Send Connector, it should be shown in the list, enabled:

Configuring accepted domains and Receive Connectors

Now we've configured outbound mail, we'll also need to configure the necessary settings to allow inbound mail.

First, we'll check that the accepted domains include our own, `lisajanedesigns.co.uk`. We'd expect them to, as it's identical to the Active Directory domain name:

We're outsourcing our mail filtering, but if we weren't we'd need to configure a few more areas, such as considerations for the Edge Roles, to ensure mail received by users is clean. In an outsourced scenario, we can instead restrict, at a firewall level, access to inbound TCP port 25 so that only the provider's IP ranges can attempt to deliver mail. Our MX records for the `lisajanedesigns.co.uk` will be set up to deliver mail to FOPE, which in turn will be configured to deliver mail to the Exchange Servers.

To allow inbound mail, we need to configure the default Receive Connector on each Exchange Server to allow anonymous clients to submit mail. Navigating to **Server Configuration | Hub Transport**, we see the **Default** Receive Connector for each server:

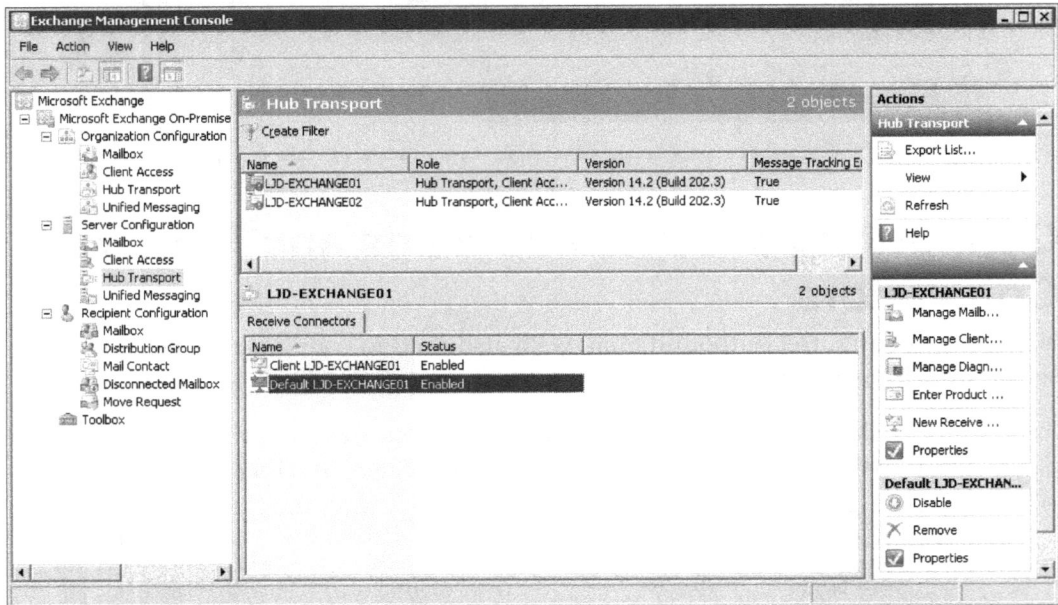

Right-click on the default Receive Connector, and choose **Properties**. Then in the **Permission Groups** tab, ensure **Anonymous users** is ticked.

Testing client connectivity

After configuring the base settings for Exchange, we should now have an Exchange organization with client access, mail connectivity, and high availability. We should now be ready to perform a few basic tests, and then connect our first iPhone to the new Exchange Server infrastructure.

Creating a test Mailbox

Before we can test anything, we need to create a test Mailbox. By default, the Administrator account on our domain has been enabled as a Mailbox. As a Domain Admin we won't be able to pair an ActiveSync device with the Administrator account due to default security settings; this is a sensible best practice so we won't change this.

To create our first test Mailbox, we navigate in the **Exchange Management Console** to **Recipient Configuration | Mailbox** and right-click and choose **New Mailbox**.

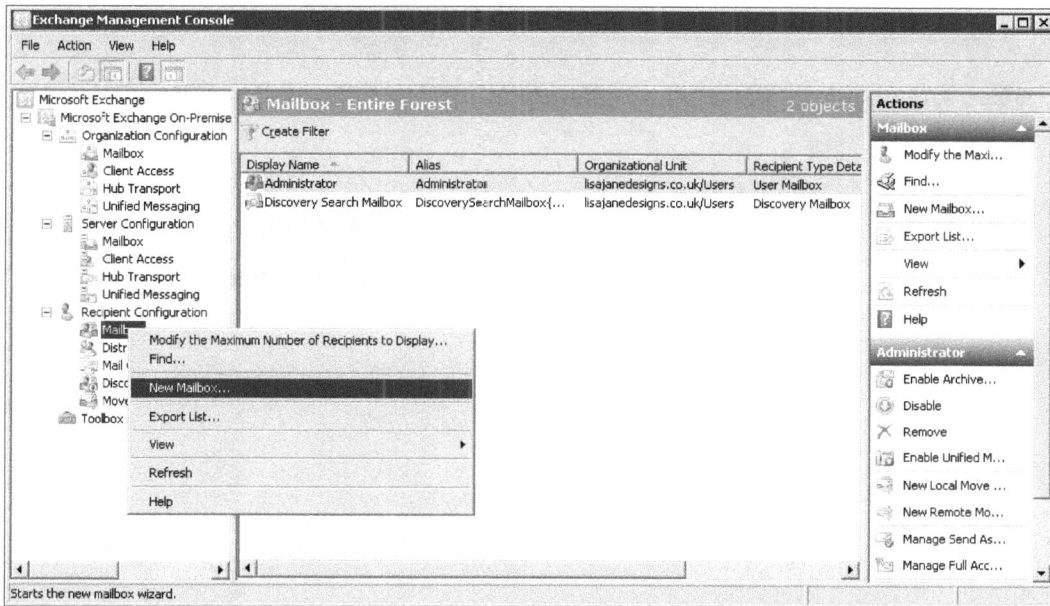

Follow the wizard through, choosing appropriate options such as the following:

- A mailbox type of User Mailbox
- Creating a new Active Directory user or enable an existing test user account
- Leave defaults for policies unchecked at this stage

Testing basic client connectivity

After creation of a new mailbox, we should be able to log in at our Outlook Web App URL, `https://mail.lisajanedesigns.co.uk/owa`, and perform a few tests, such as the following:

- Sending and receiving mail between internal and external accounts

- Connections from internal and external connections to ensure the DNS entries are set up correctly both in the Active Directory DNS and with our external DNS provider

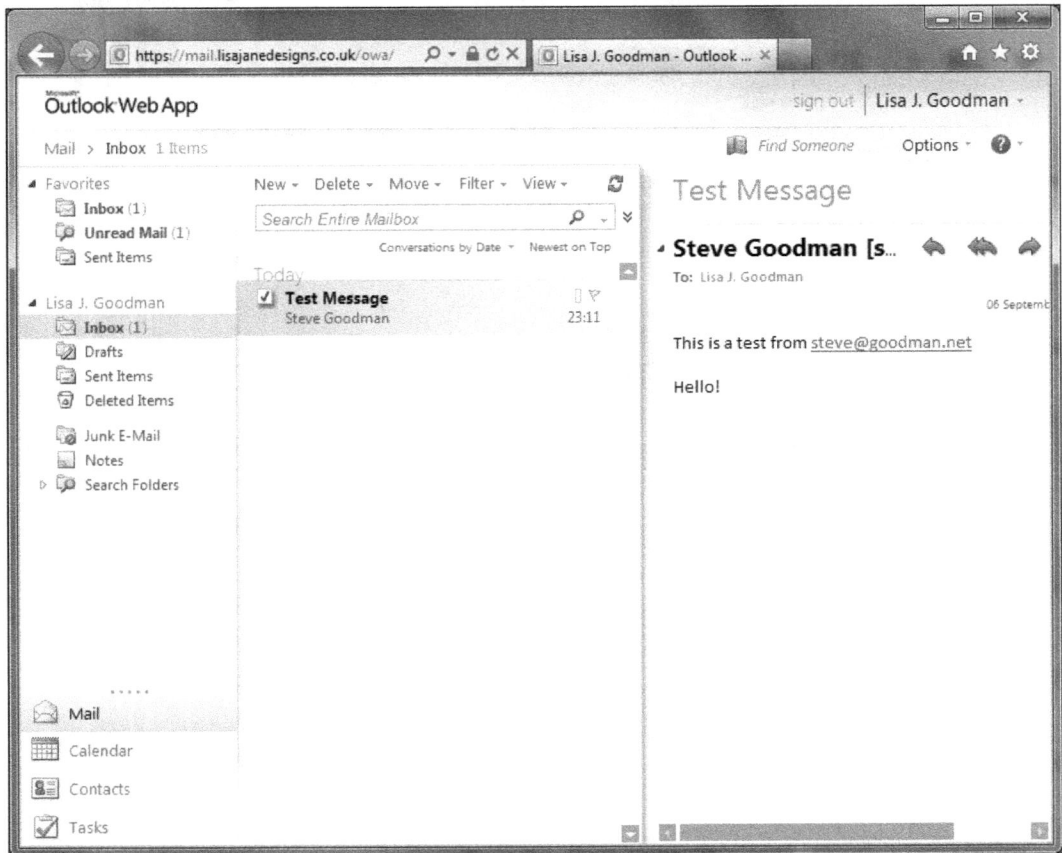

If we encounter any issues, we'll need to work through some basic troubleshooting, such as the following:

- Checking the DNS records are configured correctly both internally and externally
- Checking ports are open to receive inbound messages
- Checking the configuration and message tracking options in Forefront Online Protection for Exchange
- Checking out the mail flow troubleshooting tools in the Exchange Management Console, under **Toolbox**

Testing AutoDiscover and ActiveSync functionality

At this point, after testing we can successfully use Outlook Web Access, we need to check that AutoDiscover works correctly and ActiveSync clients can connect to the Exchange Servers over the Internet.

Microsoft provides a web-based tool, called the **Remote Connectivity Analyzer**, that simulates the process a client uses to connect to the Exchange Servers. Visit the Remote Connectivity Analyzer at the following URL:

```
http://www.testexchangeconnectivity.com
```

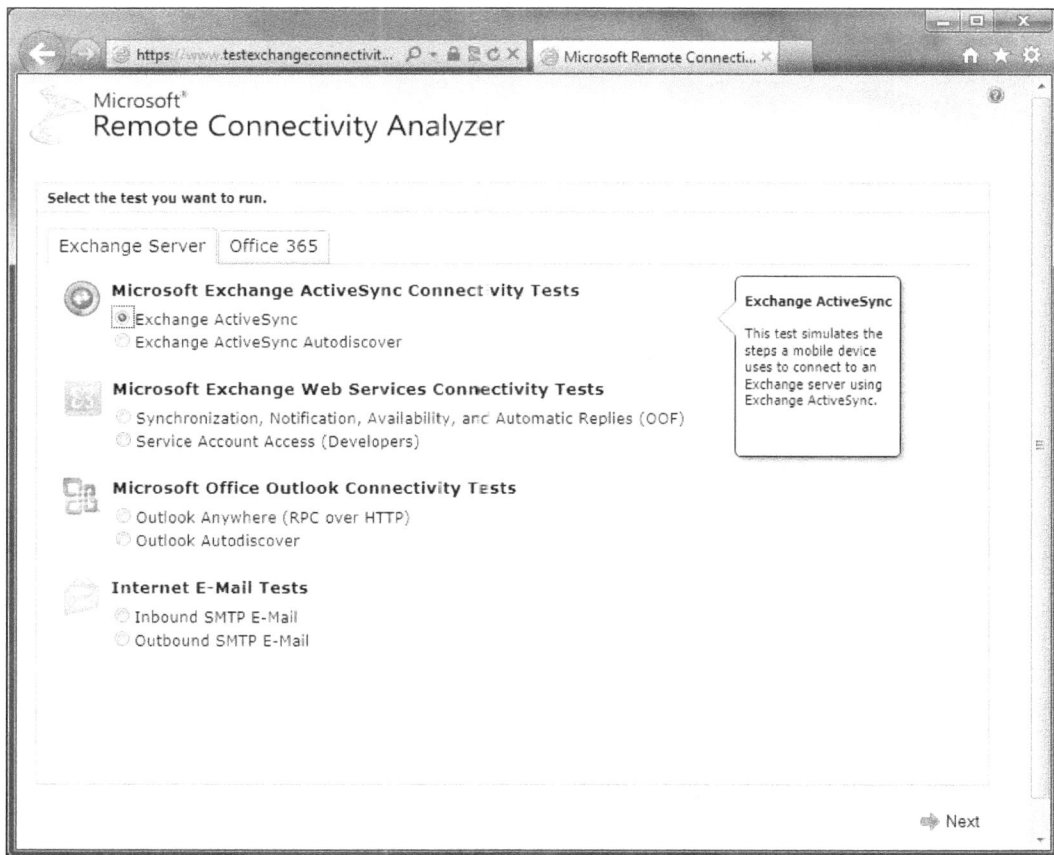

By selecting **Exchange ActiveSync**, listed under **Microsoft Exchange ActiveSync Connectivity Tests**, we are prompted for credentials to connect to the Exchange Servers. Then, the Remote Connectivity Analyzer will attempt to use AutoDiscover to simulate the lookup process and attempt to connect to the mailbox.

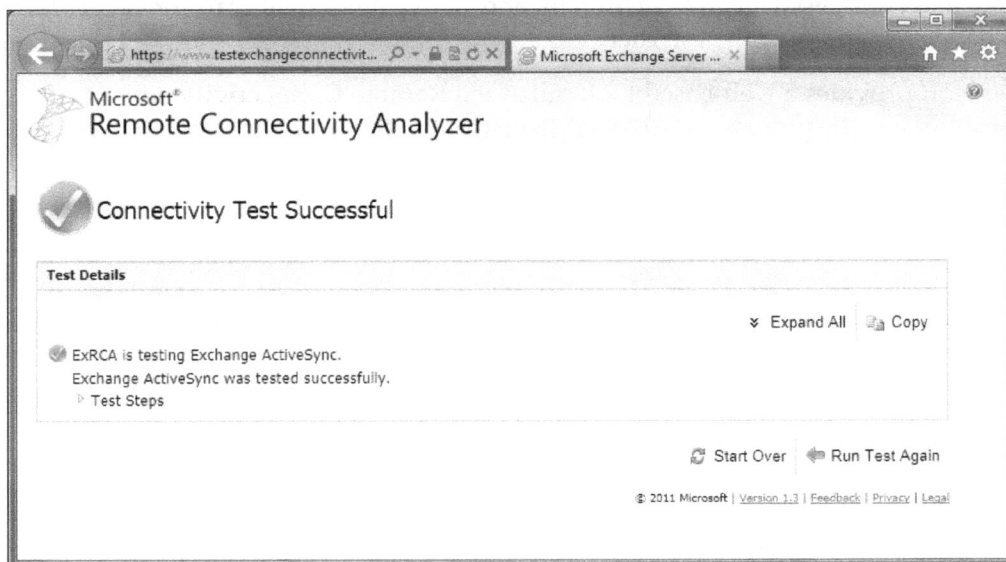

If the connection is successful, the message **Exchange ActiveSync was tested successfully** will be displayed. If the test is unsuccessful, we can expand **Test Steps** to diagnose where the test has failed and by investigating the error message, we can then correct the error and re-test. Typical reasons for failure might include:

- **Certificate errors**: such as if the SSL certificate is untrusted or invalid
- **DNS lookup errors**: for addresses such as the AutoDiscover name
- **Firewall issues**: preventing connection to the Load Balancer from external addresses

After successfully testing ActiveSync and AutoDiscover functionality, we're ready to connect our first iPhone to the new Exchange infrastructure.

Testing iPhone connectivity

To test out whether an iPhone can successfully connect to and use our Exchange Servers, we'll manually add an Exchange account to an iPhone. To add an account manually, go to **Settings** | **Mail** and choose **Add Account**, then select **Microsoft Exchange**:

Next, enter the **Email**, **Username**, and **Password** for the account. When asked for the **Domain** and **Username**, we can either enter the NetBIOS domain name (for example, LISAJANEDESIGNS) and the Windows logon username on its own, or simply enter the User Principal name (for example, lisa@lisajanedesigns.co.uk) on its own in the **Username** field:

After tapping **Next**, the iPhone will attempt to use AutoDiscover to look up the Client Access DNS name, `mail.lisajanedesigns.co.uk`. If successful, this should be displayed in the **Server** field. Choose **Save** to store the new account on the iPhone.

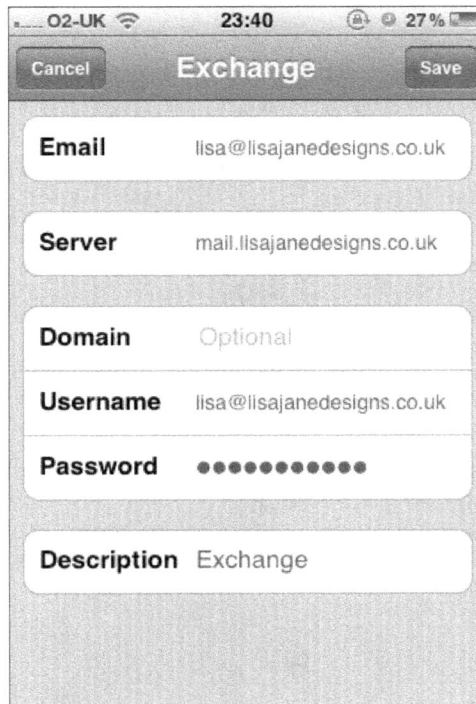

After a couple of minutes, the iPhone should complete its first synchronization with the Exchange Servers and the mail we've sent and received when testing from Outlook Web App should be shown. We'll use some of the same tests used with Outlook Web App, such as attempting to send and receive mail, and test both against internal Wireless LAN access and over an Edge or 3G data connection.

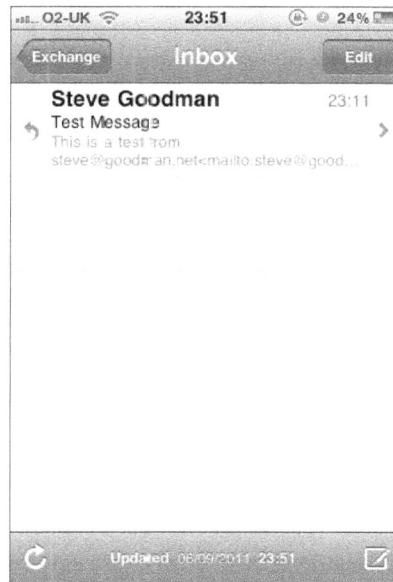

Summary

In this chapter, we've taken the design from the previous chapter, and on two Windows servers implemented Exchange according to that design from start to finish. We've covered the basics of preparing Active Directory, installation of pre-requisites, and installation of Exchange Server itself.

After installation we've configured a Database Availability Group to provide resilience and high availability for our Mailbox role. We've also configured Load Balancing to share the client load and provide high availability for the Client Access role. Combined, these features provide a very reliable Exchange infrastructure in a fairly small package.

We also went through the basics of configuring Exchange, such as creating SSL certificates, configuring Outlook Anywhere, and configuring the Hub Transport role to send and receive mail.

Finally, we've tested our Exchange infrastructure to ensure that we can not only send and receive mail between internal and external users successfully, but we've also reached an important point—we're able to connect an iPhone to our new Exchange infrastructure and use it to send and receive mail.

In the next chapter, we'll be looking at how easy Office 365 is to configure and get using.

4

Office 365 Configuration for iOS Connectivity

In the previous two chapters, we've covered the full installation and configuration of a basic but highly available Exchange Server 2010 infrastructure. However, it doesn't have to be that way. If you're prepared to sacrifice some of the control, such as determining when and how the underlying Exchange infrastructure is maintained and upgraded, then there's another option, Office 365.

Microsoft's cloud-based online-services offering provides Exchange Server 2010 along with Lync Online and SharePoint Online 2010, and is paid for through a monthly subscription. In this chapter, we're going to cover the following:

- Sign-up process for Office 365
- DNS Configuration
- Testing and Troubleshooting
- Connecting an iOS device to Exchange Online

For this chapter, we're going to consider an alternative scenario for Lisa Jane Designs — one where our fictional company has decided to instead use a hosted service for Exchange rather than build an on-premises mail server infrastructure.

The options for a hosted Office 365 installation are varied but include options to use federation that allows local Active Directory credentials to be used, directory synchronization that allows automatic account creation and updating based on local Active Directory users, and the ability to create a hybrid configuration where some accounts are hosted on-premises and some are hosted in Office 365.

One of the great things about Office 365 is that it's not an all or nothing solution; a business could start with Office 365 and move to on-premises services, start with a on-premises service and move to Office 365, or keep a combination of the two. It's not an all-or nothing solution and it's possible to move between the two with fairly little disruption. Therefore it would be reasonable for an organization to start off with Office 365 and if they outgrow it, move to an on-premises solution if it makes more sense at a later date.

The example we're using for Lisa Jane Designs is really to show the most basic scenario demonstrating how simple it is to get up-and-running with a simple Office 365 tenant aimed squarely at providing Exchange for our mobile workforce. We won't cover some of the more complex aspects, such as federation and directory synchronization. Although both features are very useful, they are a little out of the scope of what we want to demonstrate and aren't required to use the basic features.

Sign-up process for Office 365

Enrolling with Office 365 is very straightforward, and to get a flavor for what Office 365 offers it's possible to sign up for a trial account.

Three main service plans or options are available for Office 365:

Service Plan	Minimum/Maximum Users	On Premise Integration
Office 365 for Professionals and Small Businesses	1-50	No
Office 365 for Midsize Businesses and Enterprises	1-10,000+	Yes
Office 365 for Education	1-10,000+	Yes

The most basic version, for professionals and small businesses, aimed at less than 25 users is the most limited and doesn't provide some of the more advanced features, but the latter options provide the full feature set.

It's not possible to move between the professionals/small businesses version and midsize business/enterprise/education versions, so if the advanced features like federation, hybrid configurations, directory synchronization, and PowerShell management are likely to be required, it's worth starting with the option that you wish to use on a long-term basis.

For our example, we're signing up for Office 365 for midsize businesses and enterprises. We begin the sign-up process by visiting the Office365 website at `http://www.microsoft.com/en-in/office365/online-software.aspx` and choosing **Get Office 365**.

As part of the sign-up process, we'll need to provide some details, such as contact information. Create a Microsoft Online Services ID to use as the Administrator username and password, then choose a starter domain, in the form *domainname.onmicrosoft.com*.

The starter domain hosts the Administrator account and also functions as a fully-functional domain to send and receive email with—perfect for an isolated trial, but for our example company, Lisa Jane Designs, we'll be adding on the `lisajanedesigns.co.uk` domain later in the process.

After the sign-up process is complete, we'll be taken to the Office 365 Administrator portal immediately:

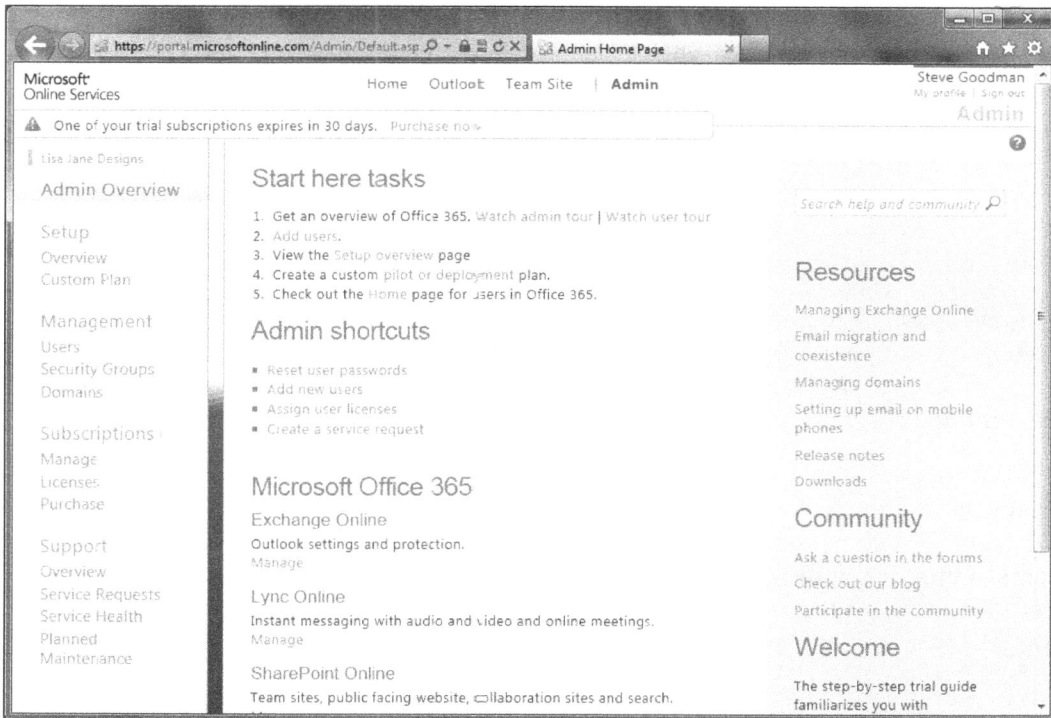

You'll see the Administrator portal is task-based, utilizing a menu on the left-hand side. The menu provides a list of tasks we can accomplish, split into **Setup**, **Management**, **Subscription**, and **Support** sections.

The main section provides the relevant tasks based on the option we've selected. The home page provides an overview of our Office 365 tenant, including the services we have available and tasks we can accomplish to complete configuration. On the home page in particular, we also see a right-hand column which provides relevant links to help get started with Office 365 and get quick access to community-based support.

Finally, at the top of the page, we can access the end-user aspects of Office 365, by clicking on the **Home** link. This takes us to the end-user view of Office 365 including links to Outlook Web Access, Lync installer, and access to SharePoint services.

If it's your first time accessing the Office 365 portal, it's worth exploring all the various administrator and end-user pages to get a feel for Office 365, and perhaps registering on the community forums as they can be a useful source of help, assistance, and knowledge. You can return to the Administrative portal at any time by visiting the following URL:

`http://portal.microsoftonline.com`

After having a look round the interface, it's time to begin our first task — configuration of the `lisajanedesigns.co.uk` domain on Office 365.

Domain and DNS configuration

The core task to enable us to make use of Office 365 for our example company, Lisa Jane Designs, is to configure the domain so we can use it for incoming and outgoing mail, and AutoDiscover purposes.

Before we start, we need access to modify the external DNS settings for our domain, `lisajanedesigns.co.uk`. In our example organization, we have a split-DNS setup with an Active Directory integrated zone for `lisajanedesigns.co.uk`, so we'll also be applying the changes to the Active Directory zone too.

We'll also need to be prepared to wait for a short time during the steps, as DNS updates can take minutes to hours to propagate. A good rule of thumb when adding DNS entries to an external DNS provider is to add a test record and see how long it takes until it can be resolved. It's also worth double checking any DNS changes before applying them, as correcting mistakes can result in longer waits for the incorrect records to expire.

To get started, our first step is to visit **Management | Domains** on the Office 365 administrative portal:

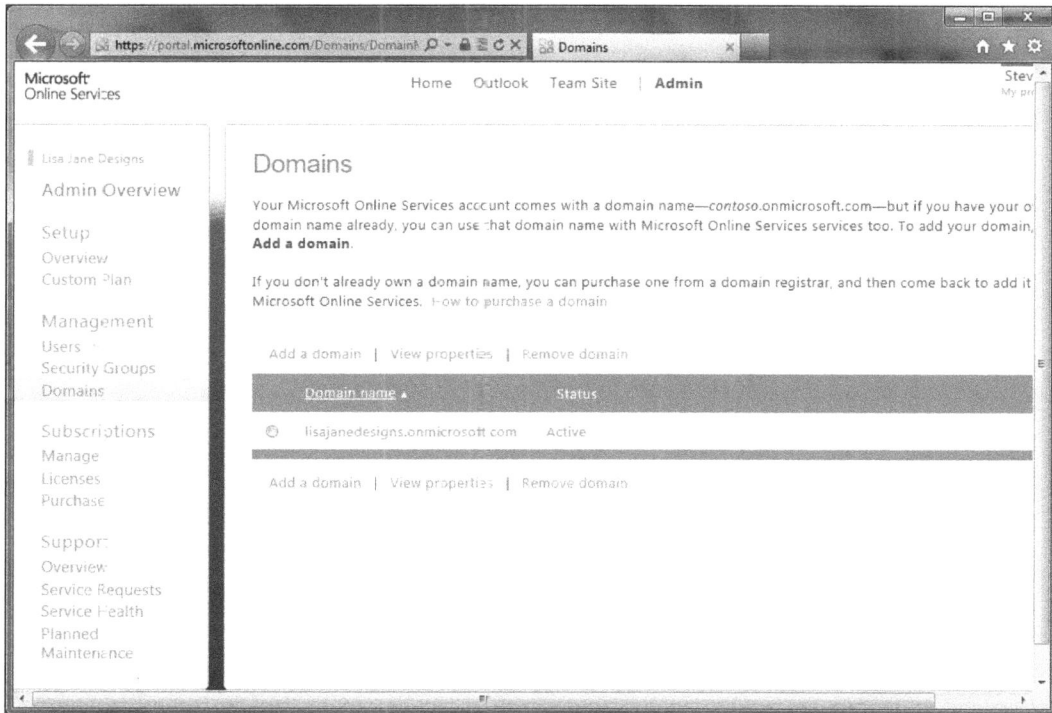

On the domains page, we see a list of the current domains associated with our Office 365 tenant. At this stage, we just see the `lisajanedesigns.onmicrosoft.com` default domain used by our Administrator account.

To add our primary domain, we simply choose **Add a domain** to launch the wizard that will assist us with addition and configuration of the lisajanedesigns.co.uk domain:

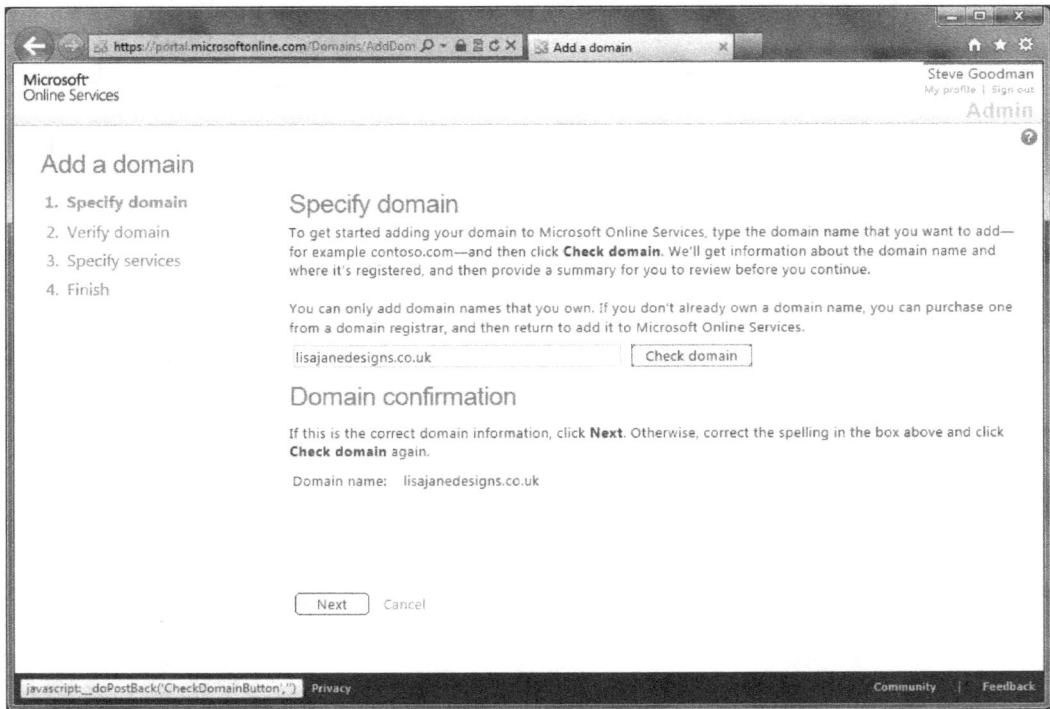

On the first page of the **Add a domain** wizard, we're asked to enter the domain we wish to add to Office 365, and press **Check domain**. By checking the domain, Microsoft validates whether the domain is registered, and ensures that it's not already in use by another Microsoft online services tenant by Office 365, Live@EDU, or Business Productivity Online Suite services.

Once the checks are complete, we'll be asked to verify ownership of the domain:

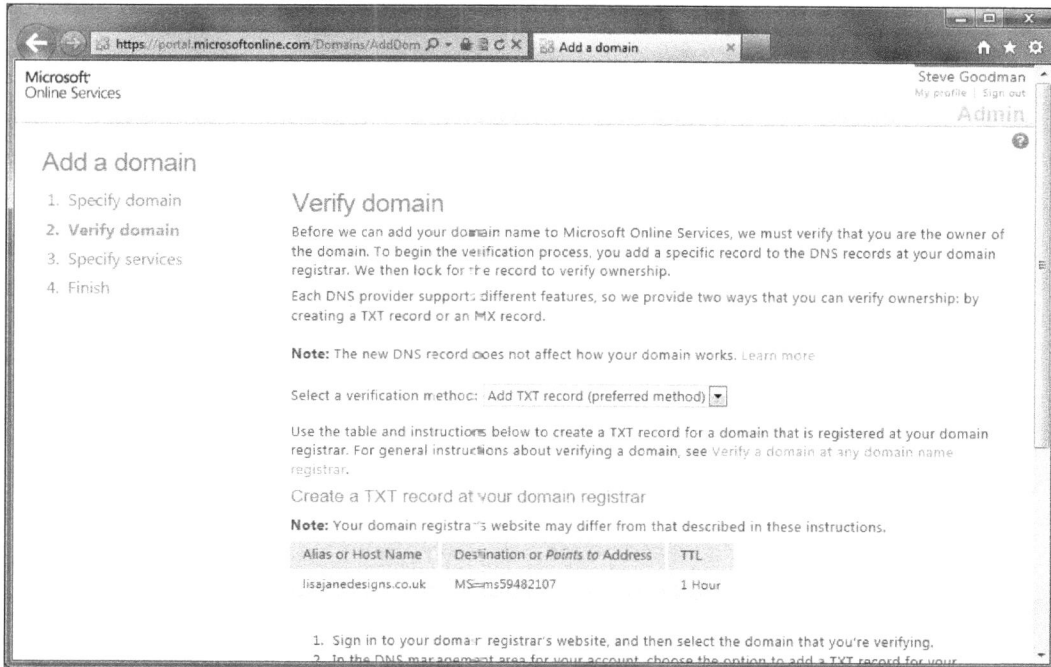

The verification process is straightforward, and involves adding either a TXT record or an MX record to our domain.

A TXT record is, as it sounds, a text record. This generally has no adverse affects on the functionality of the domain and is effectively a way of adding a "comment" to the domain. TXT records are used for a number of purposes, such as when configuring Sender Policy Framework, a technique used to reduce spam, and when configuring Federated Sharing, a way of allowing calendar and contact sharing between Exchange and Office 365 organizations.

An MX record is a mail exchanger record. MX records are used to signify which hosts are responsible for incoming mail for a domain. If the domain is already being used to host mail, then the addition of an MX record does come with some risks. The verification MX record is added at the lowest priority (signified by a high number), which means that it should be used last by mail servers attempting to send mail to the domain. It's possible that either a non-compliant e-mail server or through bad luck that other mail servers responsible for processing incoming mail become unavailable and mail is rejected, but in practice this change should have little or no effect.

For verification of our domain, we're going to opt for the TXT record:

A, CNAME and TXT records			
Name	Type	Content	Delete
@	A ▾	94.136.40.82	☐
www	A ▾	94.136.40.82	☐
	Add new entry		
@	TXT ▾	MS=ms59482107	

In the example, our external DNS control panel requires the "@" symbol to signify the record applies to the root lisajanedesigns.co.uk domain. We choose the type **TXT**, and for the content add the text value specified by Microsoft in its entirety exactly as shown on the Office 365 Administrator portal.

After waiting for the DNS records to propagate, we can return to the **Add a domain** wizard, and choose to verify that the TXT record was successfully applied.

Once the verification process is complete, we are asked to select the services we wish to associate with this domain—Exchange Online, Lync Online, or SharePoint Online. For our example, we'll just choose to configure Exchange Online:

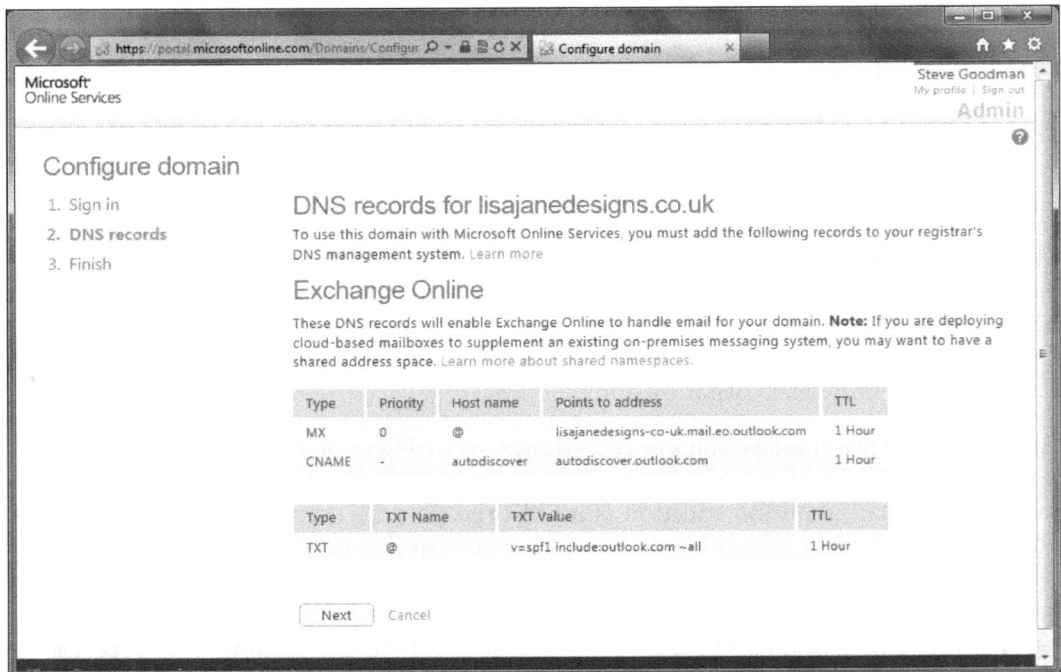

After choosing to configure the domain for Exchange Online, we'll be presented with the DNS records that are required for Exchange functionality, namely, the MX record, a CNAME (an alias record for the Auto Discover functionality), and a replacement TXT record. The TXT is used for the Sender Policy Framework functionality that effectively states that Microsoft's mail servers should be trusted when sending mail from our domain.

We'll add those to our domain as shown in the following screenshot. Note that some domain providers don't allow MX records with a priority of zero to be added (as Microsoft request), but that's okay as a priority of 5, 10, or even 20 will work just as well assuming it's the only record present:

After adding the domain we should end up with something like the following:

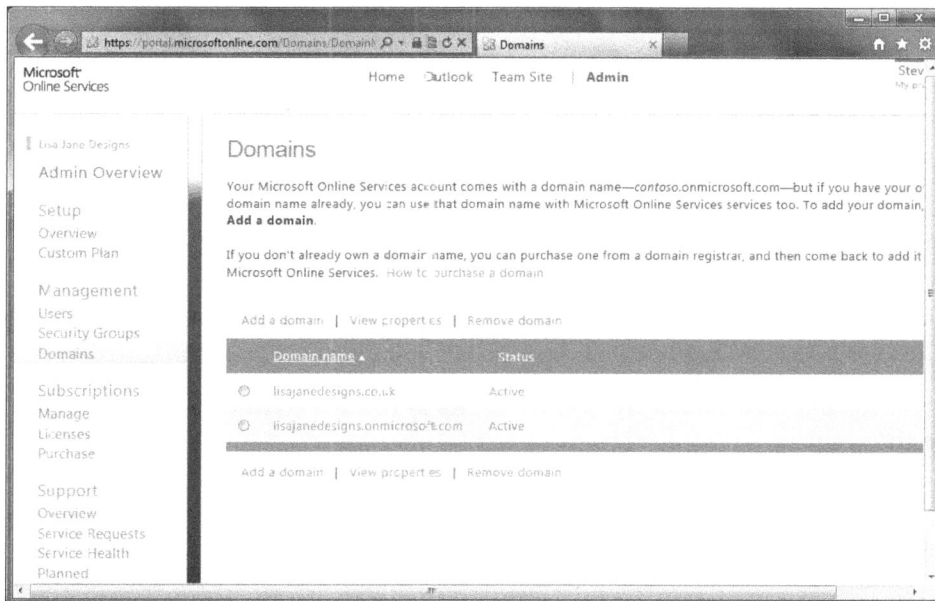

Testing and troubleshooting

After configuration of the DNS entries, we should be ready to test the Office 365 tenant and associated domain.

Checking DNS entries

After we've enabled the domain in Office 365 and configured the DNS records required, it's worth taking the opportunity to ensure that we can resolve the entries successfully. To validate the entries, we can use the built-in Windows command, `nslookup`.

We'll be looking up the three records we've added in the previous step:

```
nslookup
> autodiscover.lisajanedesigns.co.uk
Name: autodiscover.outlook.com
Address: 65.55.94.86
Aliases: autodiscover.lisajanedesigns.co.uk


> set q=MX
> lisajanedesigns.co.uk
lisajanedesigns.co.uk  MX preference = 5, mail exchanger =
    lisajanedesigns-co-uk.mail.eo.outlook.com.


> set q=TXT
> lisajanedesigns.co.uk
lisajanedesigns.co.uk  text =
    "v=spf1 include:outlook.com ~all"
```

If you've used `nslookup` before, then you might notice we've used a non-default option to look up the TXT and MX records, namely, `set q=`. This option, entered as a command at the `nslookup` prompt, sets the query type to the record type we choose; in the previous case MX, then TXT.

If the records are returned correctly, we're ready to start creating accounts and testing the service.

Creating accounts

To begin testing functionality, we need to create at least one test mailbox on our Office 365 tenant under our newly added domain, lisajanedesigns.co.uk.

Through the web browser, there are two different ways to create mailboxes. The first is in the Office 365 Administration portal, under **Management | Users** and by choosing **New | User**:

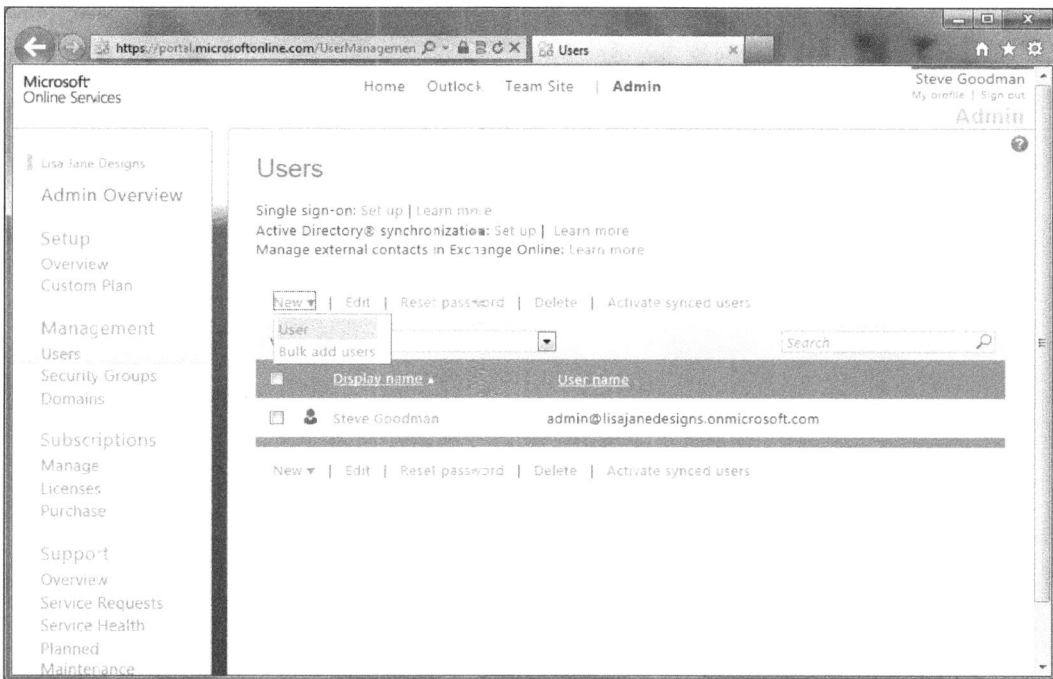

The second option, which will be more familiar to those used to Exchange Server 2010, is by means of the Exchange Control Panel. You can access this through the Office 365 Administration Portal by navigating to **Admin Overview**, then under the **Exchange Online** heading choose **Manage**. Alternatively, you can directly access the Exchange Control Panel at the following URL, replacing lisajanedesigns.co.uk with your domain name:

```
http://outlook.com/ecp?realm=lisajanedesigns.co.uk
```

The Exchange Control Panel is similar to the on-premises version, but has additional features, most importantly the ability to create mailboxes. To create a new mailbox, click **Users & Groups**, navigate to **Mailboxes**, and choose **New | User Mailbox**:

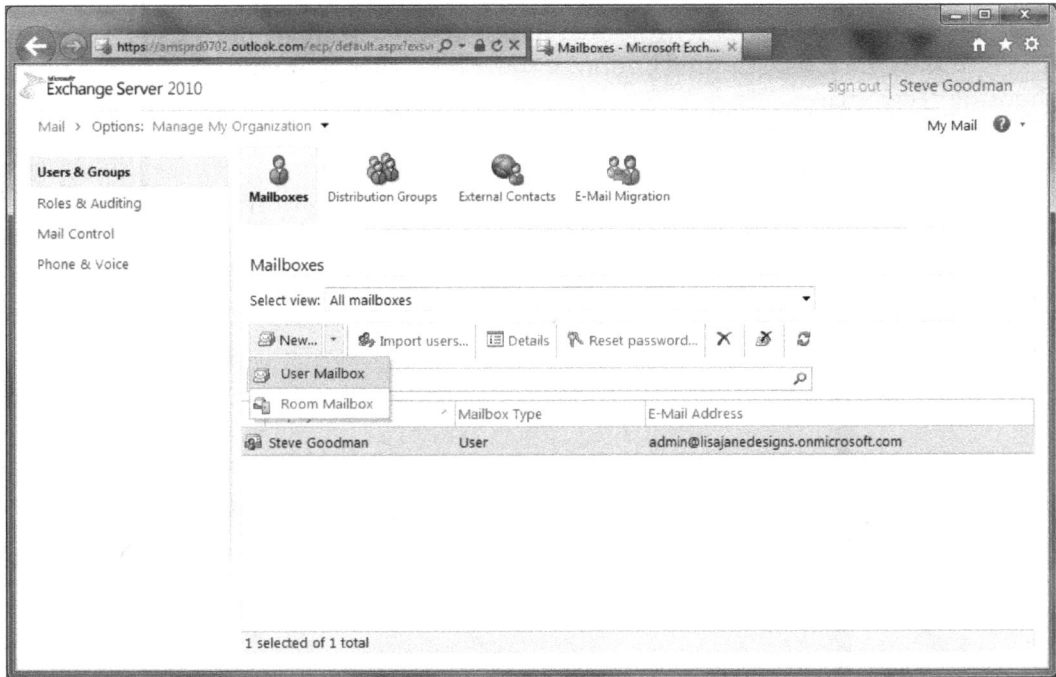

Testing the account using Outlook Web App

After creating a test mailbox, we can now attempt to log in to Outlook Web App. Exchange Online runs through the `outlook.com` domain, which is shared between Office 365 and Live@EDU. The former uses Microsoft Online Services IDs for access, while the latter uses the consumer Windows Live ID equivalent. Therefore, when distributing the URL to access Outlook Web App we append the tenant domain to allow the correct authentication service to be selected; for example:

`http://outlook.com/lisajanedesigns.co.uk`

After logging in to the service, you'll clearly see an interface similar to Outlook Web App on Exchange 2010 SP1 — the major difference to an end user is the default Office 365 branding, which can be changed through the normal template selection dialog found under **Options**.

The main purpose is to check the functionality of the service, so after sending and receiving a number of messages we see that the service is indeed functional:

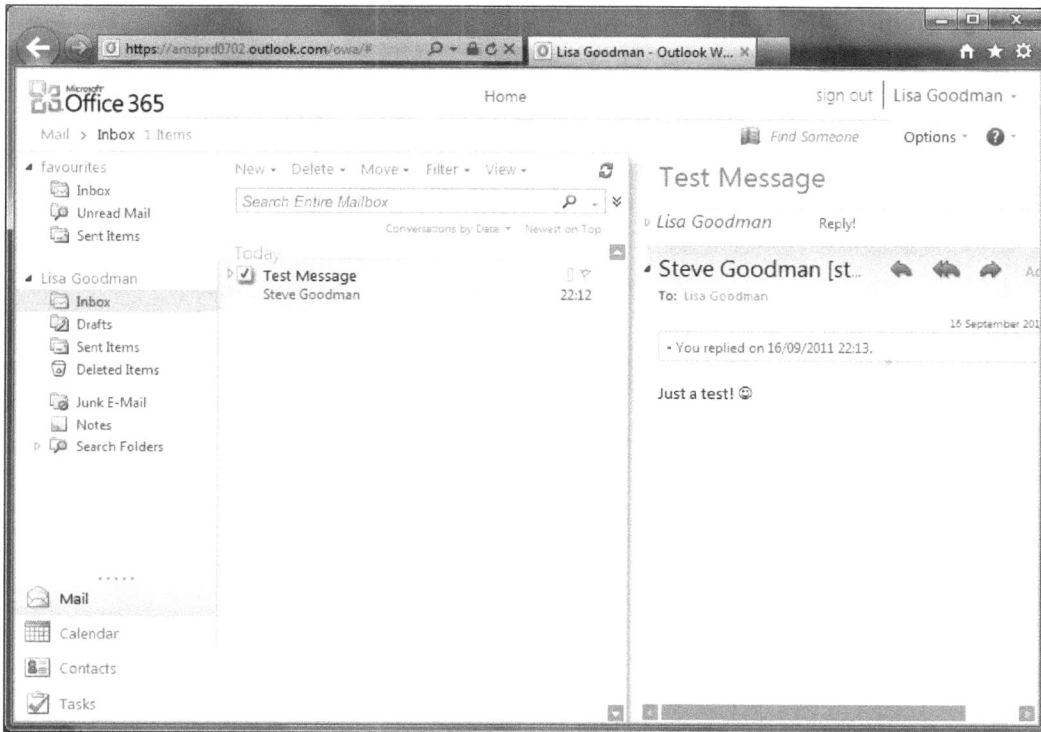

Checking ActiveSync connectivity

Before connecting our iOS device, we'll now ensure that the AutoDiscover process and ActiveSync work correctly. Although there's little reason to doubt they would — Microsoft are managing the service for millions of mailboxes and we've checked our DNS records — it's certainly worth testing connectivity beforehand to ensure the service works.

To test connectivity, we use the Remote Connectivity Analyzer — the same one used against Exchange 2010 in the previous chapter:

```
http://www.testexchangeconnectivity.com
```

On the Remote Connectivity Analyzer homepage, we select the **Office 365** tab, then select the **Exchange ActiveSync** option. On the following page, we enter our test account details and attempt the test. If the test is successful, we should be presented with information similar to the following:

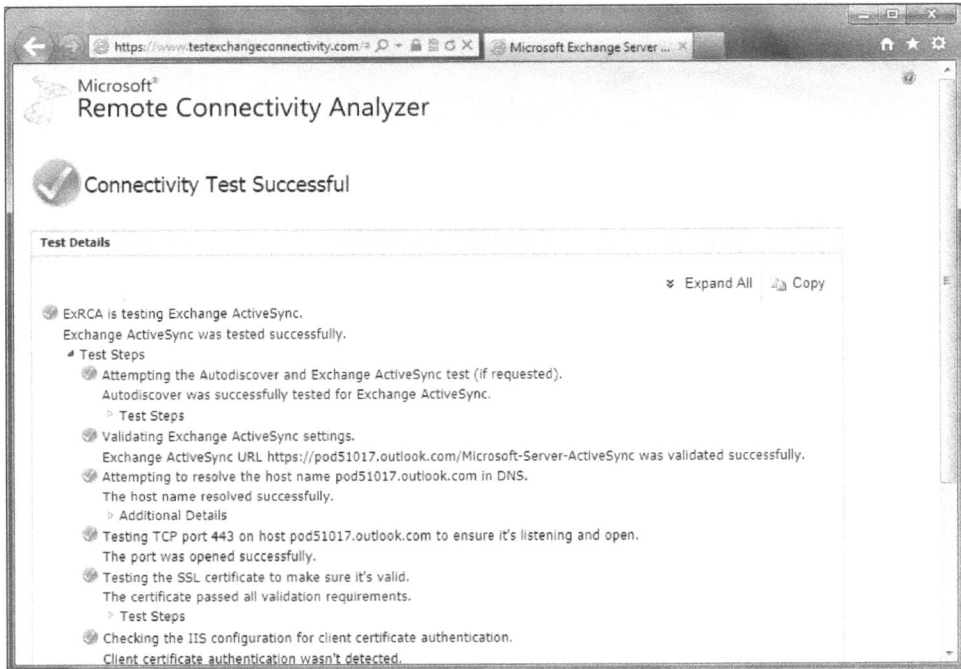

If the test fails, the first step is to investigate the error message shown by the Remote Connectivity Analyzer. If the error relates to name discovery, check the DNS entries and consider waiting a little longer for entries to propagate. If the error message appears to relate to Exchange configuration though, then it may be necessary to raise a support request through the Office 365 Administration portal.

Assuming the tests complete successfully, it should be possible to continue and configure our iOS device.

Connecting an iOS device to Office 365

Adding an Office 365 mailbox to an iPhone is an almost identical process to configuring one to work with Exchange Server 2010 — the only difference being that the server name provided as part of the Auto Discover process isn't likely to be one you already knew.

To manually add our test mailbox, navigate on the iOS device to **Settings**, then choose **Add Account...**, selecting the **Microsoft Exchange** option.

On the screen that follows, we will enter the same settings used in the Remote Connectivity Analyzer; the e-mail address, the Microsoft Online Services ID (typically the same), and the password. Then, tap **Next**:

The iOS device will now attempt to complete the Auto Discover process, and after a few moments should display a server name under the outlook.com domain:

We'll then choose **Next**, and save the settings to the device. After a few moments we should see the contents of the mailbox in the **Mail** application:

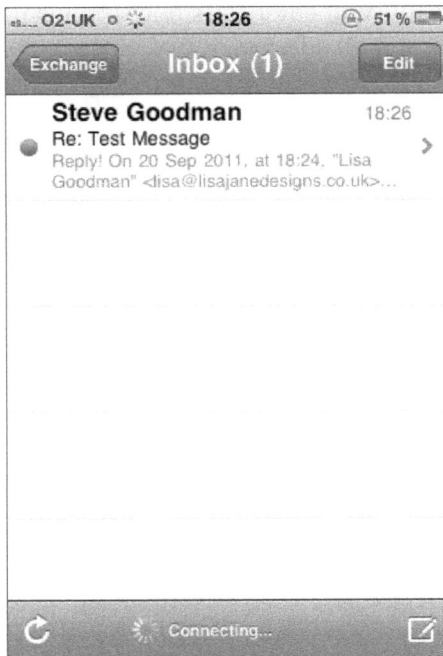

As with the Outlook Web App test, it's worth verifying everything works as expected by sending and receiving a few test messages, creating a few calendar items and contacts to ensure that Exchange Server integration works correctly, and that changes to contacts, appointments, and tasks are reflected in Outlook Web App or the full Outlook client.

If everything works correctly, we've set up Office 365's Exchange Online service to provide basic functionality for iOS devices.

Summary

In this chapter, we've walked through the straightforward process of the basic setup of an Office 365 tenant and briefly discussed the advanced options available on top.

The process involved online sign up for Office 365 services followed by instant provisioning. We then configured DNS entries to utilize the domain for our example company Lisa Jane Designs, `lisajanedesigns.co.uk`, enabling mail and Auto Discover services.

After testing the configuration and ensuring the basic functionality works, we finally connected an iPhone to the service to verify that Office 365 was working correctly with iOS devices.

In the next chapters, we'll begin to look at the more advanced features offered by Exchange and Office 365 to iOS devices, starting with device policies including what policies are available, and the impact of enabling them.

5
Creating and Enforcing Policies

ActiveSync Mailbox policies allow you, the administrator, to take control of ActiveSync devices and enforce settings, control how the device can be used, and ensure the correct security settings are correctly enforced.

This chapter is intended to give you an introduction to the security policies available in Exchange Server 2010 and Office 365 and show how each of the available security policies apply to devices like the iPhone and iPad.

We'll then cover the practicalities of implementing policies using Exchange Server and Office 365 and finally look at how you might ensure only iOS devices are used in your Exchange organization. We'll break all this up into the following sections:

- The purpose of security policies
- Security policies available
- Creating and managing ActiveSync Mailbox policies
- Restricting device types

At the end of this chapter, you should be confident in deploying policies to iOS devices, either to a selection of your users or organization wide.

The purpose of Exchange ActiveSync policies

As some of the most popular consumer devices, the iPhone, iPad, and iPod Touch present a significant risk of misuse and theft, and a common problem with most mobile devices, that they can easily be lost or misplaced.

Therefore, ActiveSync security policies have a critical purpose in helping ensure that not only can devices be restricted to conform with company policies but also be secured so that password and lockout policies are enforced.

For example, many e-mail messages contain confidential information or sensitive messages containing data covered by various legislation, such as EU Data Protection regulations, and the organization may have a duty to ensure that the data is held securely. Policies are therefore very important to ensure that information on devices is protected by security measures such as, at a minimum, numeric passcodes and having rules in place to ensure the device cannot be broken into through trial and error.

In other scenarios, such as when company policies don't allow certain features to be used, such as cameras or the web browser, it's important to be able to ensure that this policy is in force.

Exchange ActiveSync policies

Exchange ActiveSync provides a wide range of policies in Exchange Server 2010, from enforcing password policies, disabling Internet sharing, and enforcing information rights management features to configuring synchronization settings while roaming.

Like all devices on the market, it's important to note that iOS devices don't support all the features available from Exchange Server 2010; therefore, some settings will not take effect when applied.

In this section, we're going to explore the policies available to ActiveSync devices and demonstrate how these features take effect on the iOS device. First though, let's have a quick look at the policies available and their support status for iOS devices:

Exchange ActiveSync policy	Supported by iOS?
Require Password	Yes
Allow Simple Password	Yes
Minimum Password Length	Yes
Require Alphanumeric Password	Yes
Time without user input before the password must be re-entered	Yes
Password Expiration Policy	Yes
Enforce Password History	Yes
Device Encryption	Yes
Include Past E-mail Items (Days)	Yes

Exchange ActiveSync policy	Supported by iOS?
Allow Direct Push while Roaming	Yes
Allow Camera	Yes
Allow Browser	Yes
Allow attachment download	No
Maximum attachment size	No
Enable password recovery	No
Encrypt Storage Card	No
Disable SMS Text Messaging	No
Disable Wi-Fi	No
Disable Bluetooth	No
Allow Internet sharing from device	No
Allow remote desktop from device	No
Disable POP3/IMAP e-mail	No
Allow consumer mail	No
Allow unsigned applications	No
Application Block/Allow List	No
Require Signed S/MIME messages	No
Require Encrypted S/MIME messages	No
Configure Message Formats (Plain Text/ HTML)	No
E-mail Body Truncation Size	No
Include past calendar items (days)	No
Allow IRM over ActiveSync	No

Unfortunately, as you'll see in the table, the list of unsupported Exchange ActiveSync policies isn't a short one, and includes features that iOS simply doesn't support natively, like Microsoft Remote Desktop. The good news is many of these policies, along with many more iOS-specific features, can be restricted or controlled through the use of iPhone Configuration Profiles, which we'll cover later in this book, in *Chapter 7, Provisioning iOS Client Devices*.

However, we do have support for the core features of ActiveSync that most organizations need.

Require Password

One of the most basic security measures available to ensure the device can't easily be accessed is to require a password. In its basic form, enabling the basic "Require Password" policy ensures that when the end user connects an iPhone (or the device next refreshes its policy from the server), the user is prompted to select a password or pass code before Exchange data is synchronized from the server.

When the policy is enabled, the user is made aware of this with the following prompt shown on the device:

Passcode Requirement

The account "Exchange" will not download new data until a new passcode is set.

| Later | Continue |

With just the basic password requirement enabled, the user only needs to enter a password that meets the defaults set on the iOS device itself, with the exception that the simple passwords are not allowed by default.

After the policy is enabled and the phone is locked, anyone attempting to use the phone will be prompted to enter the password:

Enter Passcode

●●●●●● OK

1	2 ABC	3 DEF
4 GHI	5 JKL	6 MNO
7 PQRS	8 TUV	9 WXYZ
Emergency Call	0	⌫

Allow Simple Password

A simple password is a four character common combination, and is typically allowed on mobile devices to ensure the end user can choose an easy-to-remember password and will not burden the IT administrator with password reset requests.

The ActiveSync policy on the Exchange Server maps to the setting in the iOS device **Passcode Lock** settings page. Depending on whether the Allow Simple Password policy is enabled or disabled on the Exchange Server, the field will be enabled or disabled on the iOS device in **General** | **Settings** | **Passcode Lock**:

As you can see in the image, it's not just switch on or off in the settings pages — it's grayed out so that the end-user cannot enable or disable the setting. The Exchange Server ActiveSync policy ensures that the settings are enforced on the device.

Minimum Password Length

By changing the minimum password length, you can ensure that the code or word entered by your end-user to unlock the device is of a sufficient length to meet your security policies. When you choose a minimum length for the password on the Exchange ActiveSync policy, the user will be informed of the requirement when he/she chooses a password.

Require Alphanumeric Password

One issue with only numerical passwords is that although they are easy to enter on a device like an iPhone, there is the risk that users will choose very easy-to-guess numbers, like their date of birth, a phone number, or a memorable date. Although to someone who doesn't know the user these might be hard to guess, with some social engineering or if the device is picked up by one of the user's family or friends, it may be very simple to guess.

If you wish to ensure that the password is a little more complicated you can enforce the use of passwords that include numbers, letters, and non-standard characters (such as a hyphen, a full stop, a comma, a pound sign, and so on).

When this is enforced, the end user will be clearly informed of the password requirements and asked to enter the password using the normal text-based on-screen keyboard:

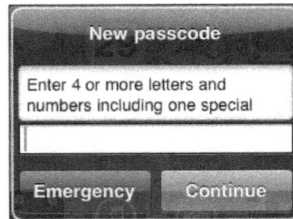

To assist the end user, who might not understand the requirements clearly, when a password is chosen that doesn't meet the requirements, the user will be re-prompted and informed what was missing.

We can see below what happens if a user just enters an alphanumeric password:

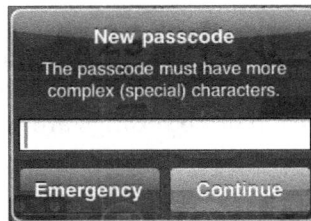

Time without user input before the password must be re-entered

If you are enabling passwords on the device, the effort and good intentions can be lost if the end user of the device can simply edit the settings of the device so that it never prompts for the password, except when manually locked or first switched on.

Therefore it's a good idea to enable a timeout using Exchange Server ActiveSync policies to ensure that if the device is left unused for a short period of time the device automatically prompts for the password.

By setting this policy, the **Auto-Lock** feature in the **General** settings of the iPhone will be changed to match the policy, and the end user will be unable to alter the setting itself:

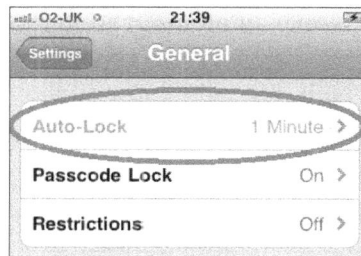

One point of note is that when enabling this policy, there is one impact it may have on end users.

If as part of their work they require the use of applications like Satellite Navigation software, a suitable timeout between requiring input and the device locking should be established. If the device locks too soon then it may disrupt their work and you may be asked to remove the policy altogether or justify its use. A suitable timeout for most organizations is five minutes.

Password Expiration Policy

The password expiration policy defines the length of time before a user needs to change their password. Similar to PC or Active Directory policies, it's good practice to require users to change the password used to access the device from time to time—at least once a year. This helps discourage the use of easy-to-guess passwords, like their date of birth or wedding anniversary.

Enforce Password History

In combination with enforcing a password expiration, a password history ensures that the user cannot simply change their password twice in succession to revert back to the code they were originally using. A typical value for the number of passwords to remember is between five and 10.

Device Encryption

By default, on devices from the iPhone 3GS onwards, the device is encrypted by default. By enabling this policy, and choosing the setting to only allow provisionable devices, you in effect only allow iPhone 3GS and later models to connect to Exchange Server.

Include Past E-mail Items (Days)

If required, you can enforce the number of days mail that the iOS device will download, and store on the device. When this policy is enabled, all other options of a certain duration (such as weeks, or all mail) are removed:

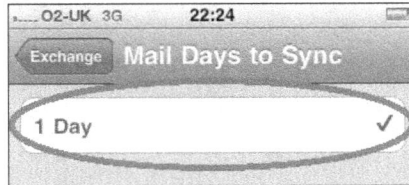

The main benefit of enabling this policy is to ensure that an end user does not use up their data allowance downloading the contents of what may be a multi-gigabyte inbox.

Enforcing the policy won't prevent an end user from accessing older messages, as they can use the search function in the Mail application to perform a server-based search against their Mailbox to access older items.

Allow Direct Push while Roaming

Roaming data charges can be extremely expensive when enabled, and even at low volumes of mail an iPhone device can easily download 5 MB over the course of a few days just by keeping Direct Push, the Exchange ActiveSync feature for push-e-mail, enabled.

By disallowing Direct Push when roaming, the end user can still access their Exchange Server e-mail. However, they must manually synchronize their inbox to see new messages.

Allow Camera

There are only two features available to iOS devices that require an Exchange Server **Enterprise Client Access License (eCAL)**, and the ability to enable or disable the use of the built-in camera is the first.

In certain environments where sensitive information is involved, such as trade secrets, or when working in environments where it may be inappropriate for a worker to be allowed the use of a camera, it is possible to disable the built-in camera facility on iOS devices.

When disabled, the camera is simply removed from the home screen.

When the camera is disabled by policy, no information is given to the end user. Apart from the obvious lack of camera functionality, the only sign that this restriction has been put in effect is hidden away in the **Settings**, under **Restrictions**:

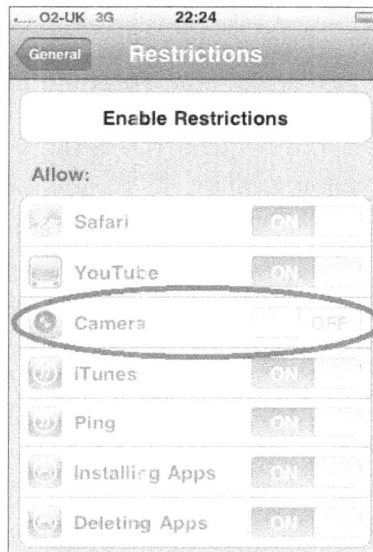

Allow Browser

The second supported feature that requires an Exchange Server eCAL is the ability to disable the use of the built-in web browser, Safari. Reasons for removing the browser might include helping prevent the end user from accessing web pages that contain malware and could compromise the device.

Similar to when the camera functionality is disabled, once the policy is enabled, the Safari Web Browser is simply removed from the homepage.

Again, the only other indicator apart from the lack of the Web Browser is that it is shown as disabled in the Restrictions settings.

Creating and managing ActiveSync Mailbox policies

In the previous pages, we've had a look at what policies we can make use of with iOS devices and we have also seen what effects enabling each policy has on the device, along with what the end user experience is like.

The next step is to understand how to actually create and manage the policies in Exchange Server 2010 or Office 365.

In Exchange Server 2010 and Office 365, an administrator can not only modify the default policy that affects all end users of the Exchange Organization, but also create and modify additional policies that can then be assigned to a subset of users, depending on the requirements. For example, we could have a default policy that required devices to lock after not being used for five minutes by default, and then add an additional policy for users of Satellite Navigation software that specified a 15 minute timeout before the device locks.

An important note on ActiveSync policies is that each additional policy does not inherit the settings of another policy, such as the default policy. Therefore, if there are common settings that must be applied across all policies they should be defined and maintained in each individual policy.

Over the course of the next few pages, we'll examine how to modify the default policy to enforce the following policy to all users:

- Only allow provisionable devices
- Set a policy-refresh interval of 12 hours
- Require an alphanumeric password with a minimum of eight characters
- Require Device Encryption, limiting support to iPhone 3GS and newer devices
- Set a time limit of five minutes without end user input before locking the device and requiring re-entry of the password
- Set a password expiration of 360 days with a history of the last five passwords

Next, we will create a similar policy with the only difference being a 15 minute timeout. We'll then assign that policy to a particular user.

To demonstrate the different ways to accomplish this, we'll perform the tasks via the Exchange Management Console, the Exchange Control Panel, and the Exchange Management Shell.

Each method accomplishes the same result, and you are free to choose any of the three methods you feel most comfortable with.

Using Exchange Management Console

The Exchange Management Console is primarily aimed at the Exchange Server 2010 administrator. Although it's possible to connect to Office 365 using the Exchange Management Console, installation requires Exchange Server to be installed in the on-premises organization.

Modifying the default policy

To modify the default policy, open the **Exchange Management Console** and navigate to **Organization Configuration | Client Access**, and then click on the **Exchange ActiveSync Mailbox Policies** tab.

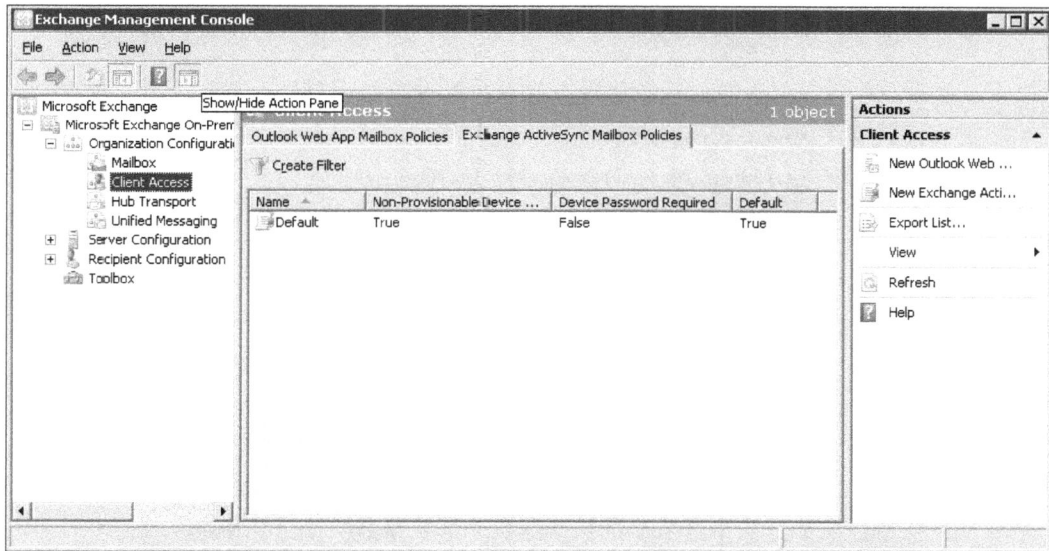

You should see the default policy listed, with the name **Default**. Right-click the default policy and choose **Properties**. Then navigate the tabbed interface and enable the settings to comply with our chosen policy:

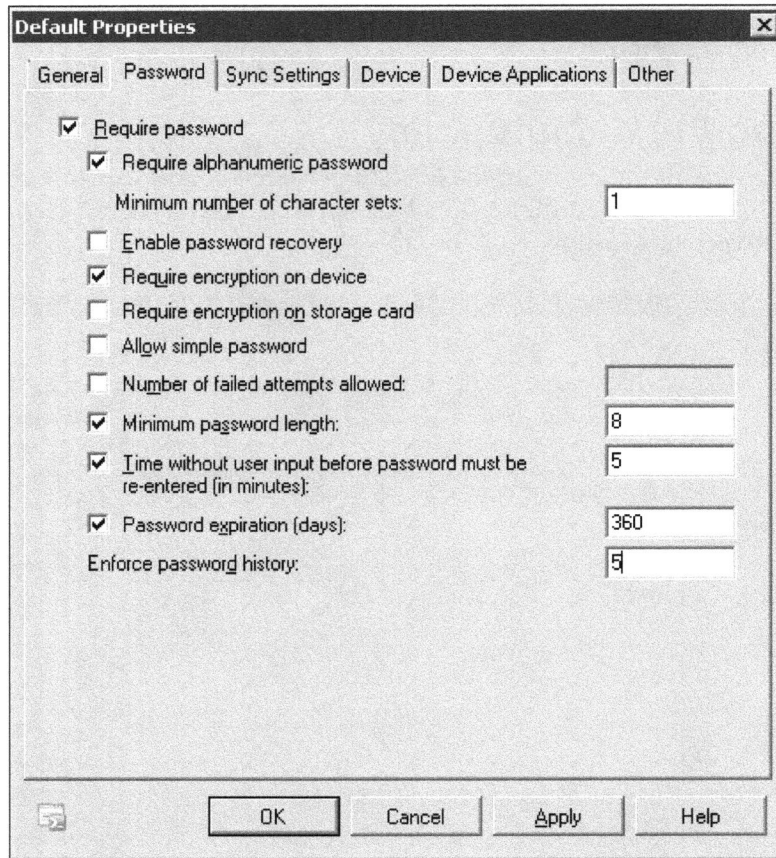

```
Default Properties                                              [X]

 General | Password | Sync Settings | Device | Device Applications | Other |

   [✓] Require password
      [✓] Require alphanumeric password
          Minimum number of character sets:            [1        ]
      [ ] Enable password recovery
      [✓] Require encryption on device
      [ ] Require encryption on storage card
      [ ] Allow simple password
      [ ] Number of failed attempts allowed:           [         ]
      [✓] Minimum password length:                     [8        ]
      [✓] Time without user input before password must be  [5    ]
          re-entered (in minutes):
      [✓] Password expiration (days):                  [360      ]
      Enforce password history:                        [5        ]




       [🔲]        [    OK    ]   [  Cancel  ]   [  Apply  ]   [  Help  ]
```

After choosing **OK** to apply the policy, all new devices connected will be forced to comply with the policy immediately, and existing devices will refresh the policy within the default 24-hour refresh period.

Creating a new policy

To create our second policy to apply to only specific users, we again navigate to **Organization Configuration | Client Access**, and then click on the **Exchange ActiveSync Mailbox Policies** tab. To create a new policy, we right-click and choose **New Exchange ActiveSync Mailbox Policy**.

The **New Exchange ActiveSync Mailbox Policy** wizard should launch and allow us to enter some of the required settings:

After creating the policy, we follow the same procedure used to edit the Default policy to apply additional settings, such as the Refresh Interval.

Assigning the new policy to a Mailbox

To assign the policy to a particular Mailbox, navigate to **Recipient Configuration | Mailbox**. From the Mailbox listing, select the Mailbox you wish to assign the policy to, and right-click and choose **Properties**:

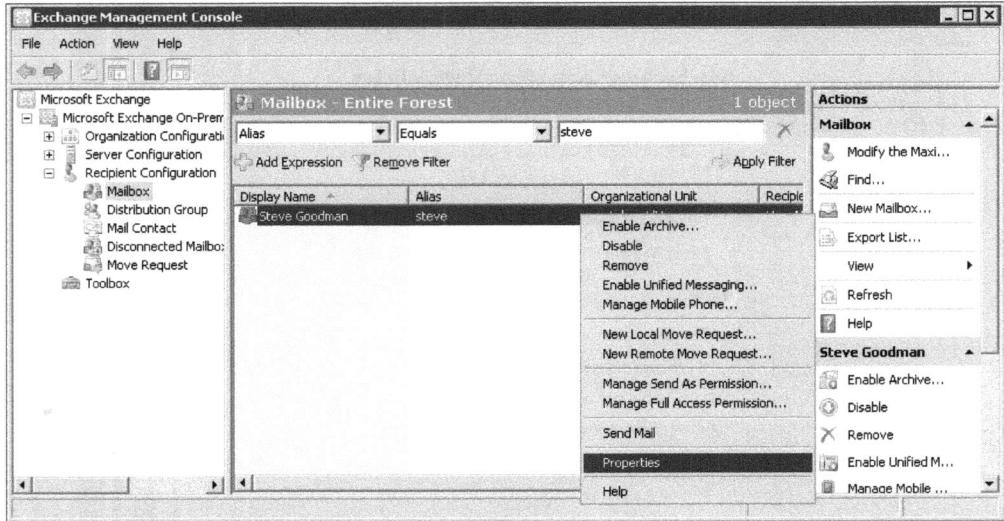

In the Mailbox **Properties**, select the **Mailbox Features** tab and select **Exchange ActiveSync**, then select **Properties**:

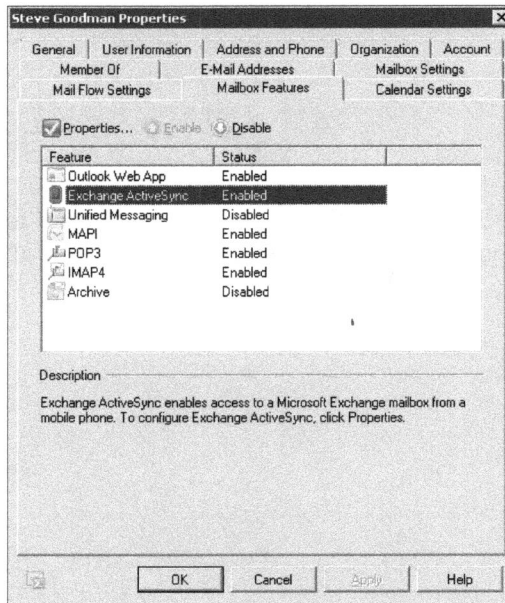

The **Exchange ActiveSync Properties** should appear and display the current policy assigned to the Mailbox:

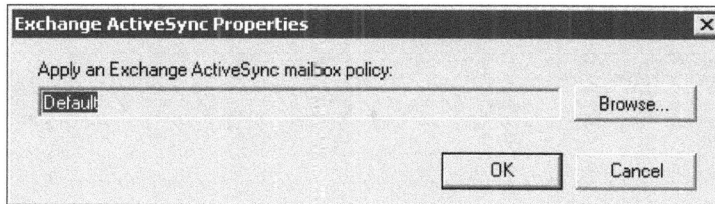

```
┌─────────────────────────────────────────────────────────┐
│ Exchange ActiveSync Properties                      [×]  │
├─────────────────────────────────────────────────────────┤
│  Apply an Exchange ActiveSync mailbox policy:            │
│  ┌────────────────────────────────────┐  ┌───────────┐  │
│  │ Default                            │  │ Browse... │  │
│  └────────────────────────────────────┘  └───────────┘  │
│                                                          │
│                        ┌──────────┐  ┌───────────┐       │
│                        │    OK    │  │  Cancel   │       │
│                        └──────────┘  └───────────┘       │
└─────────────────────────────────────────────────────────┘
```

Click **Browse** to select the new policy, then click **OK** both in the **Exchange ActiveSync Properties** and the Mailbox **Properties** to save the changes.

The Mailbox should now have the policy assigned, and if it was using the modified default policy previously, should refresh with the new policy settings within 12 hours.

Using Exchange Control Panel

The Exchange Control Panel is the web-based interface used for end user options and basic administration tasks in Exchange Server 2010 and the Exchange Online component of Office 365. The Exchange Control Panel allows the management and creation of ActiveSync Mailbox policies and the assignment of policies to Mailboxes through the web interface.

For a local Exchange Server 2010 installation, visit the following URL to access the Exchange Control Panel:

```
https://<Client Access Server Name>/ecp
```

For an Office 365 tenant, visit the following URL and log in with your Microsoft Online Services administrator ID:

```
http://outlook.com/ecp?realm=<Your Office 365 Domain>
```

For the following procedures, we'll use Office365 to demonstrate the process. However, the user interface is identical in Exchange Server 2010.

Modifying the default policy

After logging in to the Exchange Control Panel, navigate to **Phone & Voice**, and select **ActiveSync Device Policy**:

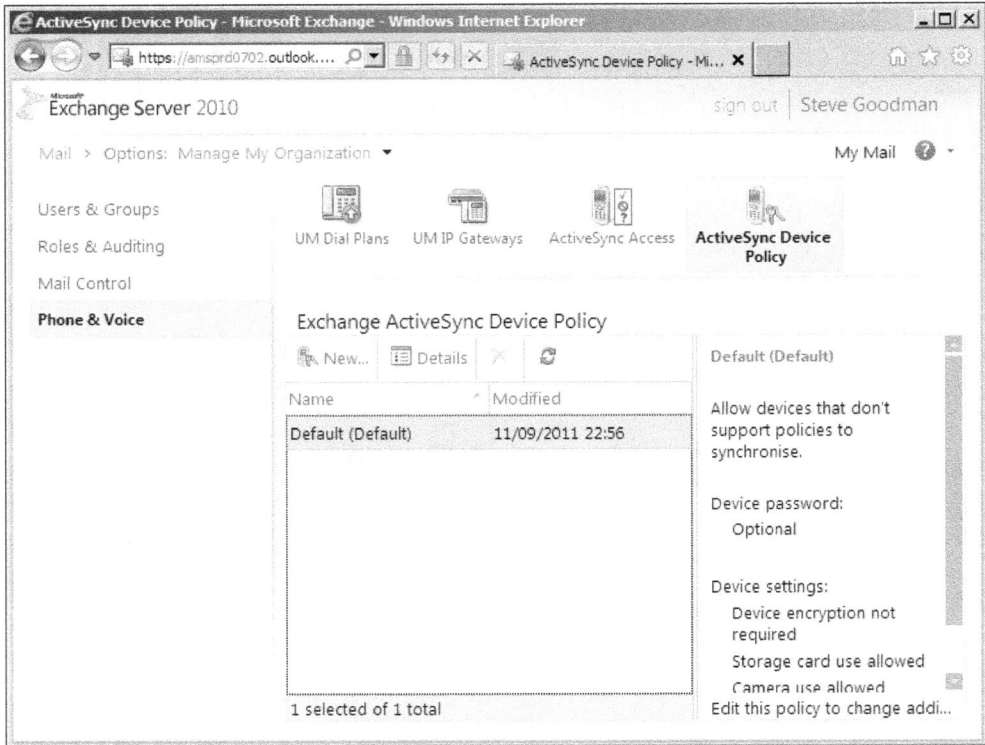

In the ActiveSync Device Policy section, you'll see the Default policy listed in very much the same way as it was shown in the Exchange Management Console, with the additional benefit that when a policy is selected, an overview of the settings is shown to the right of the policy listing.

To edit the default policy, select **Default (Default)** from the list and click **Details**. The policy settings should show in a new browser window, where we can then input the ActiveSync Mailbox policy settings to comply with our requirements:

Once the correct settings have been selected, select **Save** to apply the settings. The overview of the policy's settings should update to reflect the changes:

Creating a new policy

To create a new policy, navigate to the **Phone & Voice** section of the Exchange Management Console and click **ActiveSync Device Policy**. Click the **New** link to launch the **New Exchange ActiveSync Device Policy** window for the new policy we wish to create:

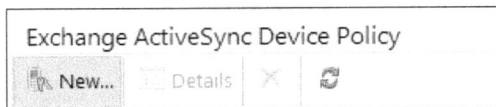

Exchange ActiveSync Device Policy

New...   Details   ✕   ⟳

In the **New Exchange ActiveSync Device Policy** window, we are prompted to input the policy settings in the same way the default policy was edited:

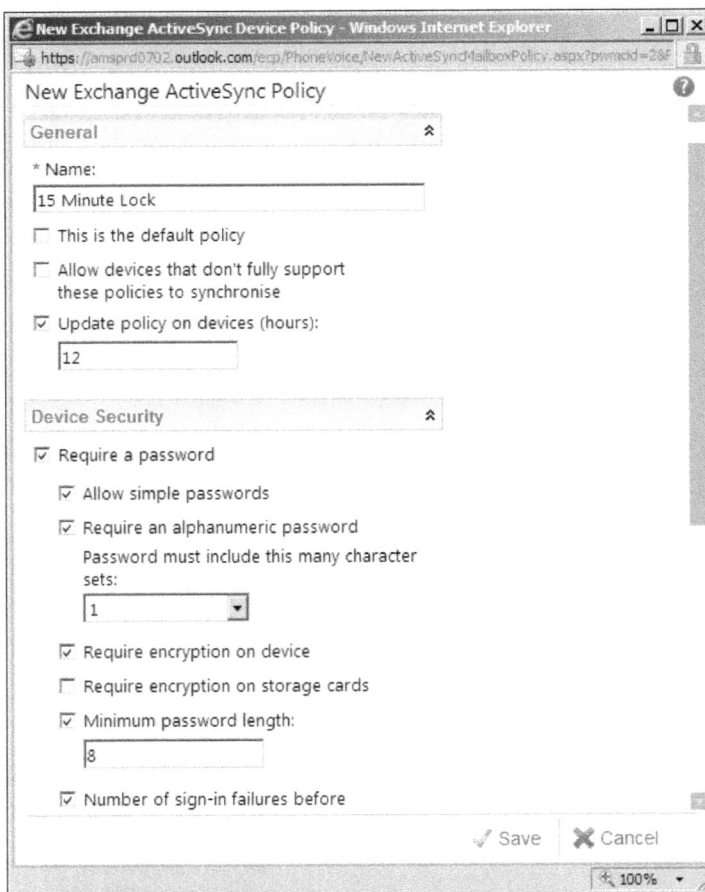

New Exchange ActiveSync Device Policy - Windows Internet Explorer

https://amsprd0702.**outlook.com**/ecp/PhoneVoice/NewActiveSyncMailboxPolicy.aspx?pwmcid=2&f

New Exchange ActiveSync Policy

General   ⌃

* Name:

15 Minute Lock

☐ This is the default policy

☐ Allow devices that don't fully support these policies to synchronise

☑ Update policy on devices (hours):

12

Device Security   ⌃

☑ Require a password

   ☑ Allow simple passwords

   ☑ Require an alphanumeric password

     Password must include this many character sets:

     1

   ☑ Require encryption on device

   ☐ Require encryption on storage cards

   ☑ Minimum password length:

     8

   ☑ Number of sign-in failures before

✓ Save   ✕ Cancel

100%

After adding the settings for our second policy, we select **Save** to store the new policy, which after saving should be listed alongside the default policy:

Assigning the new policy to a Mailbox

To assign the new policy to a particular Mailbox, we need to visit the section of the Exchange Control Panel used to manage Mailboxes and Mailbox settings. Navigate to **Users & Groups** and select **Mailboxes**.

The list of Mailboxes in our Exchange Server 2010 or Office 365 Exchange Online tenant should be shown:

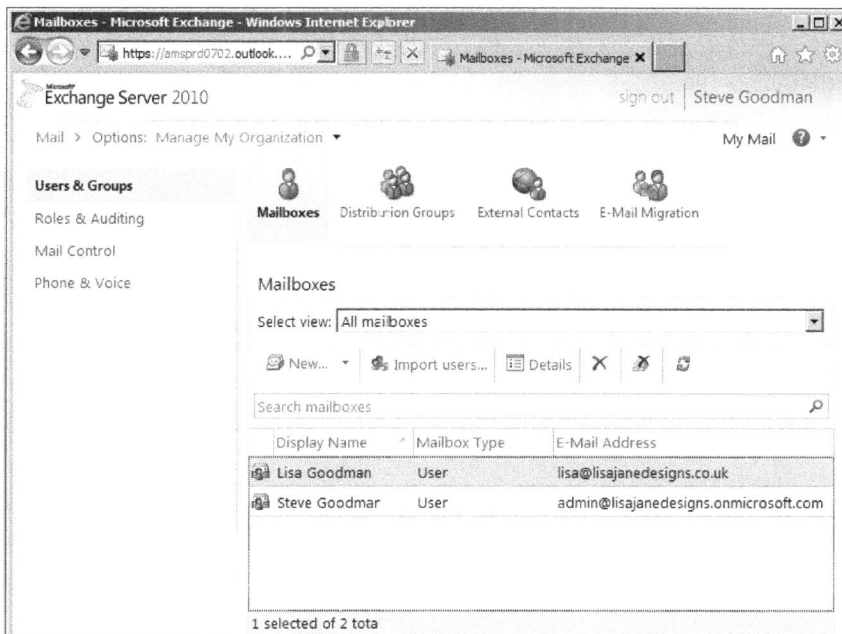

From the Mailbox list, select the user we wish to apply the policy to, and then click **Details**.

The details for the selected user should show in a new browser window. To edit the ActiveSync Mailbox Policy, first scroll down to **Phone & Voice Features** and select the **Exchange ActiveSync** item from the list, then click **Edit**:

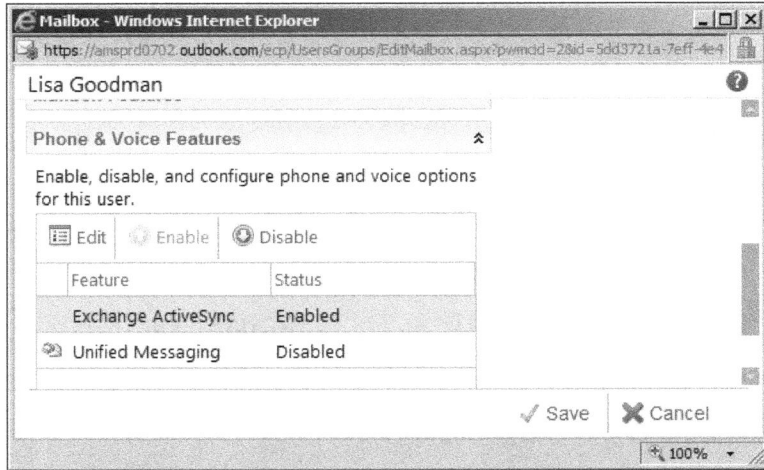

The **Exchange ActiveSync Details** browser window should open. To select a new policy, click **Browse** in the **Exchange ActiveSync device policy** section:

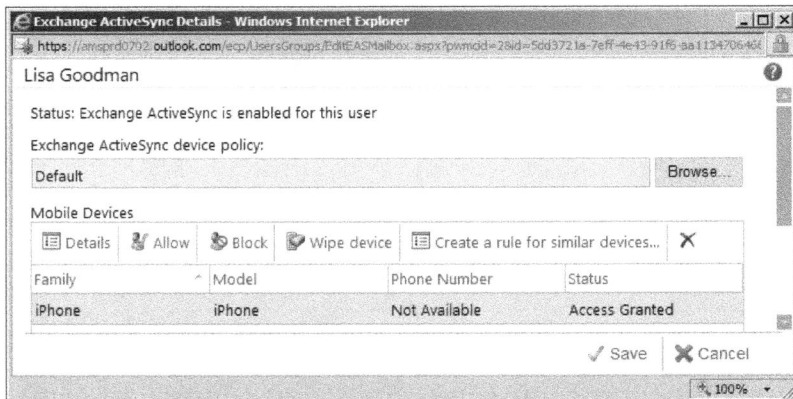

After choosing the new policy, choose **Save** in the **Exchange ActiveSync Details** window and then the **Mailbox** details window to apply the policy to the Mailbox.

Using Exchange Management Shell

If using the graphical interface feels too long winded, then the Exchange Management Shell is a great alternative.

Based on PowerShell, the Exchange Management Shell allows all actions that can be accomplished by using the Exchange Management Console or Exchange Control Panel to be performed in a command window.

In the following example we'll perform the same actions we performed in both graphical interfaces with just a few commands.

In Exchange Server 2010, the Exchange Management Shell is installed and available in the **Start** menu when installing the Exchange Management Tools, as part of any Exchange Server 2010 installation.

For Office 365, the connection to Exchange must be made manually from a PowerShell command prompt using the following two commands:

```
$session = New-PSSession -ConfigurationName Microsoft.Exchange
-ConnectionUri https://ps.outlook.com/powershell -Credential (Get-
Credential) -Authentication Basic -AllowRedirection

Import-PSSession $session
```

Modifying the default policy

To modify the default policy we'll use the Set-ActiveSyncMailboxPolicy cmdlet, but the first step is to examine the default policy itself, and check what changes are required.

Checking the default policy is accomplished by using the Get-ActiveSyncMailboxPolicy cmdlet, which we will use the | character to pipe, or pass, the result into the Format-List command to allow us to see all the default policies attributes:

```
Get-ActiveSyncMailboxPolicy Default | Format-List *
```

After examining the policy, we make the changes to comply with the settings we have chosen to implement:

```
Set-ActiveSyncMailboxPolicy 'Default' -AllowNonProvisionableDevices
$false -AlphanumericDevicePasswordRequired $true
-DevicePasswordEnabled $true -DevicePolicyRefreshInterval
'12:00:00' -AllowSimpleDevicePassword $false
-MinDevicePasswordLength '8' -MaxInactivityTimeDeviceLock '00:05:00'
-MaxDevicePasswordFailedAttempts 'unlimited' -DevicePasswordExpiration
'360.00:00:00' -DevicePasswordHistory '5' -RequireDeviceEncryption
$true
```

The default policy should now be modified and take effect on all newly-configured devices and existing devices within 12 hours.

> **Getting help with Exchange Management Shell cmdlets**
>
> For a reference of the available parameters to use with `Set-ActiveSyncMailboxPolicy` or any other Exchange cmdlet, use the `Get-Help` cmdlet with the `-Online` parameter to show the Technet help page:
>
> **`Get-Help Set-ActiveSyncMailboxPolicy -Online`**

Creating a new policy

The process of creating a new policy is very similar to the way we've modified the default policy, except that we'll use the `New-ActiveSyncMailboxPolicy` cmdlet to accomplish this, and specify a value of 15 minutes:

```
New-ActiveSyncMailboxPolicy -Name '15 Minute
Lock'  -AllowNonProvisionableDevices $false
-AlphanumericDevicePasswordRequired $true -DevicePasswordEnabled $true
-DevicePolicyRefreshInterval '12:00:00' -AllowSimpleDevicePassword
$false -MinDevicePasswordLength '8' -MaxDevicePasswordFailedAttempts
'unlimited' -DevicePasswordExpiration '360.00:00:00'
-DevicePasswordHistory '5' -RequireDeviceEncryption $true
-MaxInactivityTimeDeviceLock '00:15:00'
```

To review the new policy we've created, we can use the `Get-ActiveSyncMailboxPolicy` cmdlet to list the attributes:

```
Get-ActiveSyncMailboxPolicy '15 Minute Lock' | Format-List *
```

Assigning the new policy to a Mailbox

Finally, after creating the new policy we need to assign it to a particular Mailbox. To list the current policy assigned to the Mailbox, we use the `Get-CASMailbox` cmdlet, piped into the `Format-List` cmdlet:

```
Get-CasMailbox lisa@lisajanedesigns.co.uk | Format-List *
```

To assign the new policy to the Mailbox, we then use the `Set-CASMailbox` cmdlet, as shown below:

```
Set-CasMailbox lisa@lisajanedesigns.co.uk -ActiveSyncMailboxPolicy '15
Minute Lock'
```

The policy should immediately be assigned the Mailbox, and will take effect at the next device refresh interval, or immediately when it is first configured.

Restricting device types

By default, Exchange Server 2010 and Office 365's Exchange Online service will allow any ActiveSync-compatible device to connect to your Exchange infrastructure. This includes Windows Mobile, Nokia, Android, and iOS devices among many others.

If you're planning on supporting a selected number of iOS devices you may wish to restrict the device types that can connect with the option, to either completely block or quarantine devices that don't meet the criteria chosen.

As an example, we'll look at how to enforce criteria to:

- Only allow iPhone devices
- Quarantine any other devices that connect
- Inform an administrator of quarantined devices

Before we set up these criteria, as a pre-requisite, connect a test device of the type you wish to be able to allow. This will populate Exchange with information about the device type so it can be chosen when creating a rule.

The most straightforward way to accomplish this is using the Exchange Control Panel, navigating to **Phone & Voice**, and then selecting **ActiveSync Access**. To begin configuration, choose **Edit**:

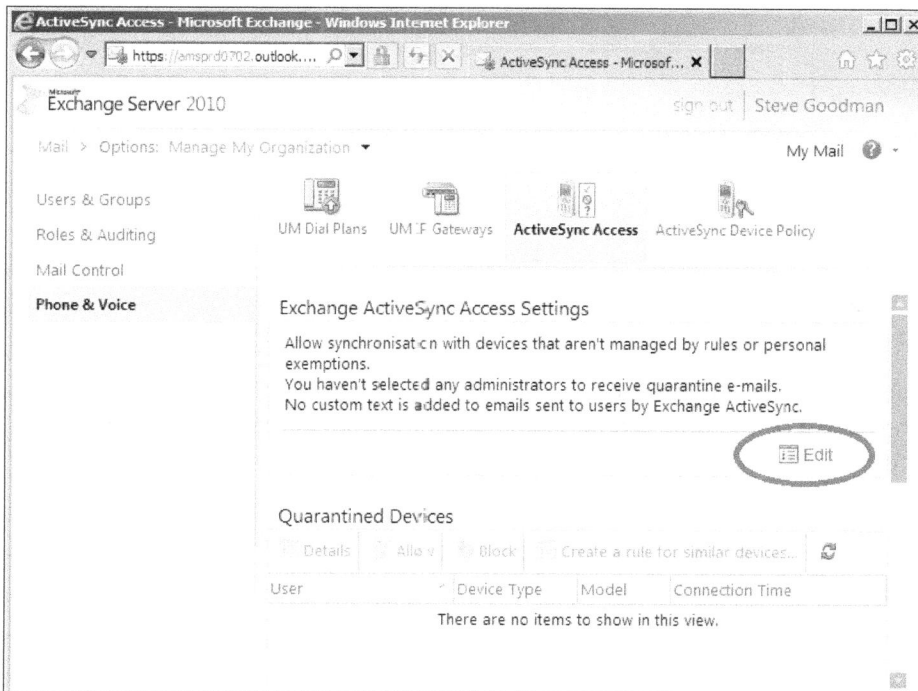

After clicking Edit, we are presented with the **ActiveSync Access** settings window, which allows us to change the default **Allow Access** to **Quarantine**.

We also add the Administrator e-mail account in the **Quarantine notification e-mails** section and provide some brief text that will be sent to any user attempting to connect anything other than an iPhone:

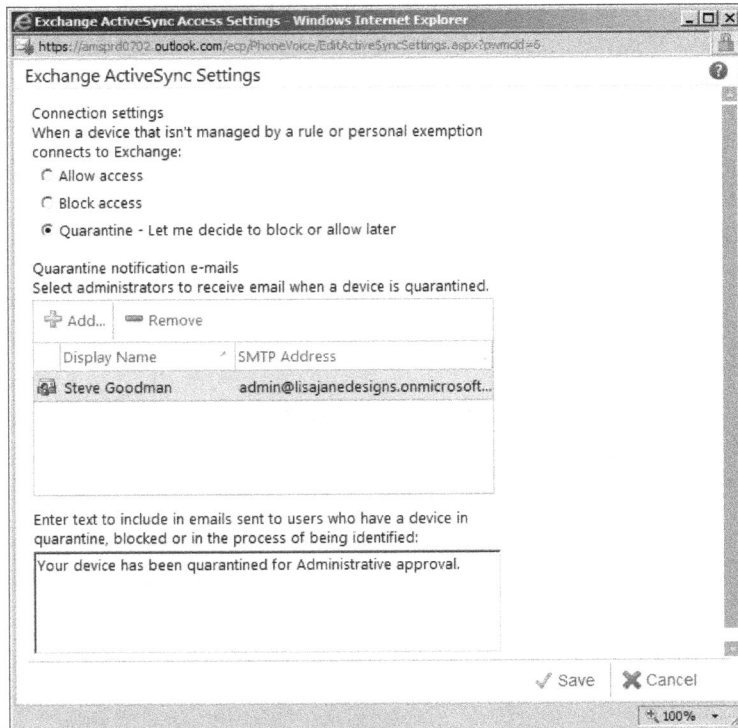

After editing the settings, we choose **Save** to apply the changes. The changes affect all new ActiveSync devices that attempt to connect, and existing ActiveSync devices will be re-evaluated for quarantine.

The next step is to allow iPhone devices to connect automatically. As we've already connected a test device to Exchange, we should be able to easily create a device access rule to allow iPhones. To accomplish this, scroll down to **Device Access Rules**, and choose **New**:

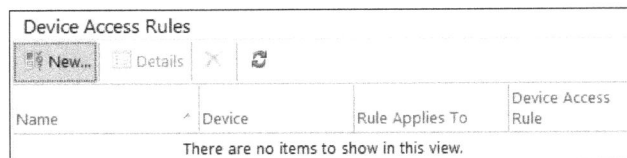

The **New Exchange ActiveSync Device Access Rule** window should open and allow us to select the criteria we wish to apply when allowing, blocking, or quarantining a device.

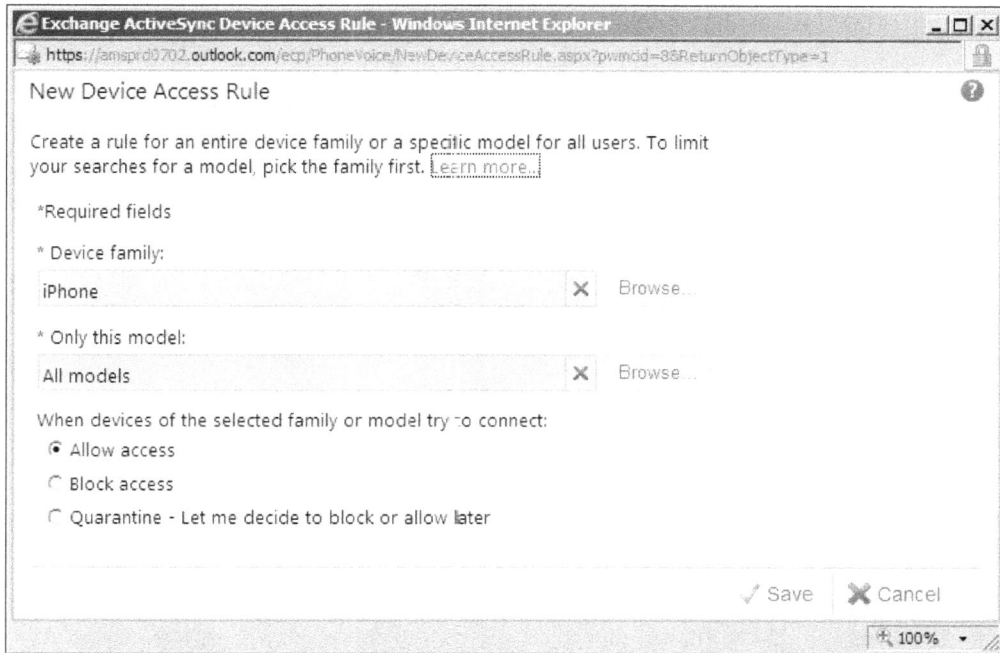

In the above example, we've used the **Browse** option to choose the **iPhone** under **Device family**. Under **Only this model**, we've chosen **All models**.

As we are quarantining other types of devices by default, we choose **Allow Access** to ensure iPhone devices can create a relationship with Exchange without administrator approval or intervention.

After entering the details, we choose **Save** to create the Device Access Rule. The new rule should be displayed in the **Device Access Rules** list:

From this point forward, new ActiveSync devices that are set up will not be allowed access to the Exchange Server 2010 or Office 365 organization unless they are either:

- iPhone devices
- Manually approved by an administrator

Should an end user attempt to connect a device that isn't an approved device, it will be shown in the list of **Quarantine Devices**:

Quarantined Devices			
▤ Details	🗸 Allow	🔌 Block	▤ Create a rule for similar devices... 🔁
User	↗ Device Type	Model	Connection Time
Lisa Goodman	PocketPC	HTC Touch...	02/10/2011 00:47

In addition, as per our policy, the defined administrator will receive notification via e-mail. The user will receive a message warning them that the device has been blocked from using ActiveSync until an administrator approves access.

Summary

In this chapter we've examined the policies that Exchange Server 2010 and Office 365's Exchange Online services can provide to give the administrator a degree of control over settings on ActiveSync devices, such as password settings, synchronization settings, and allowed features.

In the earlier part of this chapter, we've demonstrated which policies actually take effect on iOS devices and how they are presented to end users when a particular setting is configured at the server-side, which will hopefully give you confidence when deciding what settings are appropriate for your organization and how you will manage implementation of the changes when they are presented to end users.

Next, we walked through the technical steps to actually implement changes both to the default ActiveSync policy and the steps involved in creating a new policy and assigning it to a user. We covered the main ways of easily accomplishing these tasks using the Exchange Management Console, the Exchange Control Panel, and the Exchange Management Shell, the last two methods being appropriate for Office 365 environments as well as Exchange Server 2010 organizations.

Finally we've looked at what is involved when restricting the types of devices that can connect to Exchange, and covered the process to enable restrictions on ActiveSync devices and make an exception to allow iPhone devices to connect without restriction. Then we briefly examined what happens when a non-compliant device attempts to create a new ActiveSync relationship with Exchange Server 2010 or Office 365.

In the next chapter, we'll examine certificate-based authentication and cover the steps required to implement a basic certificate authority, and configure Exchange Server 2010 to accept certificate-based authentication for ActiveSync clients.

6
Configuring Certificate-based Authentication in Exchange Server 2010

Certificate-based authentication in Exchange Server 2010 allows you, the administrator, to ensure that ActiveSync clients connecting to Exchange are securely deployed and controlled, by restricting access only to devices that can present the correct certificate associated with the user's account.

In this chapter we'll be revisiting our fictional company, Lisa Jane Designs, with a view to implement certificate-based authentication for the Exchange Server 2010 organization.

In our example, Lisa Jane Designs will be looking to overcome issues with regular user password changes and also make sure that the casual user cannot connect a personal iPhone or other iOS device to Exchange Server 2010. To accomplish this, we'll be installing a certificate authority into the existing Active Directory and Exchange Server 2010 infrastructure, configuring it to ensure we can issue certificates for users, then configuring Exchange Server 2010 to use certificate-based authentication for access to ActiveSync, and to test functionality we will also temporarily configure Outlook Web App to use certificate-based authentication.

By the end of the chapter, we will have a certificate authority set up and ready to use our first user certificate; we'll use this in the next chapter to deploy the certificate to an iOS device using an iPhone Configuration Profile. If you're not looking at deploying certificate-based authentication, don't worry — it's not a pre-requisite for provisioning iPhones and this chapter can be skipped if it's not needed in your environment.

Overview of certificate-based authentication

General username and password authentication to Exchange Server 2010 ActiveSync, while good enough for most purposes, can become troublesome in environments that have complex requirements. For example, in an environment where user accounts require password changes on a regular basis.

Although a user can log into Outlook Web App or use a desktop computer to change their password, no such method exists for ActiveSync clients to achieve the same thing. In addition, the experience when a user changes their Active Directory password is less than ideal on the mobile device and can cause end user issues such as account lockouts. With certificate-based authentication to Exchange ActiveSync, the end-user no longer uses a password for authentication to Exchange, but instead uses a private and public key pair to identify the user accessing Microsoft Exchange.

This also has the benefit that by ensuring that only clients presenting a valid certificate can gain entry, a user cannot simply buy another iPhone as a personal device and connect that into the Exchange infrastructure.

Through the use of Microsoft's Certificate Services, we can create a public-key infrastructure that will allow us to generate the necessary certificates — a private key and matching public key — ready to deploy to devices. The following diagram shows a simplified overview of the process:

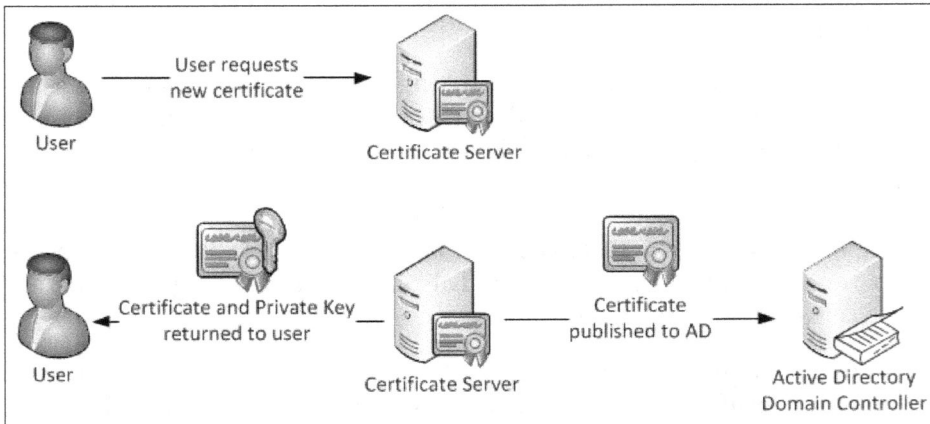

We can then configure Exchange Server 2010 so that it only allows authentication from devices that present certificates, and disallow the more common username and password authentication.

After performing this configuration, the authentication process, in simplified form, is as follows:

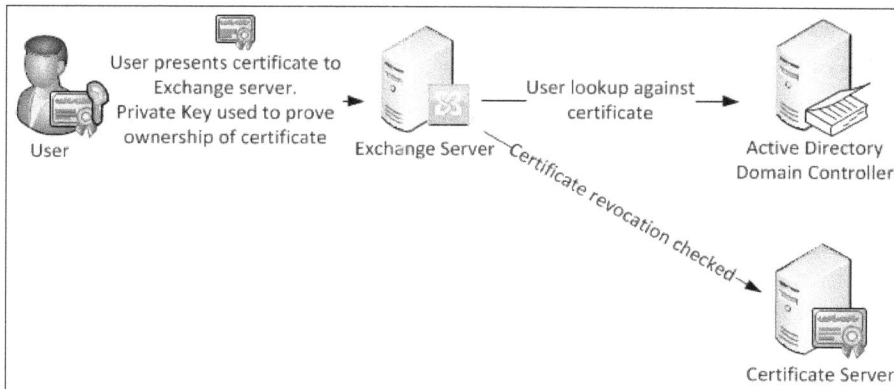

Once we are able to generate certificates and associate those with user accounts, we'll be able to use the iPhone Configuration Utility, in the next chapter, to deploy the private key to iOS devices and configure them to connect to Exchange, presenting the certificate for authentication instead of the password.

Considerations for certificate-based authentication

Implementing a public key infrastructure into your organization isn't a simple task and is one that shouldn't be considered lightly. If there are other requirements across the organization, such as encrypting files on local disks, signing and encrypting email, and deploying internal server certificates, you may wish to consider these requirements before implementing a certificate authority.

For our example company, Lisa Jane Designs, we will implement an Active Directory integrated Enterprise certificate authority. We'll be doing this for the following reasons:

- Integration and automatic publishing of certificates in Active Directory
- Built-in component of Windows Server 2008 R2
- Simple to implement and administer

Other options for implementation of a certificate based authentication include:

- Implementation of a standalone Windows certificate services server
- Implementation of an OpenSSL-based UNIX or Linux solution
- Use of third-party certificates from a commercial SSL vendor and purchase of individual user certificates

All of the above options are equally valid and the choice should be based upon the needs of your organization.

However, with those solutions, it is necessary to manually import and publish certificates into Active Directory for each user, whilst the integrated Active Directory based solution, Active Directory certificate services, allows this process to occur as part of the certificate request process.

Installation of the certificate authority

To begin our installation of a certificate authority, we first need to ensure a few pre-requisites are in place.

For our installation, we'll be using a freshly installed Windows 2008 R2 Enterprise Edition server on the internal Lisa Jane Designs network, with good connectivity to the Active Directory and Exchange Server infrastructure.

> **Which Windows Server edition version do you need?**
>
> Different editions of Windows Server 2008 R2 support different Certificate Authority features. Detailed information about features supported on different Windows Server 2008 R2 editions is available on the Microsoft TechNet website:
>
> `http://technet.microsoft.com/en-us/library/`
> `cc772393.aspx`

As we'll be installing the Active Directory integrated certificate services, our server will be joined to the same Active Directory domain as the Exchange infrastructure. This will allow us to easily create certificates for Exchange users that can be used for certificate-based authentication without further configuration.

To begin, we'll open the Windows Server 2008 R2 Server Manager, and right-click on **Roles**, then choose **Add Roles**. The **Select Server Roles** wizard should display, where we can select the role **Active Directory Certificate Services**:

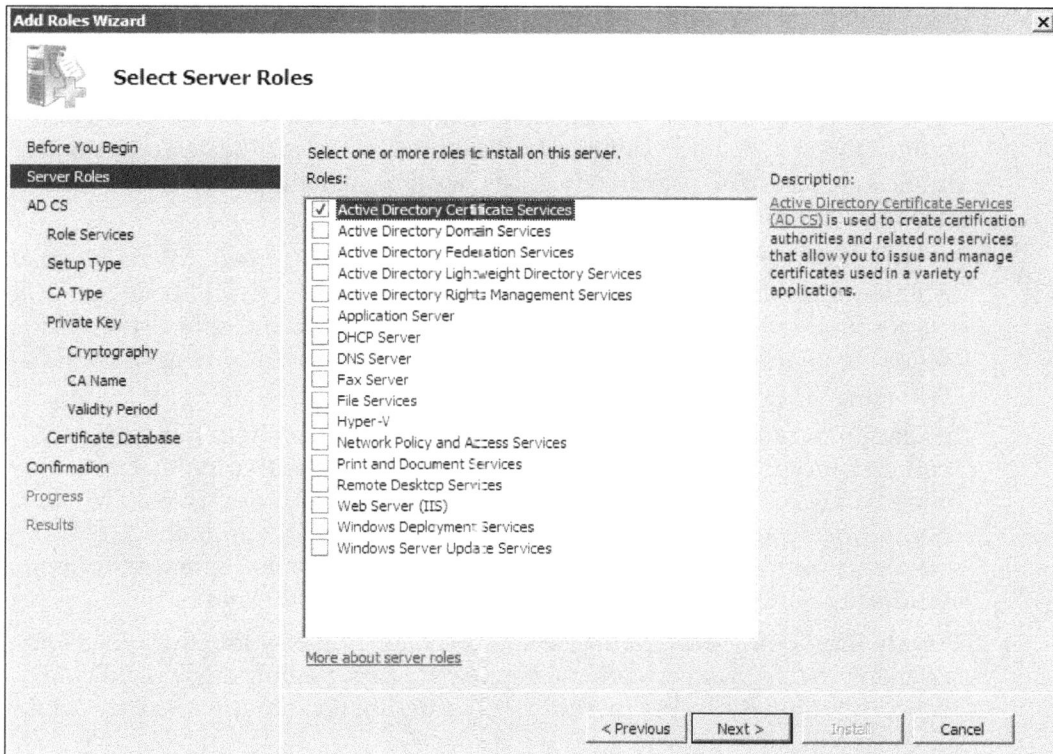

Through the Server Roles wizard, we'll then be prompted for the configuration information needed for setup of the certificate authority.

For the Lisa Jane Designs implementation of a certificate authority, we've chosen the following options:

- **Role Services**: The following services provide core certificate authority services, along with a web-based interface should we wish to allow self-service certificate generation at a later date:
    - Certificate Authority
    - Certificate Authority Web Enrolment

- **Setup Type**: To use the full features of Active Directory certificate services, including automating the publishing of certificates to user accounts in Active Directory, we've chosen the **Enterprise** certificate authority.

    As mentioned in the previous section, a **Standalone** option is available; however, choosing this option would require further configuration to publish certificates for users.

- **CA Type**: (**Root CA**) As the Lisa Jane Designs environment is built in a new Active Directory environment and no enterprise root certificate authority or public key infrastructure already exists, we'll be installing the "root", or initial certificate authority.

    As part of the installation, it will generate its own self-signed private key that will guarantee the certificates it issues. The other option would be to install a subordinate certificate authority, where a root certificate authority would be used to generate the subordinate certificate authority's private key and certificate.

    In a larger organization or business with special security requirements, it might be a consideration to install a root certificate authority, then immediately install one or more subordinate certificate authorities. The root certificate authority could then be isolated from the production network, providing a level of security against compromise. The subordinate certification authority would then be used to issue certificates.

- **Private Key**: Using the defaults, except to change the key length to 2048 bits, we choose to create a new private key. As we aren't rebuilding a certificate authority from an existing private key, we do not need to use an existing key for the certificate authority.

    The one change, from the default to 2048 bits, is based on best practices for generation of private keys; choosing a larger key character length will help protect against attempts to break the encryption of the private key.

- **CA Name**: Default name, in this case `lisajanedesigns-CERTSERVER-CA`. The default name is based upon a concatenation of the domain name and server name, with the text "CA" appended. We have no reason to alter the CA name for the Lisa Jane Designs implementation, therefore it is left using its defaults.

- **Validity Period**: The default certificate authority validity period is five years. This means that certificates issued by the certificate authority will be valid only up until the expiry date, at which point the certificate authority certificate must be renewed, although not all certificates issued to users need to be re-issued.

It is possible to specify a longer validity period; however it is worth bearing in mind that as issued certificates are revoked (perhaps due to a lost phone) the certificate revocation list will continue to grow. By choosing to set a reasonable date of five years, we know that Lisa Jane Designs will not need to maintain an ever-growing list of revoked certificates; however, it does mean that certificates issued will need to be renewed periodically.

- **Certificate Database**: (C:\Windows\System32\CertLog) For the purposes of our example organization, we are happy to leave the certificate database in its default location.

- **Web Server Role Services**: As the server will be solely used for a certificate authority, we are able to leave the default services for IIS as is, which includes common HTTP features for the proper operation of IIS, such as the ability to display static content and error pages, along with the ability to run ASP pages, used for the self-service certificate authority.

Configuration of the certificate authority

After installation completes, it should now be possible to view the certificate authority in **Server Manager**, listed under **Roles** as **Active Directory Certificate Services**.

In the following screenshot you'll see **Active Directory Certificate Services**:

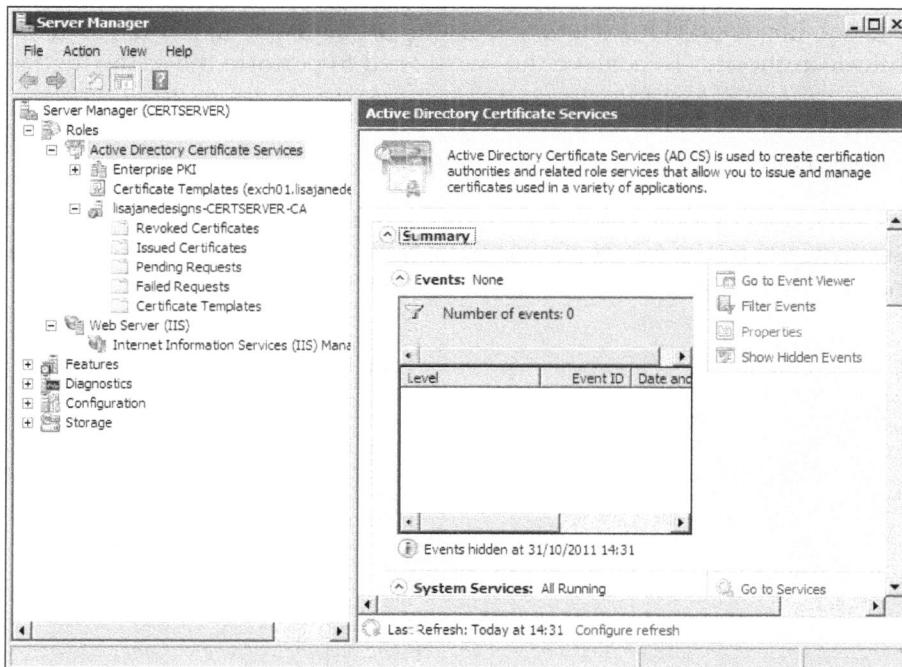

In the snap-in, we are presented with the Active Directory-stored **Enterprise PKI** and **Certificate Templates** sections, and we can drill-down to our root certificate authority itself, in our case **lisajanedesigns-CERTSERVER-CA**.

Under our root certification authority, we're able to see the following:

- **Revoked Certificates**: certificates that have once been issued to users but later rescinded
- **Issued Certificates**: certificates that have been generated and automatically issued by an administrator; or certificates that users have requested and have been approved by an administrator
- **Pending Requests**: certificate requests that have been requested by users but need to be approved by an administrator
- **Failed Requests**: certificate requests that have been denied by an administrator
- **Certificate Templates**: the templates that have been configured at an Active Directory enterprise level for this certificate authority

Through the rest of this chapter, we'll revisit this console to enable the certificate template that allows us to request certificates as an administrator on behalf of users, but for general day-to-day use we will use a different snap-in, which we'll look at later on in the chapter.

Our next step, however, is to complete the setup of the Web Enrolment features of the certificate authority. To achieve this, we'll need to perform the following tasks:

1. Request an SSL certificate from the locally installed certificate authority.
2. Assign the certificate to the Default Web Site.

To begin, we'll open the Internet Information Services (IIS) Manager, and navigate to the **Server Certificates** section, found by clicking on the root node, typically the server name (in our case **CERTSERVER**).

Double-click on **Server Certificates**, or in the **Actions** pane (located on the right-hand side), click **Open Feature**:

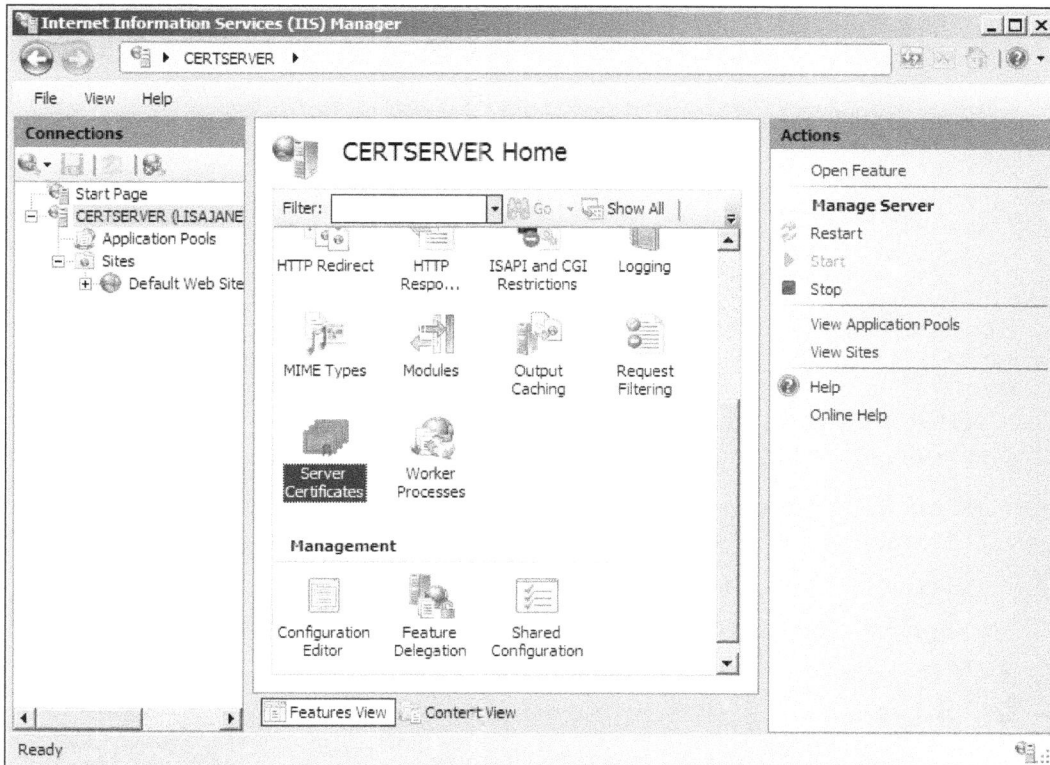

Next, you should see the following options within the **Actions** pane:

- **Import**: import a private key and certificate from a file.
- **Create certificate request**: generate a new private key and certificate signing request (CSR) file. The CSR file is typically used to request a certificate from a third-party certificate authority.
- **Complete certificate request**: after a third party certificate is issued, the certificate received is installed using this option.
- **Create domain certificate**: generate a new private key and request a certificate from an Active Directory certificate authority.
- **Create self-signed certificate**: generate a new private key and certificate signed by the server (not the local CA) itself.

Of these options, for the certificate authority, we'll be choosing to create a **domain certificate**. This certificate will be trusted by all domain-joined machines, which receive the certificate authority root certificate by group policy:

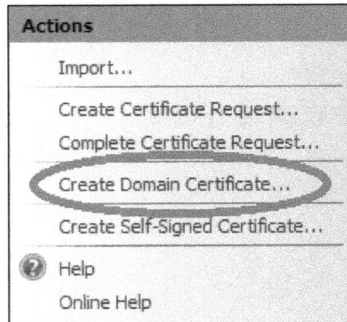

The **Create Certificate** wizard should be displayed, prompting for information about the certificate, including:

- **Common Name**: the fully qualified domain name of the certificate server — in our case `certserver.lisajanedesigns.co.uk`
- **Organization Name**
- **Organization Unit**
- **City/Locality**
- **State/Province**
- And a drop-down list to select the **Country**

The important field is the common name, and if this is specified incorrectly and does not match the name used to access the Web Enrolment service, a warning will be displayed in Web Browsers stating that the certificate name mismatches the name of the server.

After successful completion of the request, the certificate should automatically be installed on the server and immediately available to assign to the Default Web Site. To accomplish this, we'll locate the **Default Web Site** in Internet Information Services Manager and right-click on the node, and choose **Edit Bindings**:

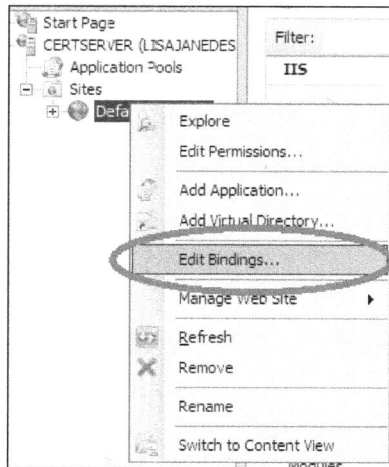

Next, we will see the **Site Bindings** list. This window displays the TCP ports, host header names, and IP addresses that the Default Web Site will listen for. By default, the site is set to listen to all requests on the standard TCP port for HTTP communication, port 80.

We'll need to choose **Add** to configure the site to use SSL:

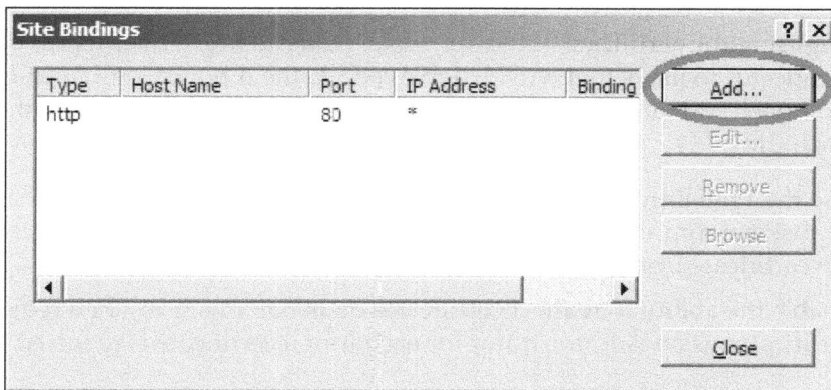

On the window that is displayed, we'll need to change the request type to **HTTPS** which automatically changes the port from 80 to the standard port for secure HTTP communication, port 443.

We then choose the certificate we created earlier from the **SSL Certificate** drop down list and press **OK**.

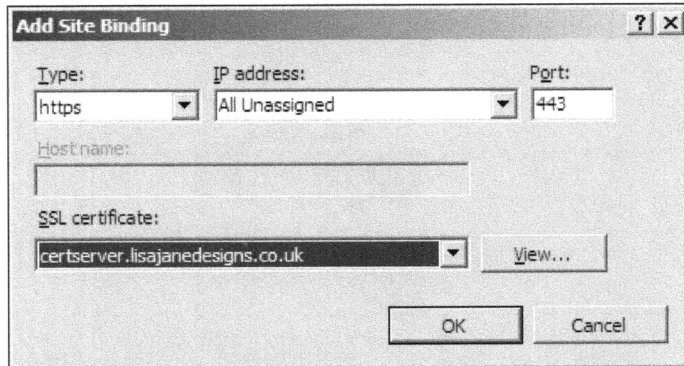

After completing these steps, the Web Enrolment features should be correctly configured for later use should they be required.

Provisioning and publishing user certificates

After configuring the certificate authority, we're ready to begin the process of issuing certificates to users that will be deployed via the iPhone Configuration Utility to iPhones and other iOS devices. To do this, we have a few different options, including:

- Use the Web Enrolment service to request end-user certificates as the user themselves approve the certificate request as an Administrator, then export the certificate from the requesting computer

- Enable the ability to request certificates on behalf of a user, then request certificates as an Administrator for each user a certificate is required for

To use the first option, the Web Enrolment service can be reached as an end user by visiting the /CertSrv URL on the certificate authority server itself. In our example server, this would be the following URL:

```
https://certserver.lisajanedesigns.co.uk/CertSrv
```

After visiting the URL, a user can then request a user certificate, which can then be approved by an administrator. However, that's not the approach we'll be taking for issuing certificates for using certificate-based authentication with iPhone and Exchange.

We'll be looking to configure and use the second option, and enable the Administrator to issue certificates on behalf of the users we wish to allow to connect to the Exchange Server 2010 infrastructure using ActiveSync. This avoids the need for the certificate request to be approved, allowing a more streamlined approach.

Creating the Enrolment Agent certificate

The first prerequisite is to enable the Certificate Authority to issue Enrolment Agent certificates, which allow us to issue a certificate to an Administrator for the purpose of requesting certificates on behalf of other users.

To enable the certificate, we need to use the Active Directory Certificate Services management span-in, which we can gain access to through navigating to the certificate authority itself via **Server Manager**, inside **Active Directory Certificate Services**, and then expanding the certificate authority node, in our case **lisajanedesigns-CERTSERVER-CA**.

Right-click on the **Certificate Templates** folder, and choose **New Certificate Template to Issue** as shown in the following screenshot:

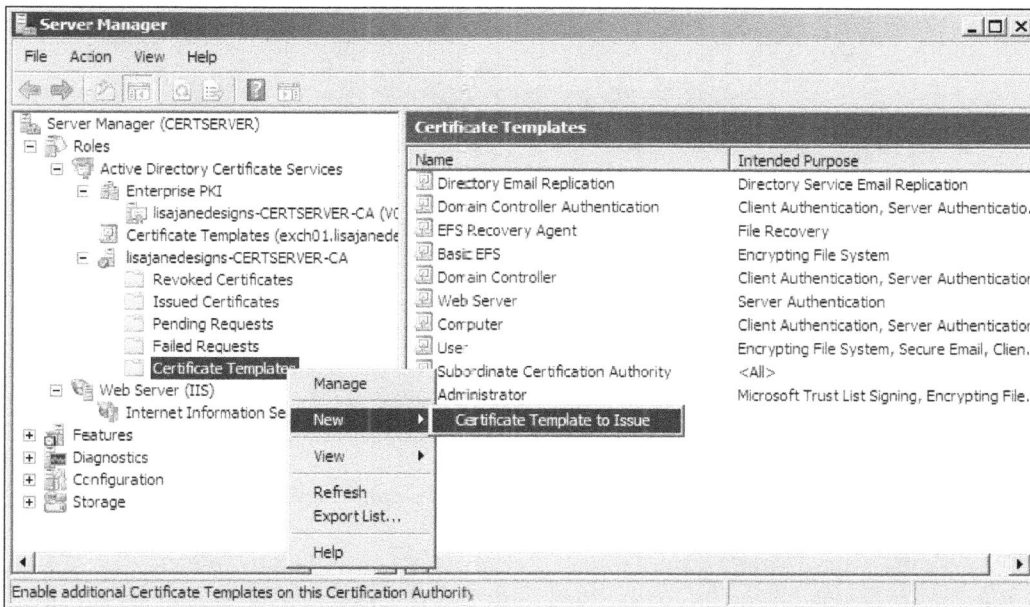

You should now be prompted with a list of available certificate templates. From the list, select the **Enrolment Agent** and choose **OK**.

The Enrolment Agent should now be shown in the list of Certificate Templates. We can now close the certificate authority snap-in, as we don't need it to create and issue certificates themselves.

For the purpose of issuing an Enrolment Agent certificate, and then to request, view, and export certificates on behalf of users, we'll be using the **Certificates** snap-in in the **Microsoft Management Console (MMC)**.

By default Windows does not provide a pre-populated MMC shortcut to access this, however it is fairly straightforward to create our own MMC snap-in with the correct settings.

To create a new MMC console with the Certificates snap-in, open the base MMC console by clicking **Start | Run** and entering mmc.exe, then press **OK**.

Next, click **File**, then choose **Add/Remove Snap-In**:

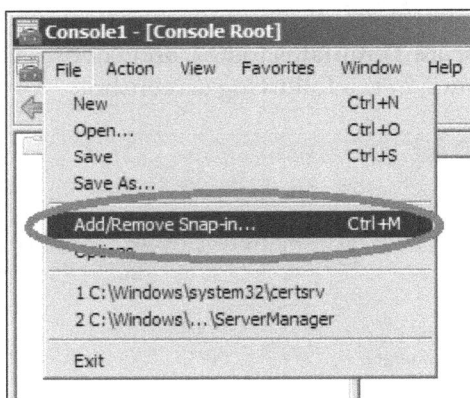

From the list that shows, choose **Certificates**, and then choose **Add**. When prompted, make the appropriate selection so that certificates for **My User Account** will be shown by this snap-in, and then choose **OK**.

> For easy access to the Certificates MMC snap-in, you can save the customized MMC console you've just created.
>
> Choose **File | Save** to save a custom .msc file. By default this will allow you to save to the **Administrative Tools** folder for easy access alongside other management tools.

The certificate snap-in should be shown, providing access to certificates associated with the current user in the **Personal** certificate store.

The first task we need to accomplish is to request an Enrolment Certificate. To request this, right-click on the **Personal** certificate store node, then choose **All Tasks | Request New Certificate**:

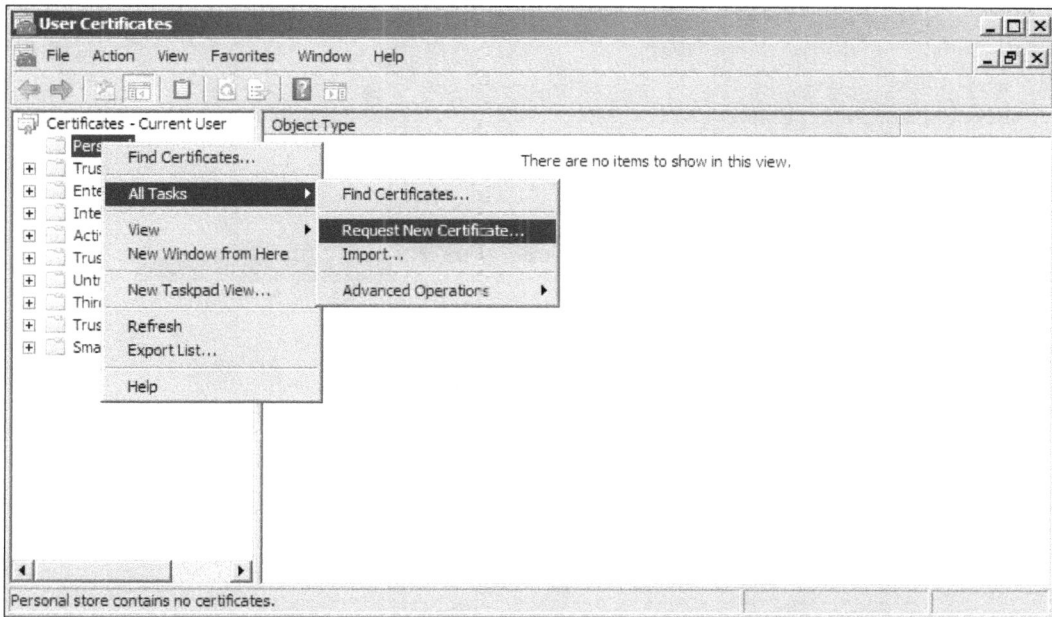

From the list of certificates, select **Enrolment Agent**, then choose **Enroll**. The certificate should be requested and if you are a Domain Admin or Enterprise Admin, the certificate should be automatically issued.

After successfully obtaining an Enrolment Agent certificate, we should now be ready to request certificates on behalf of users.

Creating a certificate on behalf of a user

Through the next few pages, we'll walk through the process of requesting and checking our first certificate for a user:

- Enroll for a certificate on behalf of a user
- Verify the certificate was successfully published to Active Directory
- Export the certificate if required for use on the workstation used to generate iPhone Configuration Profiles

After this process is complete, we should have a complete certificate that can be used for certificate-based authentication against Exchange Server 2010.

To begin, we'll stay within the Certificates snap-in, and right-click in the **Personal** certificate store, then within the **Advanced Operations** sub-menu, choose **Enroll on behalf of** to begin the process of requesting a certificate for a user:

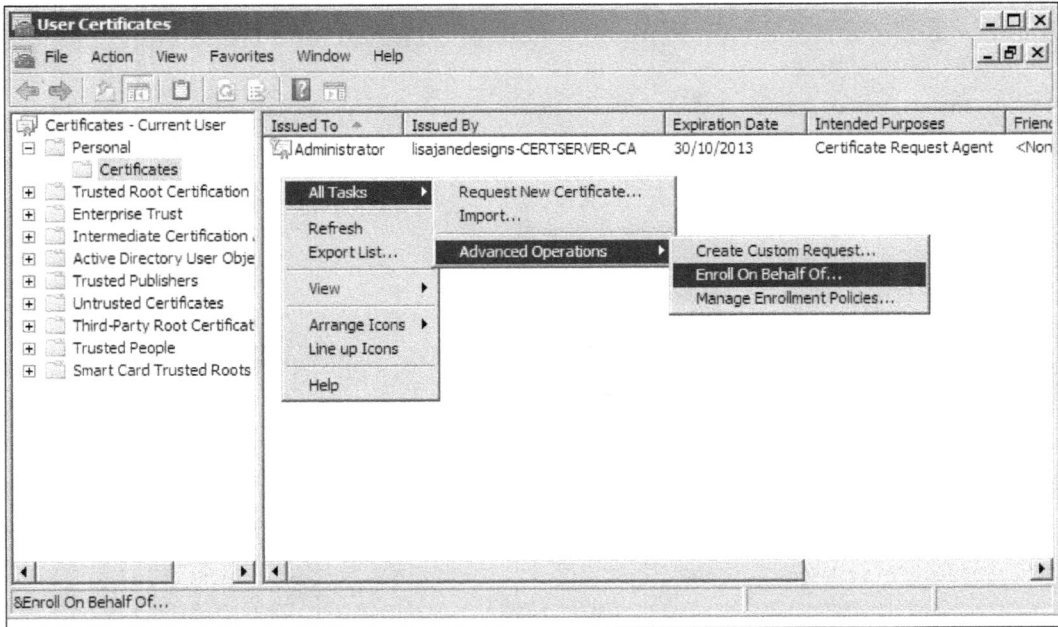

The certificate enrolment wizard should be displayed, where we can complete the following details when prompted:

- **Enrollment Agent Certificate**: select the certificate created in the above steps when prompted

- **Certificate Type**: user certificate, suitable for digital signatures, key encipherment, encrypting file system, secure email and importantly, client authentication

- **Select a User**: browse or enter the details of the user on whose behalf the certificate is being requested

After successful completion of the wizard the following should occur:

- A new private key is created in the local Personal certificate store for the Administrative user making the certificate request

- A certificate is requested from the certificate authority and automatically approved

- The certificate is published to Active Directory and associated with the user the certificate has been requested on behalf of

The certificate should also be shown within the Personal certificate store of the administrator that requested the certificate.

The next step is to ensure that the certificate has been published to Active Directory and correctly associated with the user. This process should only need to be checked the first time a certificate is requested on behalf of a user, simply to ensure that the process has been followed successfully.

To verify that the certificate has been published, using an Administrative workstation or server with Active Directory management tools installed (such as a domain controller), open **Active Directory Users and Computers**.

By default, **Active Directory Users and Computers** does not show published certificates for users. To enable this feature, click **View** and ensure **Advanced Features** is selected:

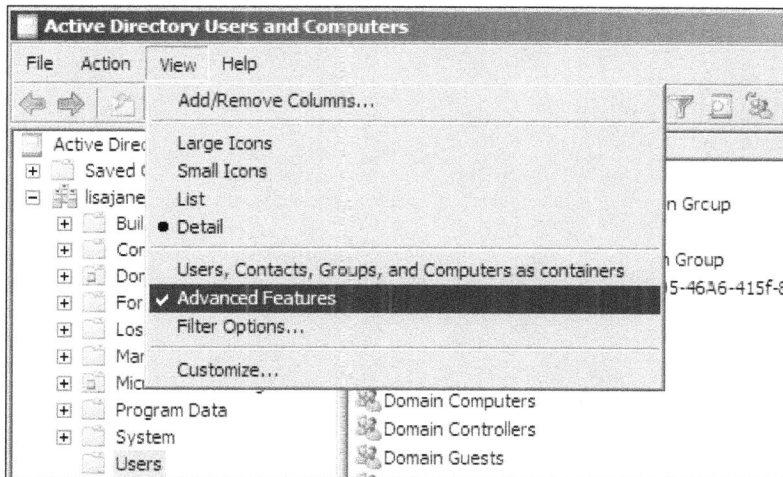

Next, locate the user we've requested a certificate for, then right click on the user and choose **Properties**. When the user's properties are shown, select the **Published Certificates** tab and examine the certificates listed. The certificate we've just created should be shown in the list.

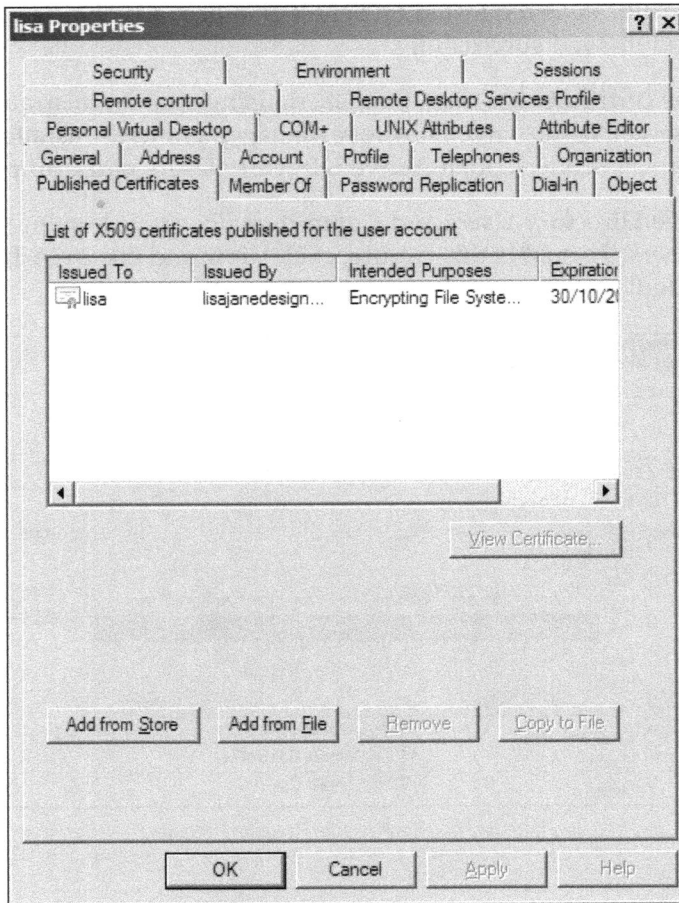

If the certificate is shown, then the process to request a certificate on behalf of a user was successful.

> If the certificate isn't shown immediately, don't worry. Active Directory replication can take a couple of minutes in environments with multiple domain controllers, and substantially longer in environments using multiple Active Directory Sites. Check replication schedules and if necessary, wait for the published certificate to replicate to the domain controller you are accessing before assuming that the operation has failed.

After checking the certificate was successfully published to Active Directory and associated with the user, we are now able to confidently state that this user, in possession of the corresponding private key and certificate, should be able to authenticate to Active Directory-based services including Exchange Server 2010; this is assuming that services they wish to use are configured correctly.

We'll now run through the process of exporting this certificate and private key to a workstation for the purposes of testing certificate authentication, and to use with the iPhone Configuration Utility in the next chapter.

For each user a certificate is requested for, the certificate and associated private key must be exported. To export the certificate, we'll revisit the **Certificates** snap-in on the server or administrative workstation that the certificate was requested from and locate the certificate within the **Personal** certificate store.

Once we've located the certificate, we can export it to a Personal Information Exchange (PFX) file by right-clicking the certificate and choosing the sub-menu **All Tasks**, then choosing **Export**:

The certificate export wizard should be displayed. When prompted, choose the following options:

- Export the private key with the certificate
- Enter an appropriate secure password when prompted
- Export as Personal Information Exchange format, selecting to include all certificates in the certification chain
- Select an appropriate file path to export the certificate and private key to
- Mark the key as exportable so that it can be exported at a later date

After export, you should now have a single PFX file which contains the user certificate, the certificate authority certificate, and the private key associated with the user certificate.

We will now move this PFX file and use standard Windows methods (such as saving to a USB key, or copying to a remove Windows Share) to move it to the workstation we will be using in the next chapter with the iPhone Configuration Utility.

If you've used the Certificates snap-in to generate the certificate on the same workstation and as the same user you'll be using to create iPhone Configuration Profiles on, then you can skip this step and the re-import steps below.

After moving the file to the workstation you'll be using to issue iPhone Configuration Profiles, log in as the user you will use to generate the profiles and locate the PFX file.

Double-click the PFX file to begin the Certificate Import Wizard. You'll be prompted for the password you used in the export step, and asked which certificate store the certificate should be imported into. Choose **Automatically select the certificate store based on the type of certificate**.

If the certificate is imported successfully, you should be shown a message box indicating the process to import a certificate was successful:

Configuring Exchange Server 2010 for certificate-based authentication

The final stage in configuring certificate-based authentication is to configure Exchange Server 2010 so that it requires user certificates as a valid authentication mechanism.

To accomplish this, we'll need to complete the following tasks on all servers hosting the Client Access Role that ActiveSync clients will connect to:

- Configure IIS pre-requisites to enable mapping of user certificates to Active Directory accounts
- Configure the Default Web Site in IIS to allow certificate mapping for authentication to be enabled
- Configure Exchange Server 2010 to only allow certificate-based authentication for ActiveSync clients

It's important to note that after configuration of certificate-based authentication for ActiveSync, ActiveSync clients such as iPhones or other iOS devices currently using username and password authentication will no longer be able to access Exchange until they are re-configured to use certificate-based authentication; therefore these tasks are best performed before you provision ActiveSync clients.

Optionally, we'll also look at how we can test functionality of certificate-based authentication from a workstation using Outlook Web App, to ensure that IIS and Exchange Server 2010 are configured correctly.

For this optional task, it's recommended to attempt this on a Client Access Server that isn't currently providing Outlook Web App services to end users. This is ideally tested before your Exchange Servers are in production, or on a server that is temporarily removed from a load-balancing array.

To set up Exchange Server 2010 to test functionality we'll perform the following tasks:

- Configure Outlook Web App to use standard authentication methods if it is currently using forms-based authentication and require client certificates
- Attempt login to Outlook Web App using the user certificate contained in the Personal certificate store on the administrative server or workstation the certificate was created on, or the workstation the PFX file containing the private key and certificate was imported to
- After successfully testing certificate-based authentication, revert Outlook Web App to the original configuration

After we've performed these tasks, we should have an Exchange Server 2010 environment configured to require certificate-based authentication for ActiveSync, and after testing certificate-based authentication to Outlook Web App have confidence that certificate-based authentication is correctly configured in Active Directory and Exchange Server 2010.

Configuring IIS pre-requisites

Our first step to configure Exchange Server 2010 is to ensure that the correct pre-requisites are configured correctly in the instance of Internet Information Services (IIS) on each Exchange Server 2010 Client Access Server that will accept ActiveSync connections.

We can perform some of this configuration using the IIS Manager user interface, however some of the configuration must be performed from the command line.

The first step is to enable Active Directory Client Certificate Authentication in the global configuration for IIS. To perform this, open IIS Manager, and navigate to the server node itself, which in our case is **EXCH01**. Click on this node, then under the **IIS** section, locate the **Authentication** options:

To change settings for the global Authentication configuration for IIS on this server, either double-click **Authentication** or choose **Open Feature** from the **Actions** pane on the right-hand side of the IIS Manager window.

The Authentication configuration should open, and present a list of authentication providers. In this list, locate **Active Directory Client Certificate Authentication**. Right click on this item in the list and choose **Enable**:

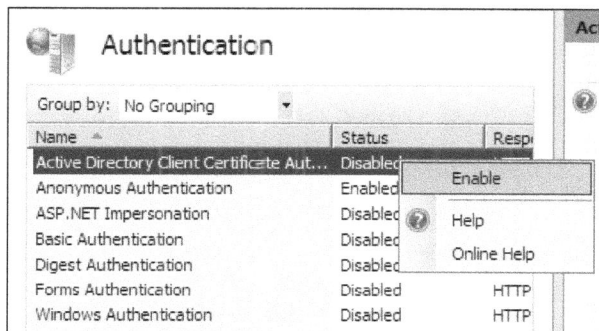

After making this configuration change, the ability for IIS to utilize user certificates for authentication should now be enabled for the server, but not enabled for the Default Web Site, which hosts ActiveSync, Outlook Web App, and other Exchange Server services.

The next step is to enable the feature for the Default Web Site. To perform this reconfiguration, open a command prompt and enter the following command on a single line:

```
C:\WINDOWS\SYSTEM32\INETSRV\APPCMD.EXE set config "Default
Web Site" -section:system.webServer/security/authentication/
clientCertificateMappingAuthentication /enabled:"True" /commit:apphost
```

After entering the command, IIS won't yet require or accept user certificates for Exchange Services, and will need further configuration within Exchange Server 2010 itself.

> If you've configured additional Virtual Directories under an IIS site other than the Default Web Site for Exchange services, including ActiveSync, you may also need to enable the feature for those IIS sites. This can be performed using the above command, replacing **Default Web Site** with the appropriate name found in IIS Manager.

Configuring Exchange ActiveSync

Our next step towards completing configuration of certificate-based authentication is to correctly enable the feature in Exchange Server 2010 on each of the Exchange servers we've enabled Client Certificate Authentication for in the *Configuring IIS pre-requisites* section.

For each Exchange Server, open the Exchange Management Console, navigate to **Server Configuration**, and select **Client Access**. Select the relevant Exchange Server from the list, and then select the **Exchange ActiveSync** tab:

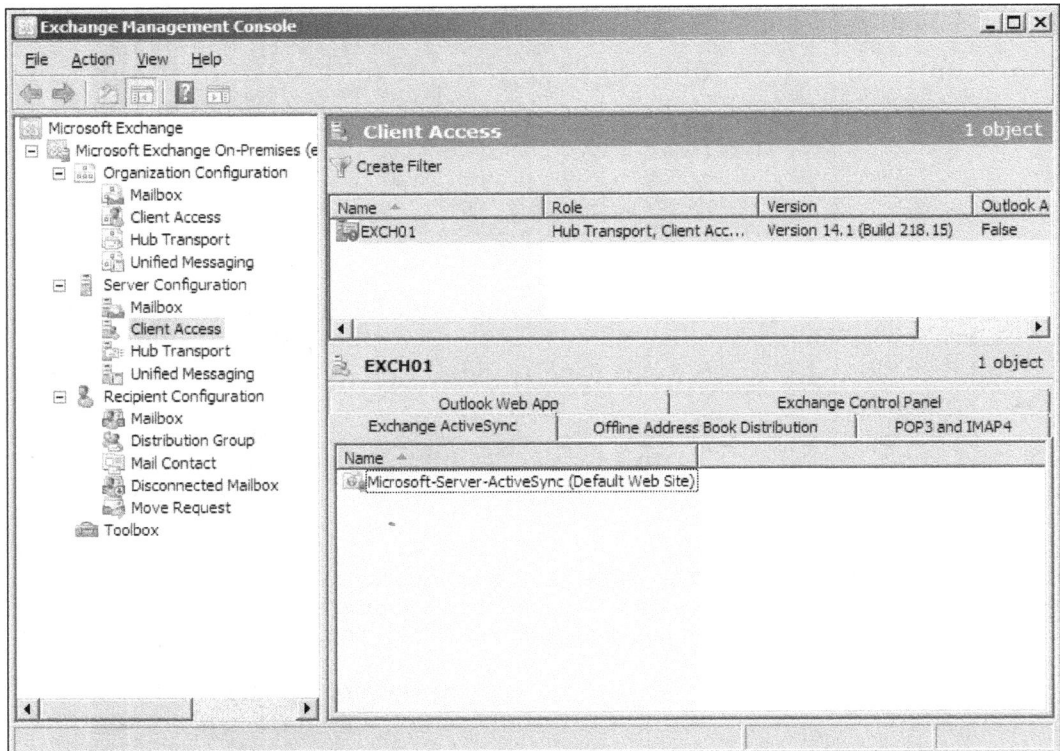

After selecting the Exchange ActiveSync tab, you should see a list of virtual directories associated with ActiveSync; typically there will be one labeled similar to the following:

```
Microsoft-Server-ActiveSync (Default Web Site)
```

Right-click this item in the list, then choose **Properties**. In the properties window that subsequently opens, select the **Authentication** tab.

In the authentication tab, change the following settings:

- Clear the checkbox labeled **Basic Authentication** so that no authentication method is selected
- Under the radio box group labeled **Client Certificate Authentication**, select Require Client Certificates

After selecting the above options, choose **OK** to save and apply the settings.

To complete the configuration, we need to apply the Client Certificate Mapping Authentication to the ActiveSync virtual directory, and then restart IIS.

First perform the IIS reconfiguration at the command line:

```
C:\WINDOWS\SYSTEM32\INETSRV\APPCMD.EXE set config "Default Web Site/
Microsoft-Server-ActiveSync" -section:system.webServer/security/
authentication/clientCertificateMappingAuthentication /enabled:"True" /
commit:apphost
```

Finally, perform a graceful restart of IIS, using the `iisreset` command:

```
iisreset /noforce
```

Please note that execution of this command will prevent client access to the IIS services, including web-based Exchange Services, for a short period of time.

After completing the above configuration steps, ActiveSync should be configured to only accept ActiveSync clients, such as iPhones, that attempt to authenticate using certificate-based authentication.

Testing certificate-based authentication using Outlook Web App

Before we attempt to provision devices it is worth testing that we can successfully connect a client to Exchange Server 2010 that is using certificates to authenticate.

Although it's not a mandatory step, we could instead choose to troubleshoot any issues when we connect iPhones to Exchange in the next chapter; we can choose to alter Outlook Web App to utilize certificate-based authentication.

In our environment at our example company, Lisa Jane Designs, the Exchange Server solution is not yet in production, therefore we will be temporarily altering the configuration on Exchange Server to perform the verification from our administrative workstation with the user private key and certificate installed.

To alter Outlook Web App to utilize certificate-based authentication, open the Exchange Management Console and navigate to **Server Configuration**, then click on **Client Access**. Select the server you wish to alter the configuration for in the list, then choose the **Outlook Web App** tab.

After selecting the **Outlook Web App** tab, you should be presented with a list of virtual directories for the specific Exchange Server — typically there will only be one, associated with the Default Web Site:

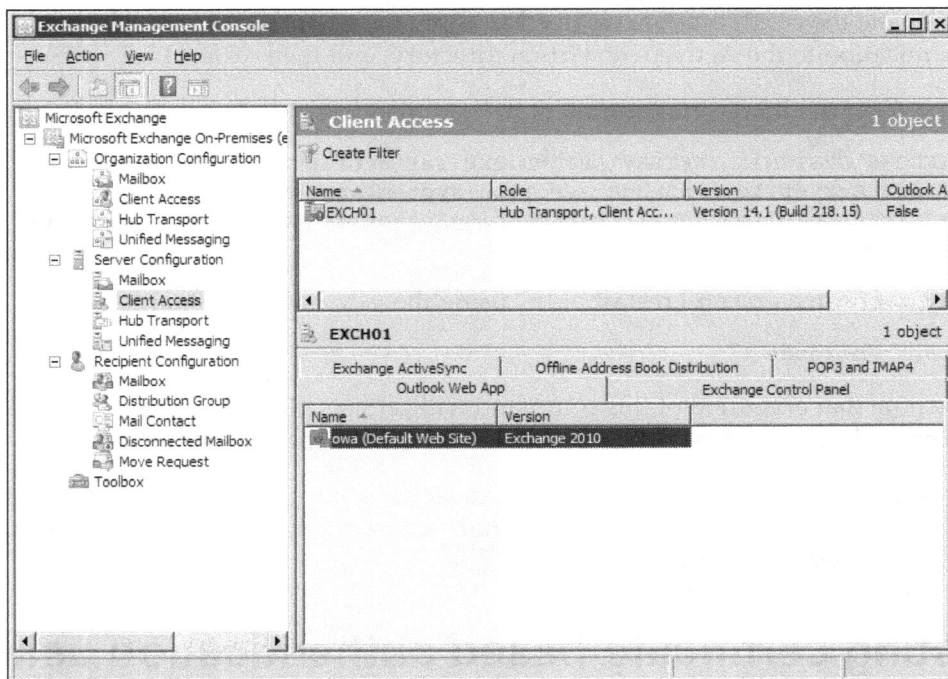

Right-click the Outlook Web App virtual directory — in our case **owa (Default Web Site)** and choose **Properties**.

Navigate to the **Authentication** tab on the **Properties** window. Before making any changes, record the current settings for Authentication methods in place, as they will be required to reverse the changes made. Next, ensure the following settings are in place:

- Select the radio button **Use one or more of the following authentication methods**
- Select the checkbox **Basic authentication**
- Clear the setting for other checkboxes including **Integrated Windows authentication** and **Digest authentication for Windows domain servers**

After altering the above settings, choose **OK** to save the changes.

Repeat the changes for the **Exchange Control Panel (ECP)** virtual directory, after recording the ECP's current settings. The ECP is used for the **Options** pages in Outlook Web App, therefore it must use the same authentication methods as Outlook Web App.

Next, open up the Internet Information Services (IIS) Manager and navigate to the **owa** virtual directory, within the server, underneath **Default Web Site**.

After selecting **owa**, choose the feature **SSL Settings** and either double-click on the icon or select **Open Feature**.

Record the current setting, which should typically be to **Require SSL** and to **Ignore** client certificates.

Change the **SSL Settings** so that **Require SSL** is selected, and that **Client Certificates are Required**:

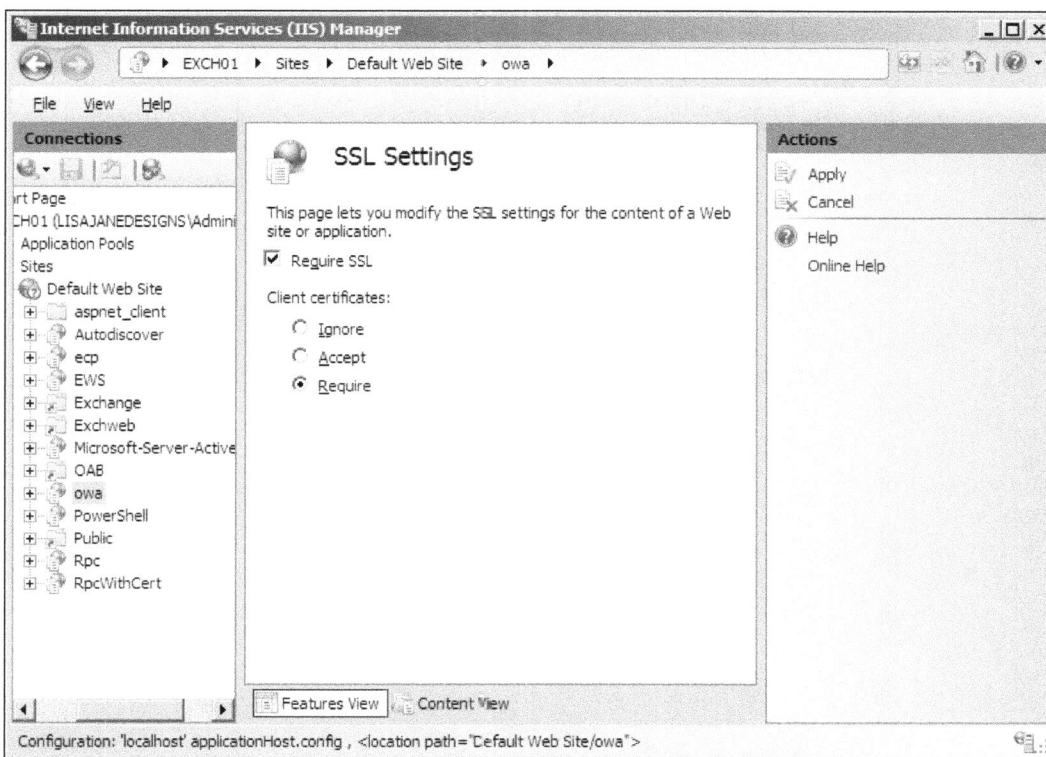

After making the changes, choose **Apply**, then close IIS Manager.

Finally, to ensure that the Exchange Server 2010 changes take immediate effect, gracefully restart IIS using `iisreset` from a command prompt:

```
iisreset /noforce
```

After restarting IIS, the configuration changes for Outlook Web App should take effect. From the administrative workstation where the user certificate is installed, logged on as the administrative user we used earlier in the chapter to import the certificate as, visit Outlook Web App, typically located at a URL in the following format:

```
https://mail.company.com/owa
```

You should be presented with an opportunity to select the certificate to use for authentication to Exchange Server 2010. Select the certificate to use for authentication, which should correspond to the user to log in to Outlook Web App as, and then select **OK**:

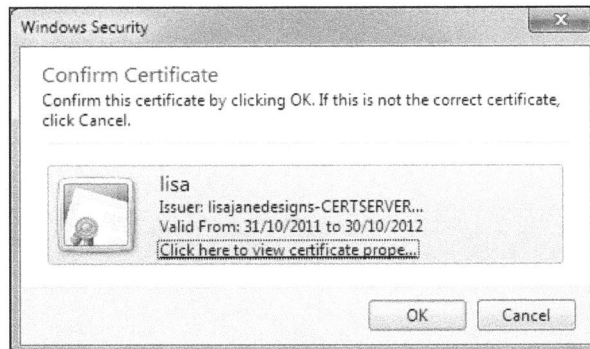

If the operation is successful, you should automatically log on to Outlook Web App without further prompts for credentials:

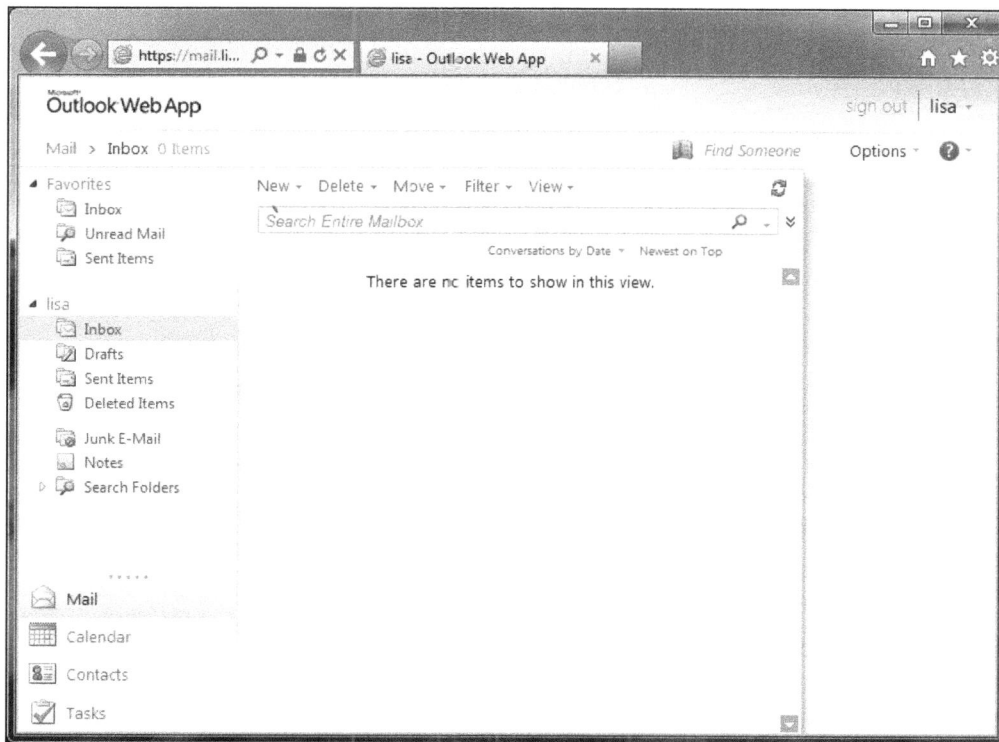

After successful login, we should be confident that the core features required for authentication to Exchange Server 2010 using user certificates are in place and function correctly.

After verification that certificate-based authentication is working, change the Exchange Server 2010 Outlook Web App and Exchange Control Panel settings back to the configuration settings recorded before making changes to Outlook Web App and the Exchange Control Panel using the Exchange Management Console.

Next use Internet Information Services (IIS) Manager to change the **owa** Virtual Directory SSL Settings back to the original settings, then apply the original configuration using the `iisreset` command shown above.

Summary

In this chapter we have implemented a simple public key infrastructure into the Exchange Server 2010 organization for the purpose of ensuring that all iPhone and other iOS devices connecting to Exchange use certificate-based authentication.

We've covered the basics of certificate-based authentication, including how it can remove the need to change passwords on the iPhone device if a security policy is in place to require regular password changes, removing some of the issues associated with keeping device password in sync with the user's Active Directory password. We've also looked at other reasons for using certificate-based authentication, including to ensure that any devices that connect using the ActiveSync protocol have been provisioned correctly using a private key and certificate, helping to prevent users from connecting personal devices to the Exchange infrastructure.

After looking at why we would use certificate-based authentication and learning a little bit about what it is, we've looked at an example use case for implementation using our example company, Lisa Jane Designs, who wish to use certificate-based authentication to stop casual iPhone users connecting their devices to the Exchange infrastructure. Based on this requirement, we've walked through the implementation of Active Directory Certificate Services, and a certificate authority, which provides the foundation of providing certificate-based authentication.

After configuring a certificate authority, we've then moved on to looking at the process of issuing user certificates as an administrator, making use of the ability to request certificates on behalf of other users, and requested a certificate for another user within the Lisa Jane Designs organization. After requesting and subsequently obtaining a certificate, we've exported the certificate and associated private key for installation onto the administrative workstation we'll be using in the next chapter to deploy the certificate using the iPhone Configuration Utility.

Finally, we've made the critical changes to Exchange Server 2010 that ensure certificate-based authentication is configured correctly and enabled for Exchange ActiveSync clients. To ensure that our certificate authority and Exchange Server 2010 can communicate correctly, we've also tested certificate-based authentication from the administrative workstation after temporarily making changes to Outlook Web App on Exchange Server 2010.

In the next chapter, we'll be looking at the iPhone Configuration Utility, which is the software used to manually create Device Configuration Profiles. We'll look at how to create configuration profiles for users, including how to deploy certificate-based authentication to iPhones and other iOS devices, and see certificate-based authentication in action on an Apple device.

7
Provisioning iOS Client Devices

In the previous chapter, we covered a fairly complex topic, certificate-based authentication, including setup and configuration of a fairly small public-key infrastructure, and made the relevant configuration changes to Exchange.

You'll be relieved to find out that this chapter is relatively easier, and for the most part relies little on Exchange Server configuration and is mostly focused on workstation-based configuration and deployment of iOS client devices.

In this chapter, you'll learn about how to provision and deploy iOS devices using Apple's iPhone Configuration Utility. This tool allows you to do more than what is possible using Exchange Server 2010 alone, including deploying certificates to iOS devices and a wealth of features to improve the restrictions that can be enforced on devices.

We'll look at how to create and manage the Configuration Profiles themselves, including how to associate user certificates with Configuration Profiles, and how to deploy the profiles to individual devices. And we'll also look at how to make it easy to deploy Configuration Profiles to user devices directly from the Exchange server.

By the end of this chapter you should understand what the purpose of the iPhone Configuration Utility is, and how it can be used most appropriately in your organization.

Overview of device Configuration Profiles

Configuration Profiles are created by the iPhone Configuration Utility and contain, in XML format, a list of configuration settings to apply to an iOS Device. Once a Configuration Profile is installed on the device, these settings remain in effect until the profile is removed from the device.

The type of settings contained in Configuration Profiles don't just apply to iOS devices in an Exchange Server environment. You can use Configuration Profiles to deploy settings for the following:

- Passcode restrictions
- Device functionality restrictions
- Application restrictions
- Security and Privacy settings
- Wi-Fi Access Point settings
- WPN settings
- POP3 and IMAP account settings
- Exchange ActiveSync settings
- Generic LDAP server settings
- CalDAV server settings
- Calendar Subscriptions
- CardDAV/Contact server settings
- Homepage web links or web clips
- Certificates and credentials
- Certificate Enrolment (SCEP) settings
- Apple Mobile Device Management server settings
- Advanced settings, such as APN settings

Once created, Configuration Profiles can be deployed to devices by a number of methods:

- By connecting iOS devices to an administrative workstation
- Over the Internet, by allowing iPhone Configuration Profiles to be downloaded from a web server to the device itself
- E-mailing Configuration Profiles to end users for self-installation
- Using proprietary or in-house iOS deployment and management solutions

In this chapter, we'll be focusing on the first two options as they are easiest to implement and give the most flexibility in terms of deployment options.

So, how does a Configuration Profile sit in terms of Exchange Server 2010 and what configuration is managed from where? The best way of looking at it is that the Configuration Profile can be used for iPhone-specific restrictions and configuration, such as how to physically get certificates onto devices and enforce restrictions on iOS-specific features, such as access to iTunes and the Application Store. Exchange ActiveSync-specific policies also get applied to the device and the combined total of the settings defined by the Configuration Profile and Exchange ActiveSync policy make up the set of policies, or restrictions, applied to the iOS device itself:

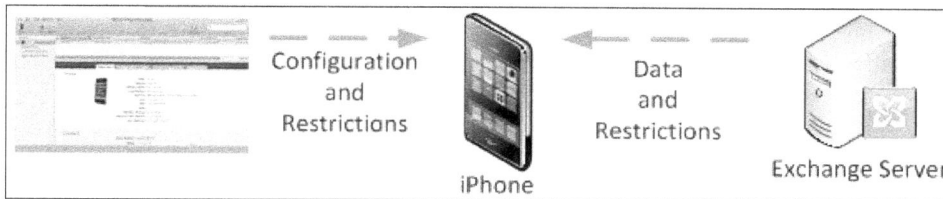

Once a Configuration Profile is deployed to a device, it doesn't automatically update; therefore it is logical to utilize Exchange ActiveSync policies where possible. If restrictions and deployment of certificates aren't especially important, the ability to ensure that a user cannot inadvertently remove ActiveSync settings through placing restrictions on the removal of the Configuration Profile may be compelling enough in itself to use Configuration Profiles for basic ActiveSync settings alone.

Finally, the iPhone Configuration Utility isn't just limited to generating and managing Configuration Profiles. Although we'll only be covering Configuration Profiles in this book, it's important to understand what else the iPhone Configuration Utility can be used for.

If your organization develops in-house applications for the iPhone, then these applications can be provisioned to devices using a feature of the iPhone Configuration Utility known as **Provisioning Profiles**. The provisioning profiles define the applications that can be installed, and once registered within the iPhone Configuration Utility, allow in-house applications to be deployed to iOS devices alongside the Configuration Profile. This can save time and effort when provisioning new devices as additional steps to manually deploy applications using iTunes or web-based distribution can be avoided.

Obtaining and installing the iPhone Configuration Utility

Apple makes the iPhone Configuration Utility available from the Apple Support website, within the **Enterprise** section:

```
http://www.apple.com/support/iphone/enterprise/
```

The iPhone Configuration Utility is available for both Microsoft Windows and Mac OS X platforms, though for the purpose of creating Exchange Server specific Configuration Profiles, particularly those containing certificates, we will be using the Windows version.

The latest Windows version can be found under the link **iPhone Configuration Utility for Windows**. At the time of writing, the current version of the iPhone Configuration Utility is version 3.4, which has full support for the latest version of iOS, version 5. For full support for all iOS 5 features and improvements over previous versions, it's recommended to download and install this version or later.

The essential pre-requisite for the iPhone Configuration Utility is the installation of the **Microsoft .Net Framework 3.5 Service Pack 1**.

On Windows 7 or later, this can be installed through **Control Panel | Programs and Features**, then by selecting **Turn Windows Features on or off**.

On earlier versions of Windows, the Microsoft .Net Framework 3.5 Service Pack 1 can be downloaded from the following URL:

```
http://www.microsoft.com/download/en/details.aspx?id=22
```

After ensuring the .Net Framework 3.5 SP1 is installed, installation of the iPhone Configuration Utility should be performed using default settings; no special configuration is required.

iTunes and device activation

If you're planning on connecting iOS devices to your administrative workstation for activation and installation of Configuration Profiles, you may also need to install iTunes. There is no independent Enterprise version of iTunes. Therefore, the consumer version should be downloaded and installed from the following URL:

```
http://www.apple.com/itunes
```

The installation of iTunes includes device drivers for the iOS devices, including the iPhone, which are used to perform activation over a USB port and to upgrade iOS devices running software below version 5 to the current version.

As of iOS 5, iPhone activation and iOS upgrade are no longer only possible via iTunes. iOS can be both updated and activated over the Internet, directly from Apple servers.

Therefore if you plan to deploy iPhone Configuration Profiles over the Internet, installation of iTunes on an administrative workstation is not necessary. For new devices in particular, the main reason for installation of iTunes is to ensure the correct drivers for devices are installed and ready.

The first scenario in this chapter, deploying individual profiles to devices using the iPhone Configuration Utility, will require installation of iTunes. Therefore if you're following the examples in this book it's recommended to install iTunes, using the default installation settings.

After installation of iTunes, an administrative workstation should be configured to launch in **Activation Mode**. This mode is for the convenience of the administrator and ensures that when a new iOS device is attached to the administrative workstation, the administrator is not prompted by iTunes to create a new relationship in iTunes with the device. Instead, the device is automatically "ejected" from iTunes after activation is performed, should it be required.

To switch iTunes to Activation Mode, launch iTunes from the command prompt with the `/setPrefIntStoreActivationMode` option set to **1**.

An example of this on 32-bit systems is shown as follows:

```
"C:\Program Files\iTunes\iTunes.exe" /setPrefInt StoreActivationMode 1
```

For 64-bit systems, the command is very similar; however, you should ensure that you replace `C:\Program Files` with `C:\Program Files (x86)`.

To verify that iTunes has been switched into Activation Mode, open iTunes and choose **Help | About iTunes**:

After installation and configuration of iTunes, connecting an iPhone or other iOS device should automatically install the appropriate drivers, shown as follows:

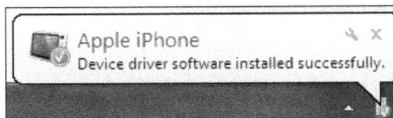

Creating Configuration Profiles for users

After installation of the iPhone Configuration Utility, you should be set to create Configuration Profiles.

In this section, we'll examine what settings can be managed through the use of Configuration Profiles, and create our first configuration profile. Later in the chapter we'll deploy the profile to a directly attached device and later on look at how we can create a more generic profile for web-based distribution to users.

After launching the iPhone Configuration Utility, you will be presented with an interface designed in a familiar Apple style, similar to Safari and iTunes.

On the left-hand side bar, we should be presented with two sections. The first is **Library** and contains the following sub-sections:

- **Devices**: displays a list of connected or previously-connected iOS devices
- **Applications**: used to import iOS applications for deployment to devices

- **Provisioning Profiles**: used to provision enterprise applications to iOS devices
- **Configuration Profiles**: the section we will focus on to create profiles for Exchange Server 2010 settings

The section is named **Devices**, and shows the currently connected iOS device.

When creating configuration settings for iOS devices the relevant sub-section, as mentioned above, is the **Configuration Profiles** sub-section.

Selecting this item from the list brings up the Configuration Profiles; by default none will be present. Click **New** from the tool bar to create our first Configuration Profile.

After creating a Configuration Profile we should now see the window split into two sections — the list of Configuration Profiles, which should display one so far, and the selected Configuration Profile itself:

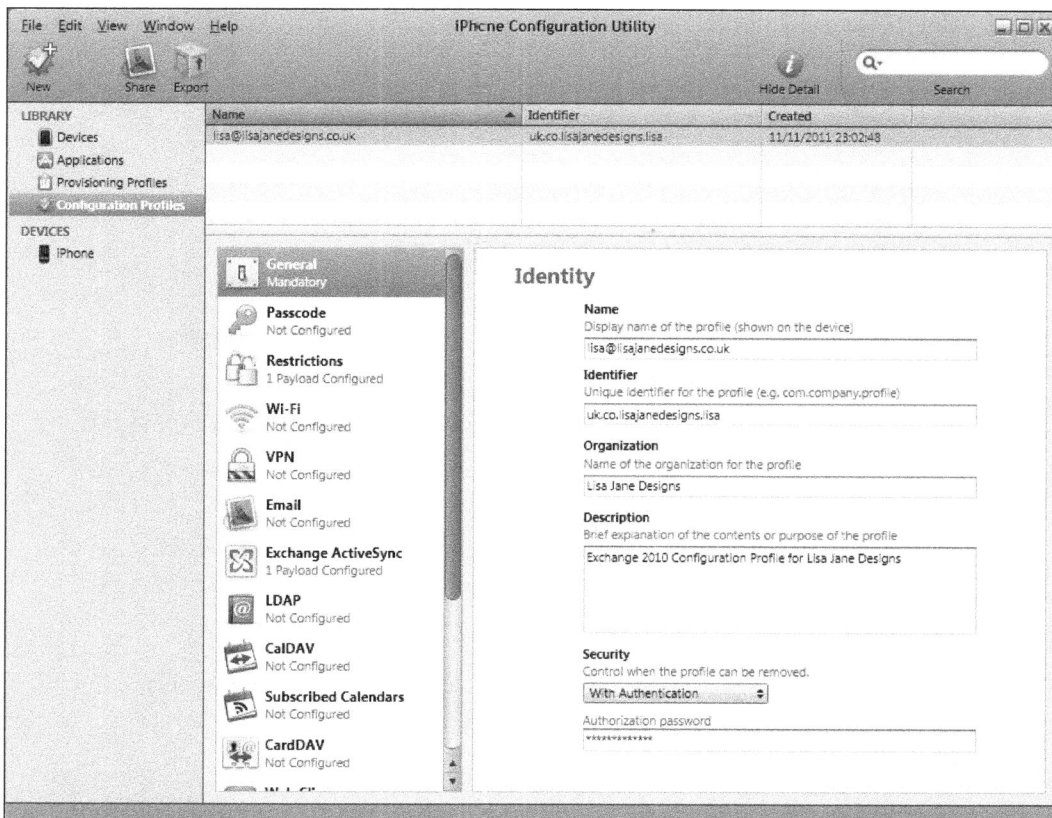

The selected Configuration Profile is shown in the bottom half of the window and uses a tabbed interface to create and adjust settings for different phone features or restrictions. By selecting each item from the tabbed list, we can either adjust the default settings, or we can create new settings where the feature configuration is not mandatory.

You'll immediately notice that some features, such as **Passcode**, are also present in Exchange ActiveSync Policies. Where the feature can be controlled by Exchange Server 2010, it's recommended to leave the setting blank or unconfigured in the Configuration Profile and allow Exchange ActiveSync to manage that setting.

For the purposes of connection to Exchange Server 2010, we'll be focusing on creating settings that apply to our Exchange ActiveSync connection and examining other device restrictions that we can configure.

General

The **General** settings primarily apply to the Configuration Profile itself, such as the profile name and removal settings:

- **Name**: The display name of the profile on the device.
- **Identifier**: A unique identifier for the profile. For example, for `lisa@lisajanedesigns.co.uk`, we can use `uk.co.lisajanedesigns.lisa`; for a generic profile we might use `uk.co.lisajanedesigns.mail`.
- **Organization**: The company name that the profile applies to.
- **Description**: A plain text description of the profile and its purpose.
- **Security**: The removal settings for the profile, with the following options:
    - **Always**: To allow the user to remove the device if they choose to.
    - **With authentication**: Allows a password to be entered (specified alongside this option) for removal.
    - **Never**: Disallows removal of the profile, unless the device is wiped.

Passcode

The passcode setting can be created and applied to the profile. However, for the purposes of connecting to Exchange Server 2010, it is not recommended.

Therefore, we'll leave the passcode settings blank and rely on Exchange ActiveSync policies to enforce password settings. This means that we only need to configure the settings in one place and have server-based control over the settings should they need to be altered in the future.

Restrictions

The restrictions section allows an iOS device using the Configuration Profile to have certain features locked or restricted on the device. These are split into the following:

- **Device Functionality**: These features allow restriction of what the in-built applications on the phone and application launcher (Springboard) can do. This includes the installation of applications, screen captures, synchronization when roaming, in-app purchase, multiplayer gaming, or the use of Siri.

  The feature that can be controlled using Exchange ActiveSync is **Allow use of camera**. Therefore if you wish to enforce this specific feature, it can be accomplished from the Exchange Server rather than the Configuration Profile.

- **Applications**: These features are similar to the Device Functionality features, and include the ability to restrict the use of the YouTube application, iTunes application, and Safari. Safari can be blocked with the use of Exchange ActiveSync policies.

  However, fine grained control over some Safari features, such as enabling JavaScript and Auto fill, is available when using Configuration Profiles.

- **iCloud**: This feature controls whether an iOS device can make use of Apple's hosted backup and synchronization offerings. By disallowing these features, the ability to automatically back up the iOS device documents and photos is not available.

- **Security and Privacy**: These settings allow configuration over whether the device can communicate with Apple for the purposes of reporting diagnostic data, and also allow control over whether the user can visit sites with untrusted or invalid SSL certificates.

  Additionally, control is available over whether a backup made by the user of the iOS device in iTunes must be encrypted.

- **Content Ratings**: Theses are most applicable if the end user of the device is allowed to install applications or download media from iTunes. Apple does not allow explicit material on the App Store; however, some applications have higher ratings due to the content they may provide access to. These settings allow appropriate corporate settings in accordance with acceptable user policies to be enforced.

You'll see in the following screenshot that for our Configuration Profile that we'll deploy to our device later, we've restricted a number of settings:

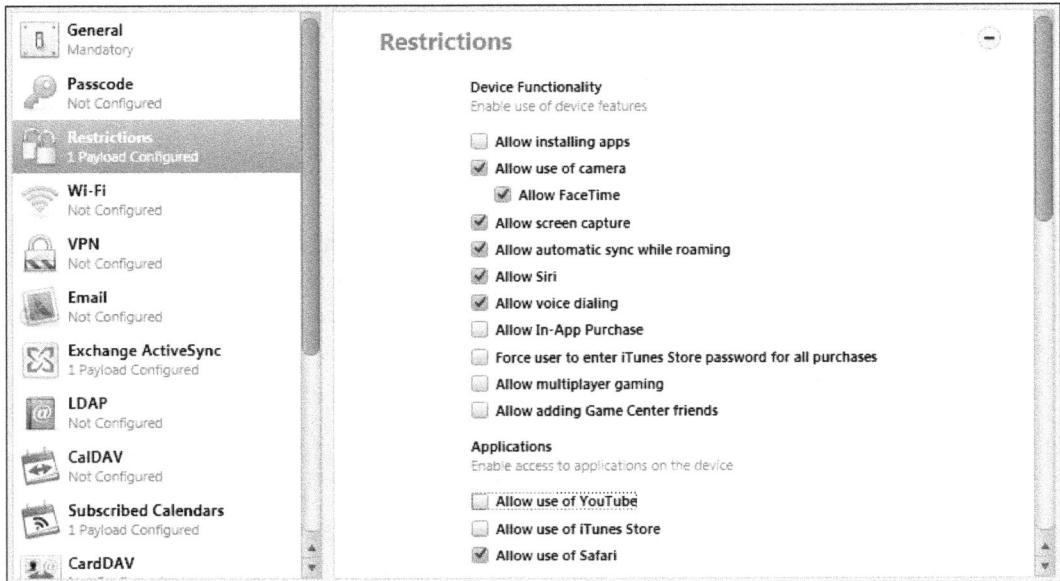

Later on when we deploy the profile to a device, we'll have a quick look at how those restrictions apply on the device itself once the Configuration Profile has been applied.

Exchange ActiveSync

As you might imagine, the Exchange ActiveSync section is especially important when creating and deploying Configuration Profiles in an Exchange Server 2010 environment.

To create an ActiveSync profile on the device, we don't need an especially long list of settings—to build the relationship with the Exchange Server we need a set of credentials, be it the username and password or certificate, along with the Exchange 2010 Server external name.

One limitation when creating Configuration Profiles is the Auto Discover feature for detecting the Exchange Server name is not available; for most environments using the on-premises version of Exchange this provides no issue as we know this already and can enter it into the configuration profile.

In an Office 365 environment, this presents a small challenge as the name is not set by the administrator and bears no relationship to the domain name of the organization.

To find the name of the Exchange 2010 Client Access server in an Office 365 environment, log into Outlook Web App using a web browser. In the address bar, you should see the server name, typically in the format, podXXXXX.outlook.com, as shown in the following example:

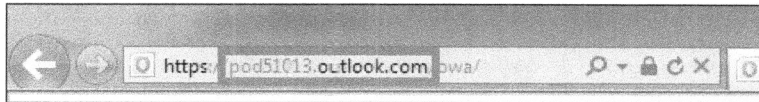

Armed with this information, or the on-premises Exchange Server external name, we can begin the configuration of the Exchange ActiveSync configuration settings:

- **Account Name**: The display name of the account on the iOS device. This can be simple, such as "Exchange ActiveSync" or reflect the organization, such as "Lisa Jane Designs E-mail".

- **Exchange ActiveSync Host**: The external name of the Exchange 2010 Server, for example, mail.lisajanedesigns.co.uk in the case of our example organization; or for Office 365 the .outlook.com name located in the previous paragraph.

- **Allow Move**: By default users are allowed to move messages between folders and between e-mail accounts. If the user configures a personal ActiveSync or e-mail account, they could feasibly move messages to their personal e-mail account. While they could equally forward the message to an external e-mail account, if they accomplish this through the move message feature on the iPhone there will be limited discover by the administrator that this has happened.

- **Use Only in Mail**: Some applications, such as the Photos app, allow e-mail messages to be composed directly from the application. This feature can be disabled by enabling this option.

- **Use SSL**: By default and in accordance with best practices, SSL communications between the Exchange Server should be enabled. If you've completed configuration of the Exchange Server using this book, then this option should be enabled.

- **Use S/MIME**: Using the user certificate created in the previous chapter, it is possible to ensure that end users send encrypted messages using the S/MIME format. For most typical environments this feature is not required; however, if you are implementing iPhones into a more secure environment which will typically have an existing Public Key Infrastructure, the requirement to send messages using S/MIME encryption can be enforced.

- **Domain, User, E-mail Address, and Password**: As you can imagine these details are critical when delivering individual user profiles; however, for generic profiles these details should be left blank. An important note is that for an individual profile that makes use of certificate-based authentication, the password field should be left blank.

- **Past days of mail to sync**: This setting reflects the setting on the iOS device that should be set as default. Combined with the Exchange ActiveSync policies, this setting can define the initial defaults set on the device, and Exchange ActiveSync policies can be used to place limits on how far back mail should be synchronized.

- **Identity Certificate**: In place of the password, once an identity certificate is enabled, it can be selected here. We'll revisit this a little later on.

For our example Configuration Profile, we'll create settings for the Lisa Jane Designs organization and enter details of the user we created a certificate for in the last chapter:

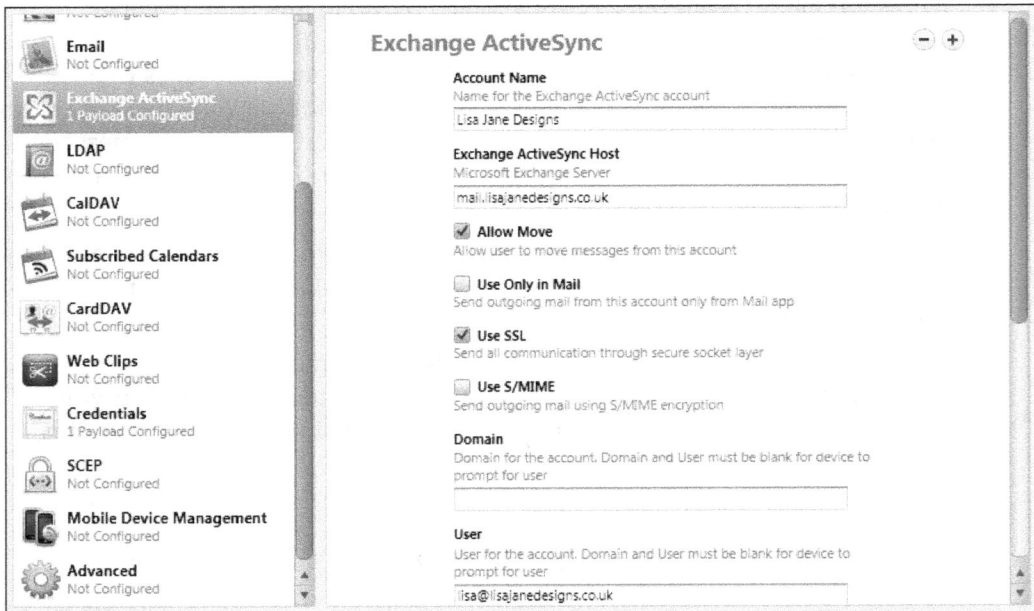

Subscribed calendars

In the next chapter we'll look at how calendar subscriptions, using the iCalendar protocol, can be used to share calendars with iPhone devices easily and simply. If, as an organization, you have common shared calendars that should be configured as standard to iOS device users, you can use the Subscribed Calendars section to add one or more calendars that are shared in the iCalendar format. The following options should be used to configure calendar subscriptions in an Exchange Server 2010 environment:

- **Description**: The calendar name shown to the end user
- **URL**: The shared calendar URL, as provided by the Exchange Server when configuring the shared calendar using the iCalendar format
- **Username**, **Password**, and **SSL** These values in an Exchange Server 2010 environment should be left blank

Credentials – embedding the User certificate

If you've implemented certificate-based authentication, covered in the previous chapter, you'll need to publish the certificate and private key to the device. That's where this section will come in handy.

In the previous chapter, one of the final steps after creating a user certificate was to import the private key and certificate into the administrative workstation that we'd use to create Configuration Profiles on. Now, it's time to put each user certificate to work and match them up with individual user Configuration Profiles.

To select a certificate, choose the **Credentials** section and select **configure**. A list of certificates should be displayed. Choose the certificate that matches the user you've configured in the Exchange ActiveSync section:

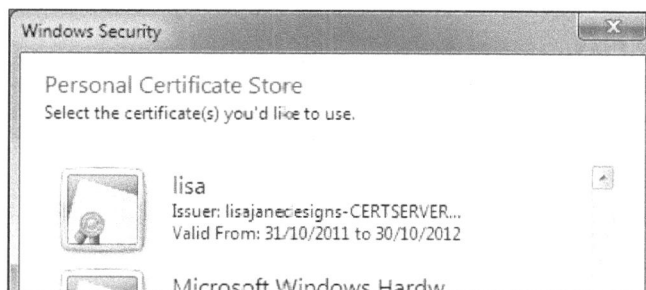

After selecting the certificate, you'll be prompted to enter a password to export it, and optionally after importing the certificate be given the chance to re-enter the password so that it can be embedded within the profile. The benefit of doing this is so that the password doesn't need to be entered on the device when you import the profile. However, it does mean that the password to the user certificate is stored within the iPhone Configuration Utility.

After importing the certificate, we now need to revisit the **Exchange ActiveSync** section. Ensure that the password for the user isn't entered, but all other user details are, and then select the imported certificate from the **Identity Certificate** option:

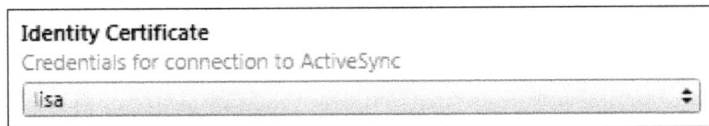

Identity Certificate
Credentials for connection to ActiveSync

lisa

After configuring the certificate correctly, the Exchange ActiveSync settings for certificate-based authentication should be complete.

Just to reiterate, if you are not using certificate-based authentication, don't worry — these settings aren't essential for use of Configuration Profiles; either enter the end user's Active Directory password in the Exchange ActiveSync settings, or if you don't have access to the password, leave the field blank to allow the end user to enter their password when they receive the device. Bear in mind by not using certificate-based authentication you are able to make use of generic Configuration Profiles covered later on in this chapter.

Other options

Let's look into other options available.

Wi-Fi and VPN

The Wi-Fi and VPN sections allow configuration of default connections to corporate wireless networks and virtual private networks. If you provide your users with VPN and Wi-Fi facilities and wish to have these connections pre-configured for users, the settings in these options may be relevant.

E-mail, LDAP, CalDAV, and CardDAV

In an Exchange Server 2010 environment the E-mail, LDAP, CalDAV, and CardDAV settings are not appropriate; E-mail accounts configured using POP3 and IMAP are not necessary when using Exchange ActiveSync. Use of an LDAP (Lightweight Directory Access Protocol) access is not required to the backend Active Directory, as Exchange Server 2010 provided access to the directory through access to the Exchange Server 2010 Global Address List. CalDAV and CardDAV protocols provide access to server-based calendars and contacts respectively, which once again are provided through the Exchange ActiveSync protocol in an Exchange Server 2010 environment instead.

SCEP and Mobile Device Management

For integrating Exchange Server 2010 and iOS devices, the use of SCEP (Simple Certificate Enrolment Protocol) and Mobile Device Management services aren't required.

Deploying Configuration Profiles to devices using the iPhone Configuration Utility

After creating Configuration Profiles for individual users and their corresponding devices, the next step is to activate the iOS device, if required, and then deploy the Configuration Profile to the device.

Device activation

Activation of devices can be performed in multiple ways in the current version of iOS—either through iTunes or over the air.

During the setup of our administrative workstation, we installed iTunes and configured it for activation-only mode. Therefore, to activate an iOS device that requires activation, like the iPhone, it can simply be connected to the administrative workstation and activated automatically at the same time as installing the configuration profile.

Alternatively, activation can occur over-the-air using a wireless network. This is configured on first boot of the device, where the user is given the option to connect to a wireless network and after connection, given the choice to activate the device. Device activation over a wireless network usually takes between one and three minutes.

Deploying the Configuration Profile

After activating the device, and creating the Configuration Profile to use, deploying the Configuration Profile using the iPhone Configuration Utility is relatively simple.

Connect the iOS device to the administrative workstation with the iPhone Configuration Utility open. The device should now show in the **Devices** section on the left-hand side of the window.

Select the device, then choose the **Configuration Profiles** tab in the centre of the main window, shown as follows:

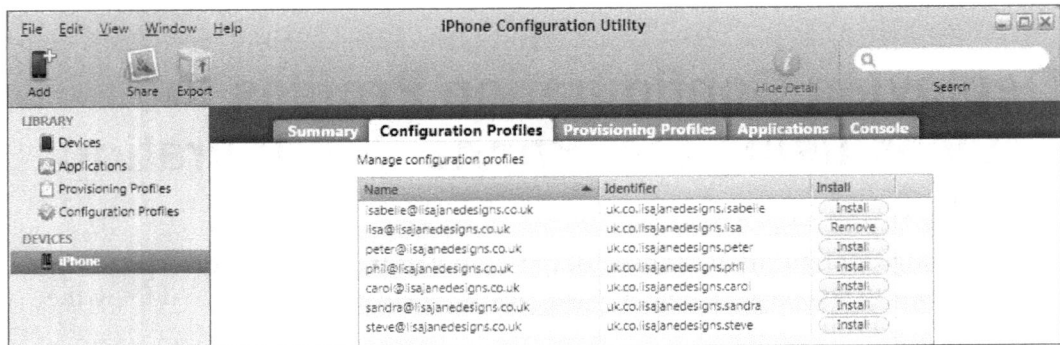

You should be presented with a list of Configuration Profiles that have been created in this copy of the iPhone Configuration Utility.

Select the Configuration Profile for the connected device—in our case the lisa@ lisajanedesigns.co.uk profile, and select **Install**.

Immediately after selecting install, the profile should be copied to the device and prompted for installation:

Choose **Install** on the iOS device to begin installation of the configuration profile. If you've allowed the user to remove the profile and specified all information required, including a username and password for ActiveSync, no prompts will be required; the only prompts for information will be to set a device PIN or password, should it be defined in the Exchange ActiveSync policy.

If you have specified options to restrict Configuration Profile removal, then you will see the following prompt warning you that the profile either cannot be removed, or cannot be removed without authorization—the password entered when you chose to restrict removal:

If you've configured certificate-based authentication, then you should have intentionally not specified a password for connection to the Exchange Server. A feature of iOS is that although this has been correctly configured and a password is not required, you will still be prompted for a password, as shown in the following image. If this is the case then it's safe to simply choose **Next** and leave the password blank:

After successful completion of the Configuration Profile deployment, the iOS device should connect to the Exchange 2010 Server and establish the Exchange ActiveSync relationship. At this point, as mentioned above, a prompt will be given for any extra information required by the ActiveSync policy assigned to the user mailbox, including prompts to choose a device PIN or password.

Immediately after applying the configuration profile, any restrictions chosen will be in effect immediately. You can see the difference between the stock iPhone before and after application of a Configuration Profile that contains restrictions:

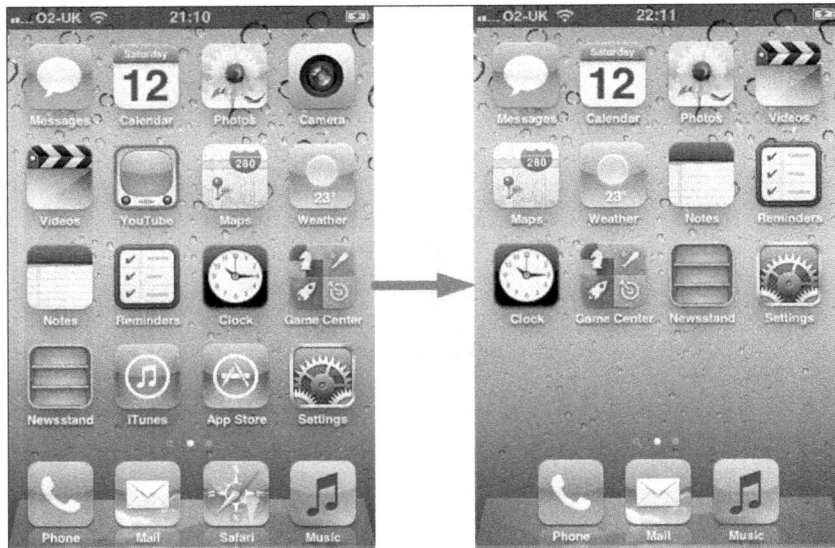

At this point the device should be ready to hand over to the end user.

Creating a generic Configuration Profile

If you'd prefer not to create individual Configuration Profiles for each and every user and device, then it may be more appropriate to examine how to create a generic Configuration Profile that can be deployed and assigned to multiple users.

To create a generic Configuration Profile, we'll add a new Configuration Profile in the same way as shown in the earlier sections, although a few settings will be set to more generic settings or left blank for completion when deployed to the device.

The first difference is in the **General** section of the profile, specifically the name of the Configuration Profile and its unique identifier. Instead of customizing it for the end user, we can give it a more generic name, shown as follows:

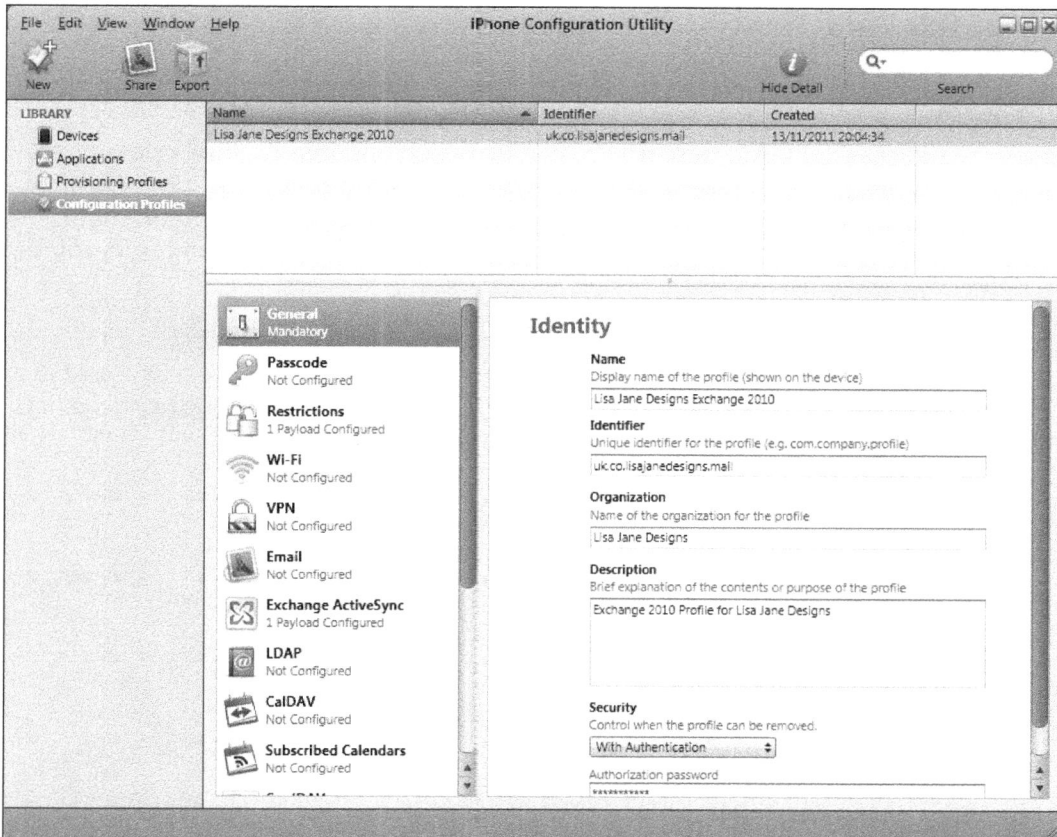

As shown in the preceding example, the **Name** of the profile is given as the organization name rather than the end user themselves. As before, this is simply to ease identification and if we are creating number of different profiles, this could signify the type of restrictions or settings the profile contains.

In the **Identifier** we've specified the external Exchange Server name in reverse, `uk.co.lisajanedesigns.mail`. This doesn't have to be the name, but choosing a consistent naming pattern will help ensure the identifiers are unique and easy to reference.

In the **Exchange ActiveSync** settings we enter the same settings used to create an individual profile, with the following exceptions:

- The **Domain, User, E-mail Address,** and **Password** fields must be left empty
- Certificate-based authentication cannot be used; therefore, **Identity Certificate** must be left unconfigured

All other settings for Exchange ActiveSync, and of course other settings, can be completed in the same way as a Configuration Profile tailored for an individual device or end user.

After creating the configuration profile, you have two options. The first option is to deploy the Configuration Profile by directly connecting devices to an administrative workstation and using the method described earlier to deploy the Configuration Profile directly to the device. Or, we can export a copy of the Configuration Profile to a file.

The exported configuration profile, a `.mobileconfig` file, will be copied to an appropriate web server, such as the Exchange Server 2010 Client Access Servers later on in this chapter. To perform this task, select the Configuration Profile from the list and choose **Export** from the tool bar:

Upon selecting **Export**, the **Export Configuration Profile** window should be displayed. Choose **Sign Configuration Profile**, and then select the **Export** button to select an appropriate location to store the file:

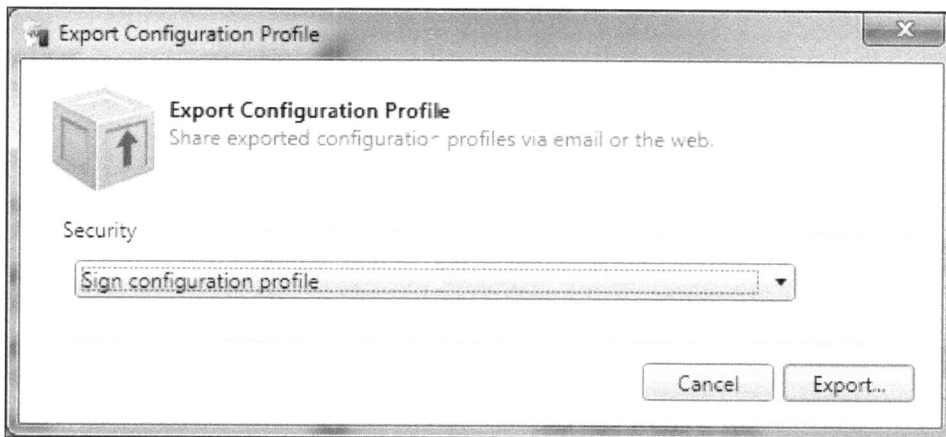

After exporting the configuration profile, store it in a safe place ready to copy to the Exchange Server 2010 Client Access Server(s) later on in this chapter.

Deploying a generic Configuration Profile from the Exchange Server

In the previous part of the chapter we've created a generic Configuration Profile to deploy to users over the Internet. The method to do this is fairly straightforward; the Configuration Profile is uploaded once to a web server — in our case our Exchange Client Access Servers. Next, each iOS device that requires the settings contained in our Configuration Profile to be applied to the device visits a specific URL to install the configuration profile. Finally the Exchange ActiveSync relationship is created with the Exchange Server infrastructure.

The following diagram shows a simple overview of this process:

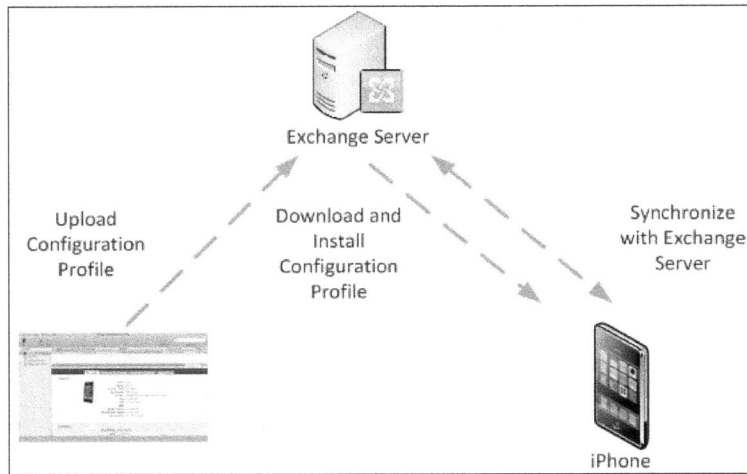

Configuring IIS

Before we're able to deploy Configuration Profiles via the web, we need to make a change to the IIS server settings on each Exchange Client Access server that will serve the Configuration Profile files.

The `.mobileconfig` file extension used is not, by default, registered in IIS. Therefore when the file is requested, IIS does not understand what MIME type to stamp the response with when it is served to clients.

Thankfully, registering the MIME type is relatively easy. On each Client Access Server that will serve the Configuration Profiles, launch Internet Information Services (IIS) Manager, then select the server name node. Choose **MIME Types** from the main window and select **Open Feature**:

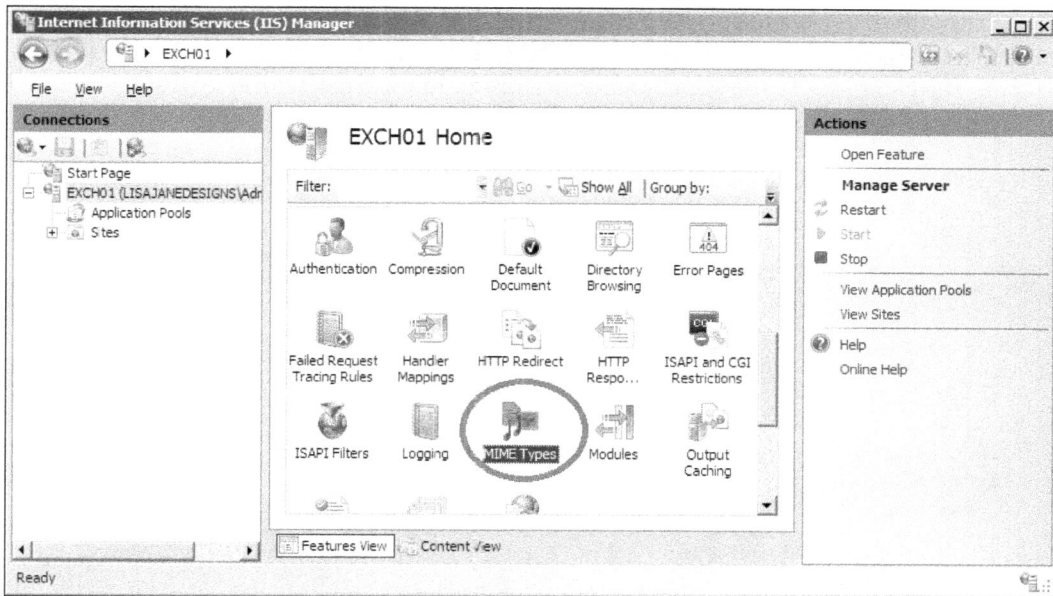

After selecting **Open Feature** you will be presented with a list of file extensions registered with IIS. Choose **Add** to create a new entry, and enter the following information:

- **File name extension**: `mobileconfig`
- **MIME type**: `application/x-apple-aspen-config`

You'll see how this should be entered in the **Add MIME Type** window:

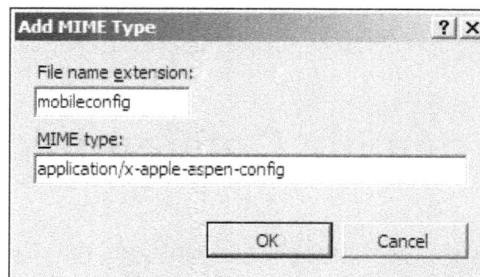

After entering the settings, choose **OK** to add the new MIME type and repeat the process on each Client Access Server that will serve the Configuration Profiles. These settings only need to be applied once to each Client Access Server.

Next, copy the Configuration Profile exported earlier to an appropriate location on each Client Access server. If you're using a load-balanced array then it is logical to copy the same file to the same location on each to ensure that the load balanced external URL can be utilized when clients attempt to retrieve the profile.

In the example below, we've copied the exported Configuration Profile `lisajanedesigns.mobileconfig` to `C:\inetpub\wwwroot`:

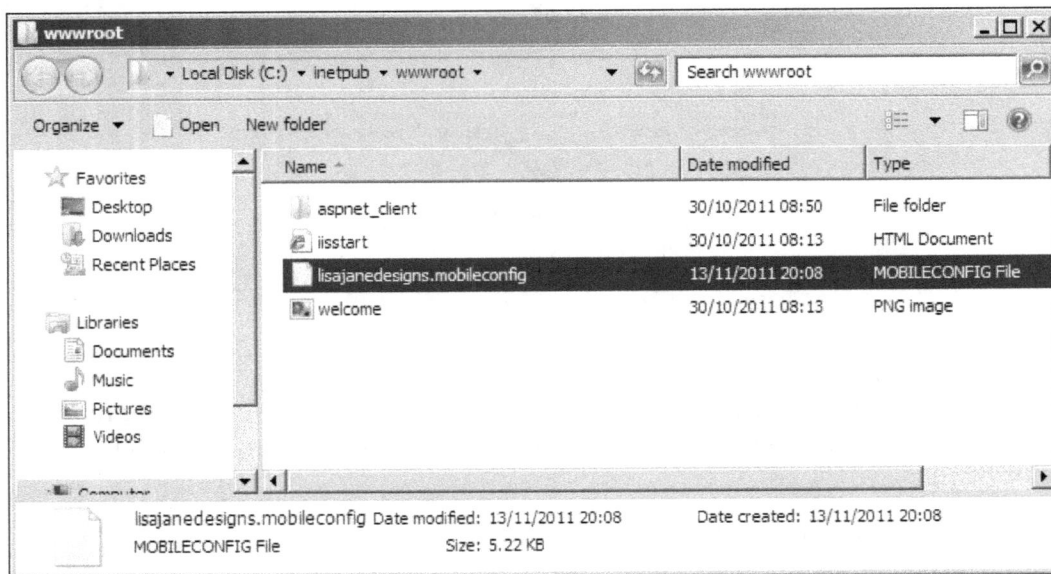

Each time you update the Configuration Profile you need to ensure you export it and copy it to each Client Access Server. Unless changes are required in the future, you may only need to perform this task once per Client Access Server.

Installing the generic Configuration Profile on devices

It's a fairly straightforward task to install the Configuration Profile on iOS devices — it's as simple as opening Safari and entering the URL into the browser. You might find this ideal as it allows the delegation of the device configuration to either end users (as an alternative to using AutoDiscover to locate settings) or to other IT support staff who can also handover the new devices to end users.

In our example organization, Lisa Jane Designs, we uploaded the Configuration Profile to the `C:\inetpub\wwwroot` directory, which represents the "root", or topmost, directory in the web server. Therefore, to access the Configuration Profile we will attempt to access the following URL in Safari:

```
https://mail.lisajanedesigns.co.uk/lisajanedesigns.mobileconfig
```

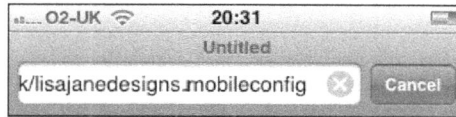

One point of note is the use of `https` to access the Configuration Profile. While it provides no benefit for accessing the Configuration Profile itself, typically your Exchange 2010 Client Access Server will be configured to only service requests made using the https protocol.

Upon attempting to access the Configuration Profile in Safari, it should automatically present itself for installation:

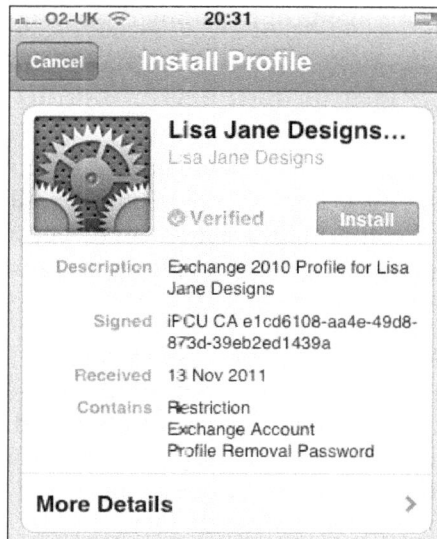

After choosing **Install**, you should be prompted for the user-specific information that wasn't entered when creating the generic configuration profile:

After entering the user specific information—namely e-mail address, domain, username, and password, the Configuration Profile will be installed. The iOS device will then attempt to establish the relationship with the Exchange Server, using the ActiveSync protocol and apply any Exchange ActiveSync policies (such as PIN requirements) within a few moments of installing the configuration profile.

Summary

In this chapter we've looked at how we can create and deploy Configuration Profiles to iOS devices using the iPhone Configuration Profile. We've covered the steps required to install and configure the software correctly on an administrative workstation and had an in-depth look at the settings and restrictions you can deploy using Configuration Profiles.

In particular we've looked at two different ways to deploy Configuration Profiles to iOS devices. The first method was to create profiles for individual users, and optionally embed user certificates to enable certificate-based authentication to be used. Then, by directly connecting the iOS device to the administrative workstation we not only activated the device automatically using iTunes, but also installed the tailored Configuration Profile directly onto the device.

The second method, which we've looked at later in the chapter, is achieved by making use of a more generic Configuration Profile that does not contain user-specific configuration. After creation of the profile, we've then implemented changes on the Exchange 2010 Client Access servers to allow the generic Configuration Profile to be downloaded over the Internet onto iOS devices.

By the end of this chapter you should be confident in how to make best use of the iPhone Configuration Utility and understand the different methods you can use to deploy Configuration Profiles to end users; however, it's worth noting that use of Configuration Profiles might not be required in your organization if you don't need certificate-based authentication or the ability to enforce specific restrictions on devices.

In the next chapter, we'll be looking at the options available for working with shared mailboxes and shared calendars in an Exchange environment, the challenges you might face, and how to overcome them.

8
Sharing Mailboxes and Calendars

The ability to share mailboxes and calendars in Exchange Server 2010 is a feature used by many companies and is typically a key feature of Microsoft Exchange to enable better collaboration in a business environment.

In this chapter, we'll be examining what functionality shared mailboxes can provide and look more into the settings they are typically used in and how clients connect to them.

As it's not all plain-sailing when connecting iOS devices like the iPhone to a Shared Mailbox, we'll examine the type of problems you will come across when attempting to provide access to Shared Mailboxes to mobile users, and how you can overcome those issues with a variety of different methods.

Calendaring is another key business tool and one of the core functionalities in Exchange that sets it apart from competing products.

Microsoft has a much more complete story when it comes to sharing calendars with non-Microsoft platforms like Apple mobile devices, and Exchange Server 2010 has the ability to share Calendars with iOS devices quickly and simply. Later in the chapter we'll look more at what functionality is provided when sharing Calendars, and we'll look at how to enable the functionality in Exchange Server 2010.

We'll also look at how end-users can share calendars with each other and with iOS devices, and how you can connect iOS devices to shared calendars both manually and automatically. We'll revisit how to approach this task using the iPhone Configuration Utility.

By the end of this chapter you'll understand more about how shared mailboxes and shared calendars can be used in Exchange Server 2010 and how to roll out this functionality to your mobile users.

Overview of shared mailboxes

The concept of a shared mailbox is straightforward — an entire Exchange Mailbox can be shared among multiple users who are all able to access and act on messages, calendar items, and contacts within the shared mailbox.

Typically these can utilize dedicated shared mailboxes which have e-mail addresses assigned to them, or access between user mailboxes can be granted and managed in the same way, such as access by a Personal Assistant or Secretary to a Manager's mailbox.

A dedicated shared mailbox is often associated with a role or a function within a business, such as a sales team, and it provides an ideal way to ensure that messages sent to a team are stored within a central mailbox, rather than stored in individual mailboxes.

The following diagram shows how the mail flow is received by the shared mailbox and can stay within the shared mailbox only, and is accessed as a secondary mailbox by mailbox users:

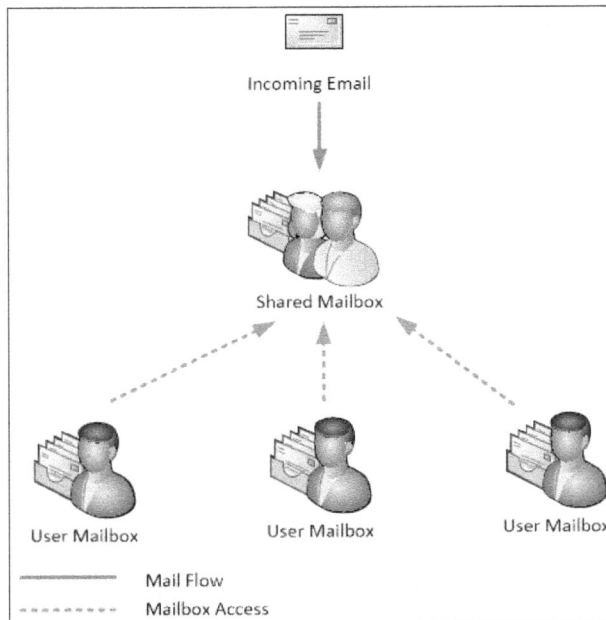

This isn't the only way available in Exchange Server 2010 to manage central team-specific e-mail addresses. Exchange Server also has the ability to create and define Distribution Groups which can fulfill a similar, or even the same purpose. The major difference is the mail flow does not stop at the distribution group level but fans out to send a separate, individual copy of each message received by each member of a distribution group in their personal mailboxes, as depicted by the arrows in the following diagram:

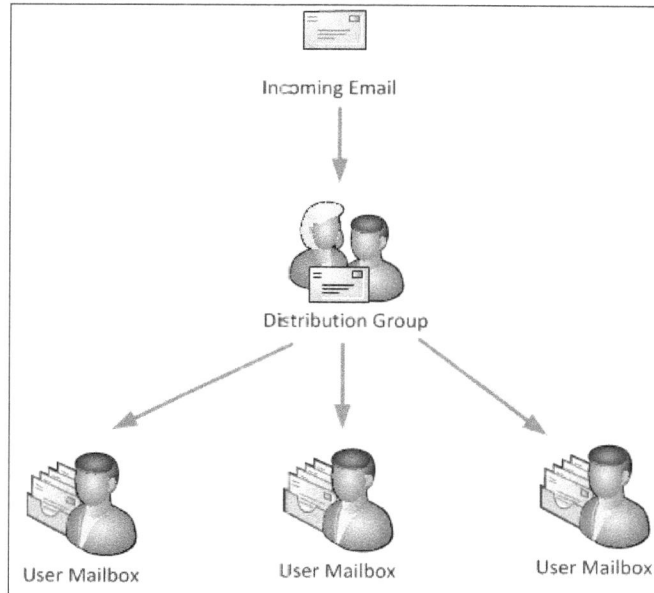

Distribution Groups and Shared Mailbox may sound like they fulfill the same role but a shared mailbox has the following distinct advantages:

- E-mail to a central address, such as "sales" is stored within a single mailbox which can be organized appropriately; for example, sub-folders for mail dealt with by different team members or actions for follow up are shared between all mailbox users with access to the mailbox.

- When employees leave, history for the central address is kept within the shared mailbox, removing the need in many cases to extract or grant access to a former employee's mailbox.

- Messages sent to a shared mailbox do not consume individual user quotas and can have distinct limits, retention policies, or a personal archive.

- When a message is sent to a distribution group, multiple copies of the message are created and stored for each eventual user recipient. Because Exchange Server 2010 no longer makes use of Single Instance Storage this means a 10 MB message sent to a Distribution Group could consume, uncompressed, many times its original size.
- Shared Mailboxes provide the full features of Exchange mailboxes to end users allowing a team to also use the shared mailbox for a shared calendar or contacts.

Of course, Distribution Groups shouldn't be replaced with Shared Mailboxes in all cases; for example, internal company communications can benefit from the use of location, role, or company-wide Distribution Groups to disseminate information. The deciding factor for using a Shared Mailbox above a Distribution Group is often based around questions like the following:

- Should everyone act on, or read the message sent to the e-mail address? If the answer is yes, then a distribution group may be the answer. If not, and just a single response is all that will be required, then a shared mailbox may be the answer.
- Are messages sent to the address aimed at individuals or a specific team? If the messages are aimed at individuals, such as disseminating information to a team, then a distribution group may be the answer; if the sender is requesting a service from anyone in the team then a shared mailbox may be the answer.

Of course one size doesn't fit all and the above are just suggestions. You could even mix and match Shared Mailboxes and Distribution Groups based on your needs. If we go back to our example company, Lisa Jane Designs, we could consider giving our Sales Team both:

- **A Shared Mailbox**: (`sales@lisajanedesigns.co.uk`) Published on the external website, customers e-mail the sales team with enquiries about purchasing products, and when orders are placed online notification messages are received by this address.
- **A Distribution group**: (`sales-dg@lisajanedesigns.co.uk`) Used by the sales team themselves, the distribution group is used by the team to ask everyone questions, such as enquiring if anyone has experience with a particular topic and distributing sales figures.

If you're a long-term Exchange Administrator or have experience with previous versions, you'll no doubt have noticed that we've not mentioned Public Folders, which can provide many of the same features offered by Shared Mailboxes.

As with Exchange Server 2007, support for Public Folders has been de-emphasized, and in Exchange Server 2010 in particular, the support for Public Folders within Database Availability Groups is not in parity with the near real-time, reliable replication offered by Mailbox Databases.

Additionally, with no straightforward method to connect mobile clients to Exchange Server Public Folders, it's hard to recommend them in a modern Exchange environment, and going forward it's worth avoiding them where possible.

Challenges associated with shared mailboxes

Unfortunately, it's not completely straightforward when it comes to allowing your users access to shared mailboxes from mobile devices. The model of granting permissions to a shared mailbox to other users, then allowing access using their normal credentials doesn't extend to ActiveSync clients.

This presents challenges because it means that even if you grant a mailbox user access permissions to a shared mailbox, they can't simply add it to their iOS device as an additional mailbox and begin to access the shared mailbox on the move.

Additionally, some of the great features associated with shared mailboxes, such as the ability to automatically map shared mailboxes in Outlook when a user is granted permissions, don't extend to iOS devices either; so there isn't a way to get a user setup with access to a mailbox from a mobile device without further configuration, either by the system administrator or the end user themselves.

However, these challenges are small and don't necessarily have to represent a roadblock on the journey to getting users connected to shared mailboxes. In the next section we'll have a look at how to accomplish this.

Creating and connecting users to shared mailboxes

We now understand a little bit more about the business issue shared mailboxes are designed to help us overcome, how they compare to other technologies available within Exchange Server 2010, and what challenges we'll face when we're looking to get iOS devices like the iPhone connected. Next, we'll get some hands-on experience making use of shared mailboxes.

Going back to our example organization and the example earlier in the chapter, Lisa Jane Designs is looking to make use of shared mailboxes initially to provide a single Sales Team shared mailbox.

Over the next few pages, we'll perform the following tasks:

- Create a new shared mailbox for the Sales Team
- Grant permissions to end users to allow access using standard clients
- Test client-connectivity using clients like Outlook and Outlook Web App
- Modify the shared mailbox to allow access from iOS and other ActiveSync devices
- Connect an iPhone to the shared mailbox manually
- Use the iPhone Configuration Utility to automatically connect a mobile device to a shared mailbox

Creating a shared mailbox

Naturally, the first step on our road to making use of shared mailboxes is to create one, which is performed using Exchange Management Shell. Unfortunately it's not possible to create a shared mailbox using the graphic Exchange Management Console, but fear not—creating a shared mailbox using the shell is a straightforward task.

A shared mailbox by default is comprised of an Active Directory account that is used to hold the attributes of the mailbox, similar to all Exchange mailboxes. The primary differences between the shared mailbox and a normal user mailbox are:

- Shared mailboxes are created as disabled user accounts with no password
- Active Directory attributes are set to signify the mailbox is a shared mailbox primarily for display and management purposes in the Exchange Management Console and Exchange Management Shell

The shared mailbox we'll be creating for the Sales Team will have the following key attributes:

Display Name	Account Name	Email Address and User Principal Name
Lisa Jane Designs Sales	sales	sales@lisajanedesigns.co.uk

Using the above attributes, we'll look to create the shared mailbox, which we'll perform using the Exchange Management Console.

To begin, open the Exchange Management Shell:

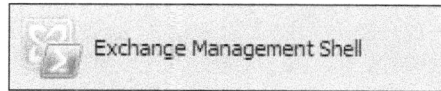

Next, we'll create the shared mailbox by entering the following command using information from the preceding table:

```
New-Mailbox -DisplayName "Lisa Jane Designs Sales" -Name sales
-UserPrincipalName sales@lisajanedesigns.co.uk -PrimarySmtpAddress sales@
lisajanedesigns.co.uk -Shared
```

In the above command we've specified details for the account, including its Display Name, the User Principle Name, the Primary SMTP Address, and the Name attribute which will be used for the Canonical Name on the Active Directory object itself, the Exchange alias, and the Pre-Windows 2000 logon name (SAM Account Name).

After executing the command, the Active Directory account is created and the mailbox is immediately created in Exchange Server.

Of course we can continue to edit the account or examine it further using the Exchange Management Shell, but we can use the Exchange Management Console to view and edit properties for the shared mailbox.

We'll have a quick look at how the shared mailbox appears in the Exchange Management Console to quickly examine the differences that make it easy to identify mailboxes of this type.

Launch the Exchange Management Console and navigate to **Recipient Configuration,** then select **Mailbox**:

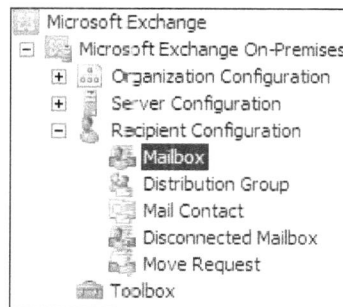

On the right-hand side of the Exchange Management Console the list of mailboxes in the organization will be displayed. You'll see the new shared mailbox listed:

Isabelle Goodman	isabelle	lisajanedesigns.co.uk/Users	User Mailbox
Lisa Goodman	lisa	lisajanedesigns.co.uk/Users	User Mailbox
Lisa Jane Designs Sales	sales	lisajanedesigns.co.uk/Users	Shared Mailbox
Steve Goodman	steve	lisajanedesigns.co.uk/Users	User Mailbox

The first thing you'll notice is that in the **Recipient Type Details** column, the recipient type is listed as **Shared Mailbox**; and if you look closely, you'll see that the icon for a shared mailbox is subtlety different, with multiple user icons representing the intention that it is to be used for multiple user access:

Granting permissions

The next step after creating the shared mailbox is to grant user access to it; in these steps we don't actually allow ActiveSync access to the mailbox but we do allow other clients to access the shared mailbox using clients that fully support accessing shared mailboxes using each user's logged in credentials.

There are two distinct parts to granting permissions to access and making use of a shared mailbox:

- Granting users full access permissions to read and modify the shared mailbox itself
- Granting users permissions to send as the shared mailbox e-mail address when creating new messages or replying to mail

The delegation of permission to send as the shared mailbox address is optional, and doesn't interfere with the ability of a user to access the shared mailbox itself.

The first step we'll accomplish is granting the full access permissions to the users we wish to have access to the shared mailbox. To begin, we'll right-click the shared mailbox in the Exchange Management Console and choose **Manage Full Access Permission**:

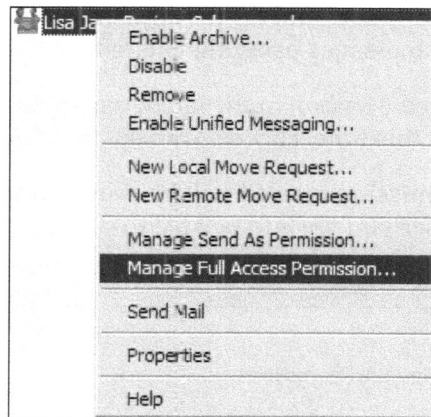

After choosing this option, the Manage Full Access Permission wizard should display. Choose **Add**, and then select each user you wish to be able to access the Shared Mailbox:

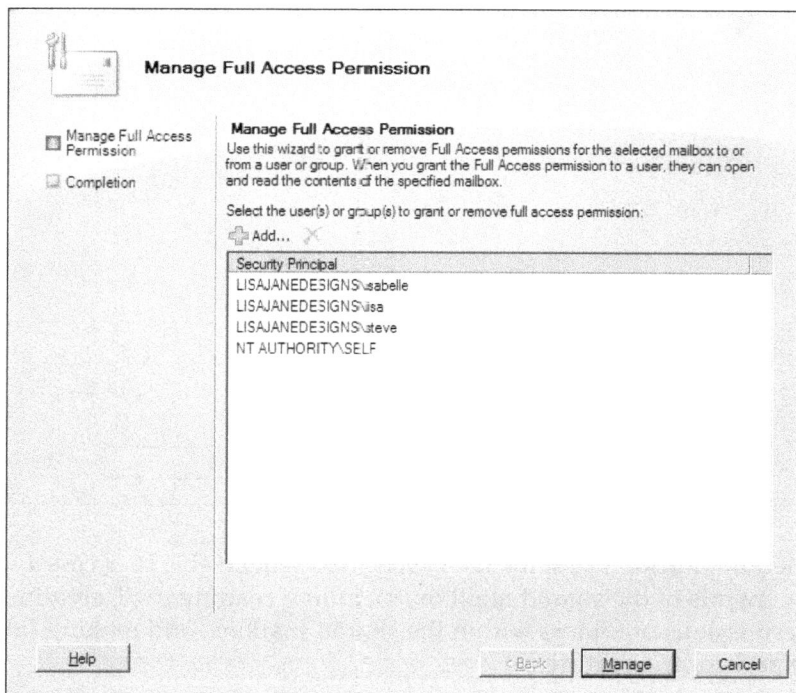

When you've selected the correct users, choose **Manage** to apply the changes to the shared mailbox.

The next, optional step is to grant Send As permissions to each user who will be able to reply to and create new messages using the Shared Mailbox e-mail address.

Again, right-click the Shared Mailbox in the list of mailboxes in the Exchange Management Console, but this time, choose **Manage Send As Permission**.

The **Manage Send As Permission** wizard will be shown, and as completed in the previous step, add each user you wish to be able to send as the address of the Shared Mailbox:

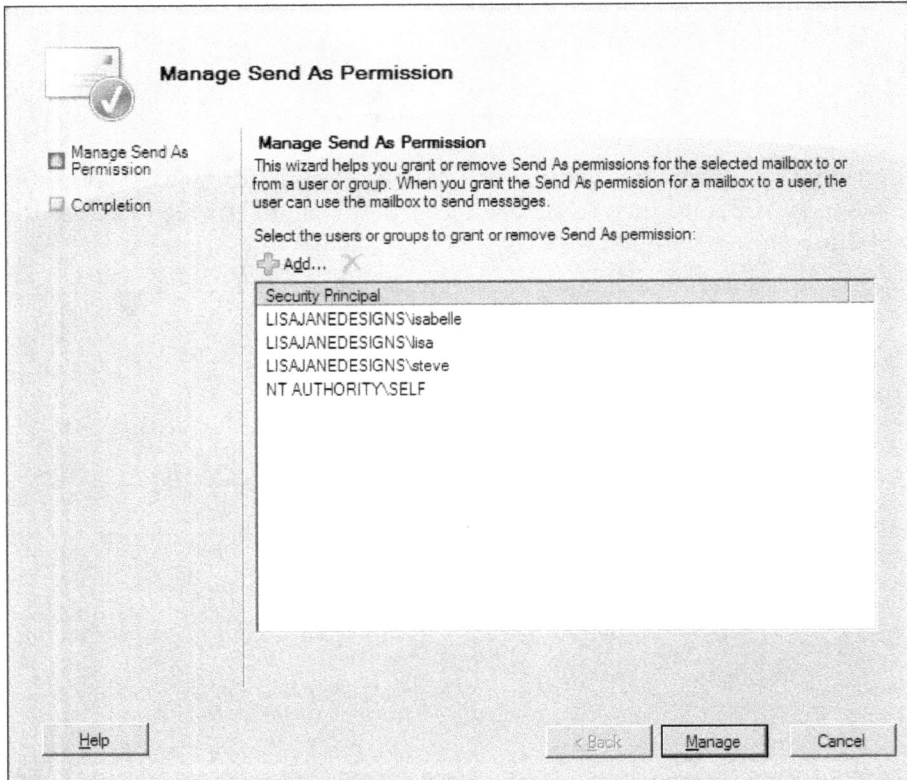

After completion of these steps, the users specified will be able to access and modify the contents of the shared mailbox, including reading mail, creating folders, changing permissions of folders within the shared mailbox, and making full use of calendaring and contact features.

Accessing the shared mailbox using Outlook

As you might expect, Microsoft has a fairly complete story when it comes to accessing Shared Mailboxes using their own native client, Microsoft Outlook, and improvements to the experience of accessing shared mailboxes have been made when using newer Outlook clients such as Outlook 2010 in conjunction with Exchange Server 2010 SP1 or later.

When Full Access permission to the shared mailbox, attributes on the Active Directory object representing the shared mailbox are added with a list of users who have access, in addition to the actual permissions themselves. This list is used by the Outlook client when it determines which additional mailboxes to open as well as the user's own personal mailbox. The result means that after granting a user full access to a shared mailbox, the shared mailbox will automatically be opened in each user's mailbox each time they open Outlook:

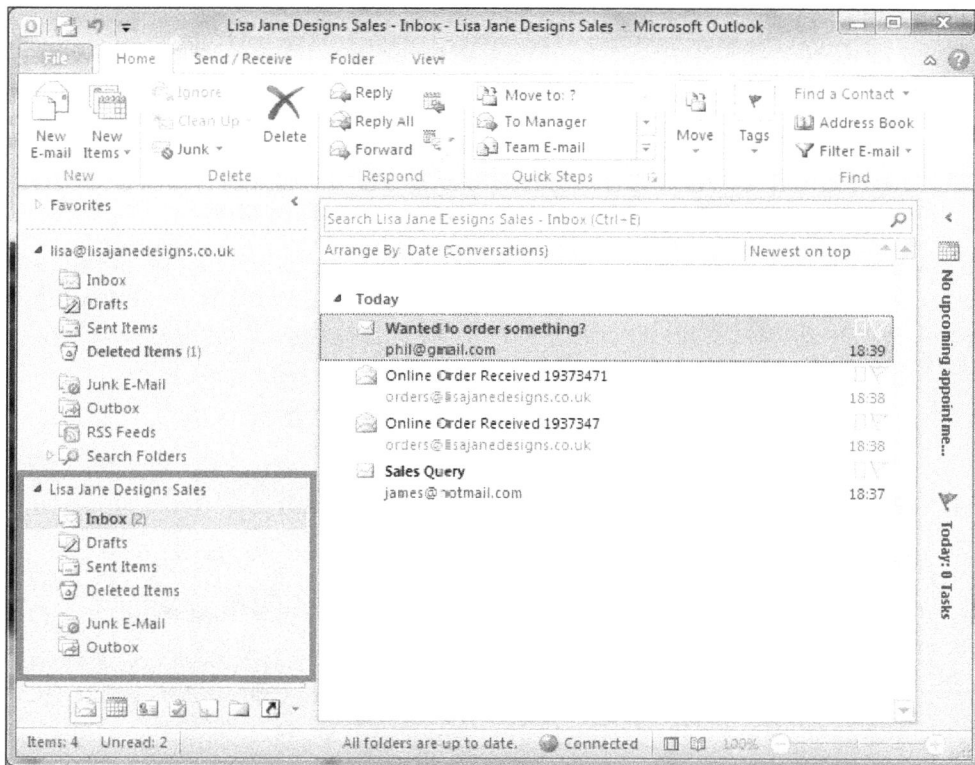

As you'll see in the image above, the shared mailbox is shown underneath the user's personal mailbox and is managed in an identical way to the user's personal mail, calendar, and contacts.

If permissions to send as the shared mailbox have been granted, upon replying to a message in a Shared Mailbox, the **From** address will also change to reflect the Display Name of the Shared Mailbox:

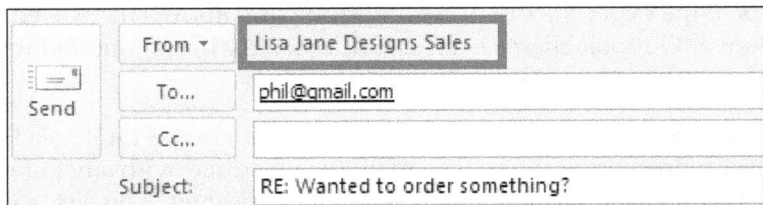

Accessing the shared mailbox using Outlook Web App

We've seen how easy it is for Outlook users to access shared mailboxes, and the common theme we'll see over the next few sections is it gets slightly more complicated each time.

In Outlook Web App, the ability to automatically open shared mailboxes the user has access to, isn't present; however, it's very simple to open either just the inbox of the shared mailbox for an Outlook-like view, or the entire shared mailbox itself.

We'll start by accessing Outlook Web App and attempting logon as one of the users we've granted access to the shared mailbox to. After login, to open the Inbox folder of the shared mailbox, right-click the user's Display Name on the folder tree, and choose **Open Other User's Inbox**:

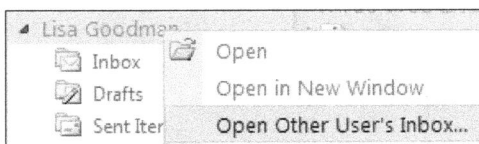

Next, enter the Display Name, e-mail address, or alias of the shared mailbox, or click **Name** and select it from the Global Address List:

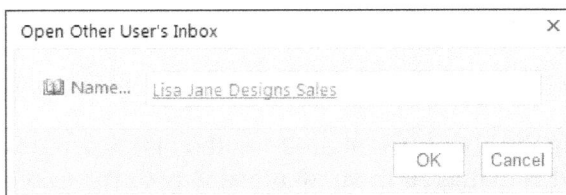

The shared mailbox should display in the folder tree list on the left-hand side of the Outlook Web App window, similar to how it's shown in Outlook:

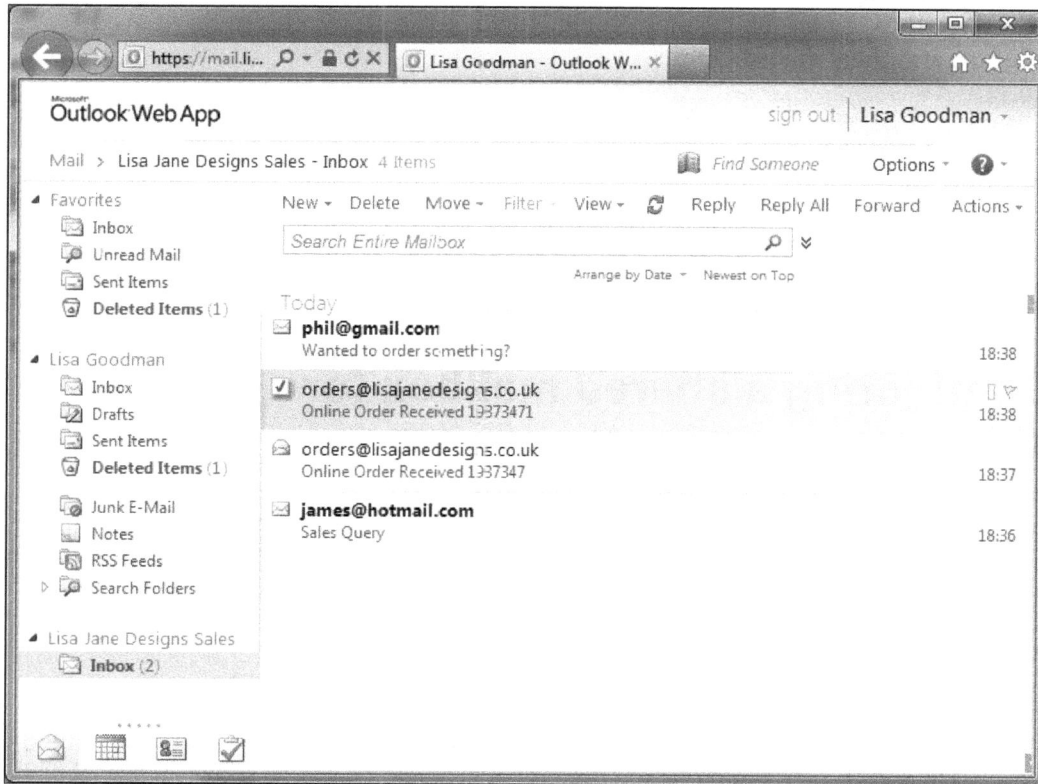

It's a similar story with calendaring; simply choose the Calendar view in Outlook Web App, then right-click **My Calendars** and choose **Add Calendar**:

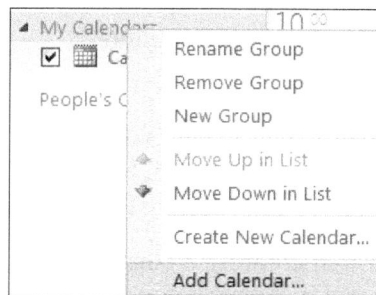

Finally, to open the full shared mailbox itself, including the ability to change the shared mailbox options, such as rules and out of office messages, click on the Display Name of the user in the right-hand corner of Outlook Web App, and choose **Open Other Mailbox**. Enter the Display Name, e-mail address, or alias of the shared mailbox, and then choose **Open**:

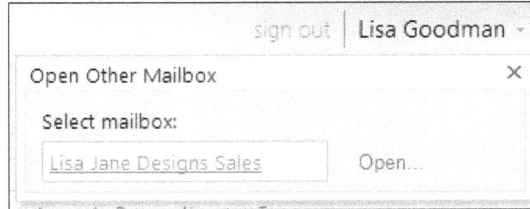

Configuring a shared mailbox for iOS device access

We've seen how to create a shared mailbox, grant permissions to users, and then how to access the shared mailbox by conventional methods; what we really want to do now that we know we can access the shared mailbox is access that shared mailbox from iOS devices.

As mentioned earlier in the chapter, there are a few obstacles in our way:

- No support for conventional shared mailbox access via ActiveSync
- The Active Directory account for the shared mailbox is created in a disabled state with no password

Therefore, we need to look at implementing a workaround solution to gain access to the mailbox by performing the following tasks using Active Directory Users and Computers:

- Creating a password for the shared mailbox
- Enabling the shared mailbox user account

These steps will enable us to treat the shared mailbox like any other Exchange Server mailbox and make use of the ability in iOS devices such as the iPhone to open multiple Exchange mailboxes using the ActiveSync protocol.

It's worth noting at this point that creating a password on the account doesn't necessarily mean we have to use it. As we'll cover later, using the techniques in the previous chapters to configure certificate-based authentication, we could instead use certificates to avoid the use of passwords. However, to enable the account itself we must create a password for it.

To begin, open Active Directory Users and Computers from an Administrative workstation that has the Microsoft **Remote Server Administrative Tools** installed, or from a domain controller, and navigate to find the Active Directory object that corresponds to the shared mailbox:

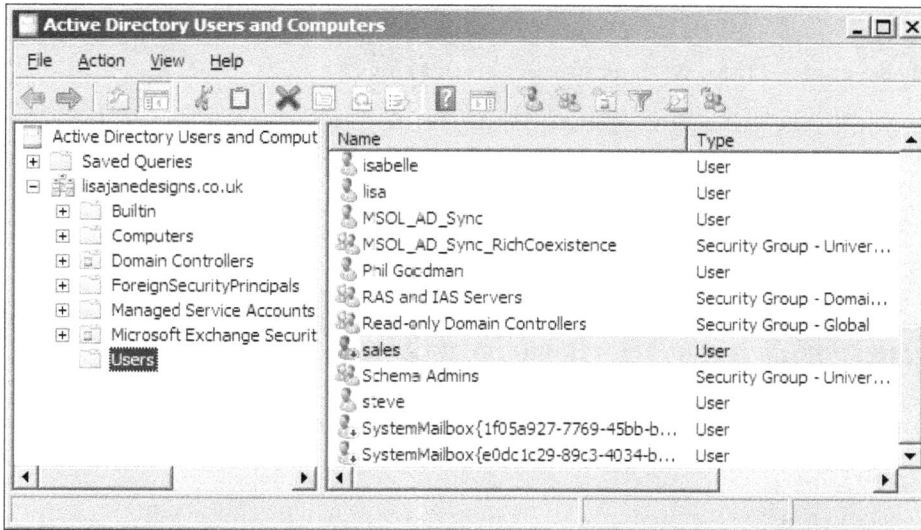

You'll see our shared mailbox in the preceding image. In Active Directory, there is nothing to signify it as a shared mailbox, and it has a single user icon like any other user. The only distinguishing feature (until we enable the account) is that it shows as a disabled user, and of course has the Canonical Name we specified at the time of account creation.

First, we'll set an appropriate password for the account, using the standard **Reset Password** option available when right-clicking the user object:

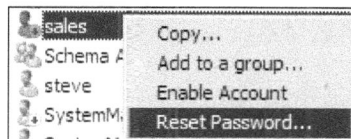

After choosing a password, we can then enable the account, again by right-clicking on the user object but choosing **Enable Account**.

Verify access to the shared mailbox via Outlook Web App using its own credentials (in our case, using the **sales** username and the password we've just set) to ensure that the previous steps have been completed successfully.

Methods to connect iOS devices

After configuring the shared mailbox's associated Active Directory user object to have a password set and the user account enabled, we can now look at the options available for connecting an iOS mobile device to the shared mailbox in addition to the user's personal mailbox.

In the following section, we'll examine two options:

- Connecting to an iOS Device manually, by creating a second Exchange ActiveSync account on the iOS device
- Connecting an iOS Device using an iPhone Configuration Profile, which allows you, as an administrator, to deploy access to the shared mailbox at the same time as provisioning the iOS device

Connecting an iOS device manually

The configuration and setup of a shared mailbox on an iOS device such as an iPhone is near identical to synchronizing a user's standard mailbox and is achieved by creating a new Exchange ActiveSync profile.

As we've covered this extensively in earlier chapters, we'll only briefly look at this process. To add a new account, navigate to **Settings** then **Mail, Contacts, Calendars** on the iOS device, then choose **Add Account**:

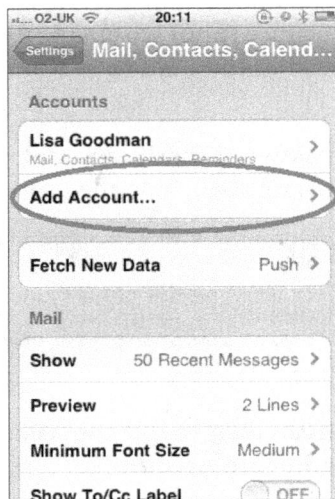

Follow the normal process of configuring the shared mailbox, taking care to specify the shared mailbox e-mail address, login name, and password rather than the user who has access to the mailbox.

After successfully adding the shared mailbox, when you next open the **Mail** application, you will be presented with multiple mailboxes to choose from:

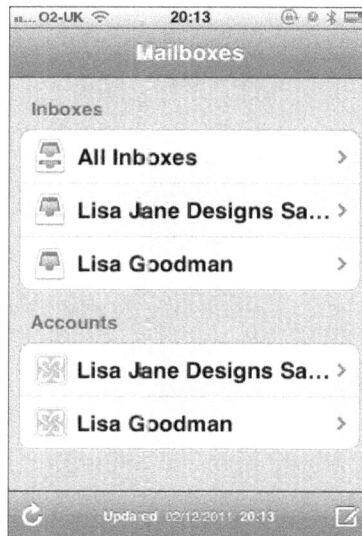

The user of the device can then either choose **All Inboxes** to show a combined view of both their mailbox and the shared mailbox, with replies to messages from each being sent from the corresponding mailbox—either the user's personal address if the message was addressed to them, or sent from the shared mailbox.

Connecting an iOS device using an iPhone configuration profile

The second option (which is more suitable for an environment where you are provisioning devices using the iPhone Configuration Utility) is to add the shared mailbox to the iPhone Configuration Profile at the time of creation.

To utilize the iPhone Configuration Utility to provision shared mailbox access to an iOS device at the same time as configuring the user's personal mailbox, begin by creating an iPhone Configuration Profile in the same way as covered in the previous chapter.

When we configure the Exchange ActiveSync settings, enter the user's settings as normal, then choose the Add symbol as shown in the following screenshot:

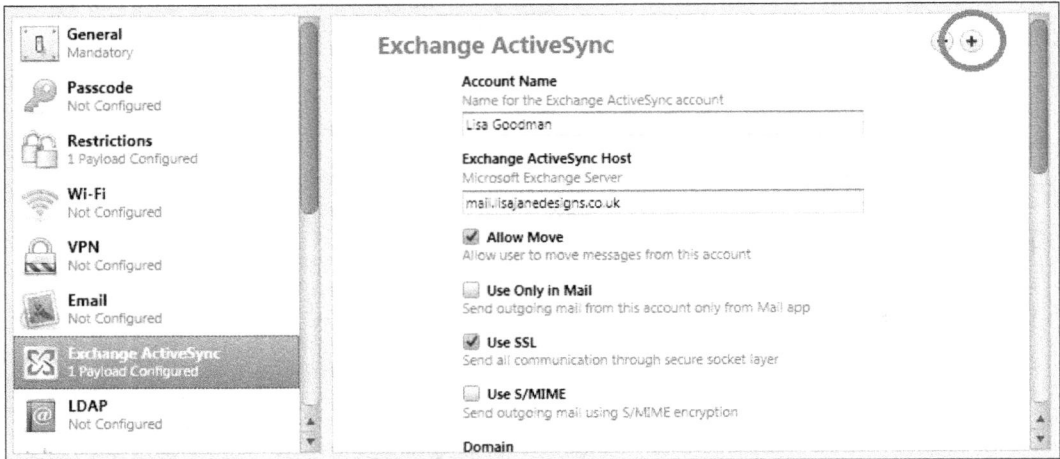

This will add a second Exchange ActiveSync account to the list, which is configured with individual options specific to the shared mailbox:

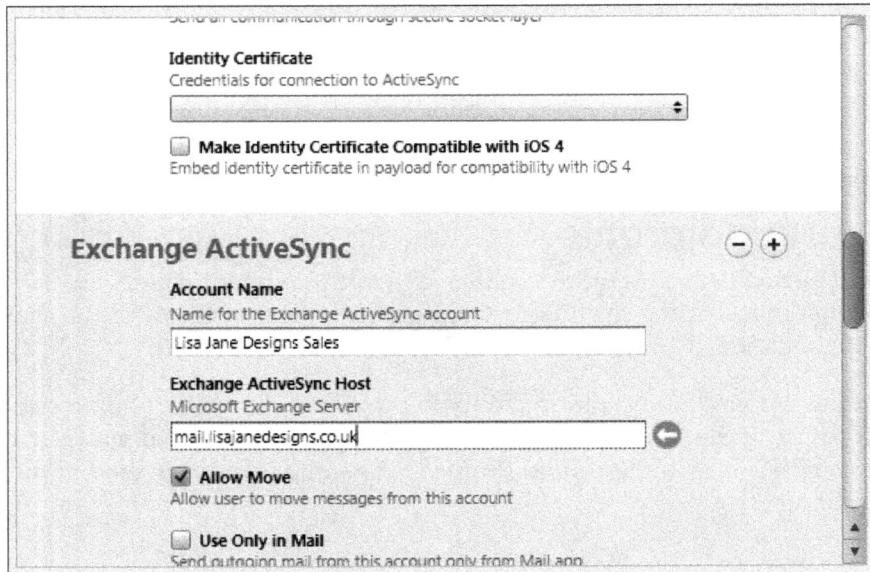

After configuration of the iPhone configuration profile, we can then deploy the profile to the device using the same methods we would for a single mailbox configuration profile.

Furthermore, should you be using certificate-based authentication, approach the configuration of the shared mailbox in the same way as you would for an individual mailbox, then when configuring the profile, add both the user certificate and the shared mailbox certificate when configuring **Credentials**, then select the appropriate authentication certificate to match each Exchange ActiveSync account.

Unfortunately, there are some issues that are not easy to overcome. When using shared mailboxes in this way, the password to the shared mailbox account may be exposed to end users. As they are effectively by-passing the permissions granted individually and accessing the mailbox directly using the shared mailbox account, revoking permissions is unfortunately a complex process.

This is performed by changing the password to the account and distributing the password to the end users who are still allowed access, so they can re-enter the password when prompted by the iOS device, or by altering the iPhone Configuration profile and re-distributing it to affected users. For certificate-based authentication, it's more complex as not only does the certificate need to be revoked using Active Directory Certificate Services, the new certificate must be configured on end user devices.

When making the choice between manual configuration and using an iPhone Configuration Profile, consider whether you wish to distribute the password to the Shared Mailbox directly to end users. If you prefer not to, then it's recommended to make use of an iPhone Configuration Profile.

Overview of iCal calendar sharing

One of the new features in Exchange Server 2010 SP1 and higher is the ability to share calendars using the industry-standard iCalendar protocol.

iCalendar is a format supported by most calendar clients, including iOS devices like the iPhone and other clients such as Apple iCal and Mozilla Thunderbird. It's also supported by hosted providers like Google Calendar and other mail servers such as Zimbra or Lotus Notes. Although a late entry to the field from Microsoft it is nonetheless a welcome addition, and it makes sharing calendars very simple between Exchange Server users who also have iOS Devices.

Naturally there are some caveats to take note of. Most importantly, Exchange Server 2010 is simply providing iCal access to the calendar that is shared; it's not providing a modifiable interface based on the CalDAV protocol. The iCal access is read only.

Secondly, sharing is not based upon the standard Outlook sharing tools. If you use the default calendar sharing options in Outlook to share a calendar with a colleague, the Calendar link in a message informing the user that the calendar has been shared will not open the calendar on the iOS device. To share a calendar using iCal, the user has to publish their calendar rather than use the familiar Outlook sharing tools.

However, once these peculiarities are understood, iCal Calendar sharing in Exchange Server 2010 is easy to use and makes it simple for an end user to share calendars with one another, and also straightforward to publish common calendars through iPhone Configuration Profiles.

In this final part of the chapter, we'll look at how to configure iCal calendar sharing in Exchange Server 2010 and examine how it is published, look at how to share or, to be precise, publish calendars using Outlook and Outlook Web App, and then complete the configuration by examining how to connect iOS devices to calendars both on an ad-hoc basis and by using the iPhone Configuration Utility.

Configuring iCal calendar sharing

By default, iCal calendar sharing isn't enabled in Exchange Server 2010; therefore to allow users to share calendars using the iCal protocol we need to perform a few simple configuration steps to enable the features for end users:

- Ensure that iCal calendar publishing is enabled on the Outlook Web App virtual directory
- Configure the Exchange Server sharing policies to allow calendar publishing by users

In addition to the above, we also need to ensure that certain parameters, such as the External URL are set for the Outlook Web App virtual directory. If you've set up your Exchange Server using the methods described in the earlier chapters in this book, you're all set.

For users of products like Microsoft's Forefront Threat Management Gateway 2010 or ISA Server 2006, you'll also need to consider your publishing rules, in particular to ensure that unsecure HTTP traffic can reach the `/owa/Calendar` directory.

Enabling Calendar Publishing

By default in Exchange Server 2010, Calendar Publishing is enabled at the Outlook Web App virtual directory level; however, it's worth ensuring that it's enabled.

To check if Calendar Publishing is enabled on all owa virtual directories, launch the Exchange Management Shell and enter the following command:

```
Get-OWAVirtualDirectory | ft Identity,CalendarPublishingEnabled
```

After entering the command, examine the output, in particular checking that CalendarPublishingEnabled is set to True:

```
[PS] C:\Windows\system32>Get-OWAVirtualDirectory | ft Identity,CalendarPublishin
gEnabled

Identity                                         CalendarPublishingEnabled
                                                 -------------------------
EXCH01\owa (Default Web Site)                                         True
```

If the value is set to False for any Outlook Web Virtual Directory, enable it, replacing the value for Identity with the value listed against the corresponding Identity field, using the following command:

```
Set-OWAVirtualDirectory -Identity "EXCH01\owa (Default Web Site)" -Calend
arPublishingEnabled:$True
```

After enabling Calendar Publishing, which is effectively enabling Anonymous authentication to the /owa/Calendar directory, users will not immediately be able to share their calendars by publishing them using the iCal protocol; we'll configure the ability to do so in the next section.

Configuring Sharing Policies

After ensuring that the functionality is enabled at the Outlook Web App Virtual Directory level, it is necessary to configure sharing policies in Exchange Server 2010 to enable the Calendar publishing functionality to be available to end users.

Sharing Policies enable the Exchange Administrator to allow or restrict the ability to share calendar and contact information with external users via a variety of different methods, from sharing between Exchange Server 2010 organizations and Office 365 tenants to the functionality we'll be using, that is, Calendar Publishing.

By default a single Sharing Policy is created in Exchange Server 2010, called the Default Sharing Policy, which is enabled and applied to all users. Additional policies can be created to accommodate different user needs, which are assigned to mailboxes as required and override the Default Sharing Policy.

To configure Calendar Publishing for our example organization, Lisa Jane Designs, we will reconfigure the Default Sharing Policy to allow Calendar Publishing to be available to anonymous users.

Using the Exchange Management Console, we'll navigate to **Organization Configuration** and select **Mailbox**. In the Mailbox section, the **Sharing Policies** tab is selected as shown in the following screenshot:

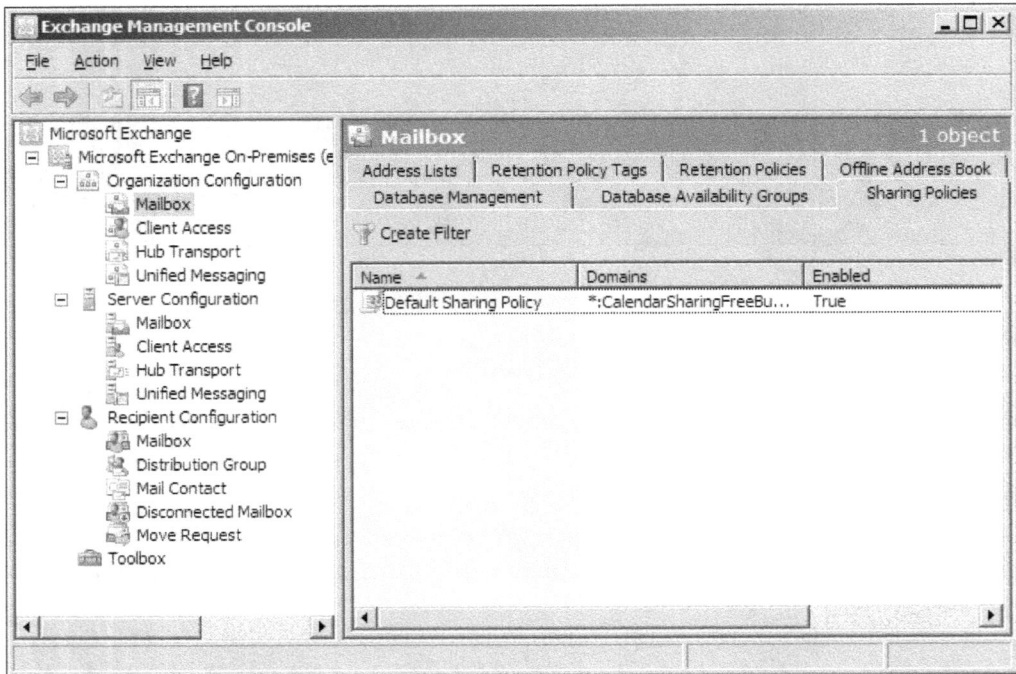

In the Sharing Policies section, the Default Sharing Policy is shown. To reconfigure it to allow Calendar Publishing, right click on the policy and choose **Properties**.

In the properties window, select **Add** and enter the following details when prompted:

Domain	Actions
Anonymous	Calendar Sharing with free/busy information plus subject, location, and body

After adding the new pseudo-domain into the sharing policy, the properties should reflect the information entered:

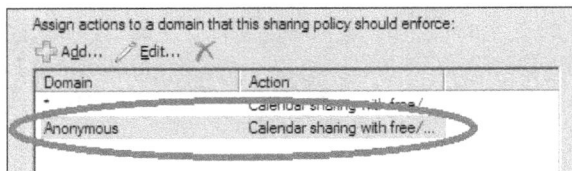

Once we are happy with the information entered, select **OK** to save and apply the properties to the Default Sharing Policy. If the new pseudo-domain has been entered correctly, the Exchange Management Console will display the following warning, confirming that the action was applied successfully and Calendar publishing is now enabled:

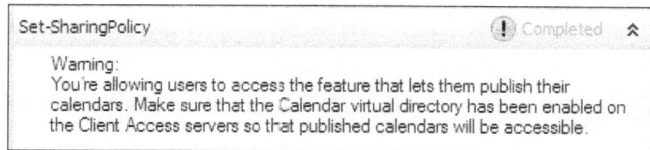

> Set-SharingPolicy   (!) Completed   ⌃
>
> Warning:
> You're allowing users to access the feature that lets them publish their calendars. Make sure that the Calendar virtual directory has been enabled on the Client Access servers so that published calendars will be accessible.

As is common with most configuration parameters specified at the Organization level in Exchange Server 2010, the settings are stored within Active Directory. Therefore, it may be necessary to wait for Active Directory replication to occur before the changes are available to end users or can be tested.

Sharing iCal calendars

The options to share, or publish calendars using the iCal format are available to end users via Outlook Web App or via Microsoft Outlook 2010. In reality, both use the same interface to configure publishing options; however, accessing these options differs between Outlook Web App and Outlook 2010.

Using Outlook Web App to publish a calendar

To publish a calendar for sharing with iOS devices in Outlook Web App, log in as normal and navigate to the calendar.

Above the main calendar displayed, the option to **Share** should be available as a drop down menu. Click **Share**, and then choose **Publish this Calendar to the Internet**:

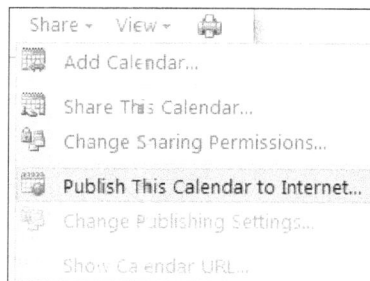

> Share ▾   View ▾   🖨
>
> 🗓   Add Calendar...
>
> 🗓   Share This Calendar...
>
> 🗓   Change Sharing Permissions...
>
> 🗓   **Publish This Calendar to Internet...**
>
> 🗓   Change Publishing Settings...
>
>   Show Calendar URL...

Next, configure the relevant settings that the person or people who should have access to the calendar should see, along with an appropriate access level. Pay particular attention to the access level, as this is the setting that defines whether the calendar is public or "restricted". A public calendar can be discovered by any entity that knows the username or format of usernames in the organizations. The "restricted" access level generates an encoded URL string that makes it extremely hard (but not impossible) for an unauthorized user to discover the URL that can display the calendar.

Once you have configured the appropriate settings, choose **Start Publishing** to enable the iCal sharing facility for the Calendar. The links to subscribe to and view the calendar should be displayed as follows:

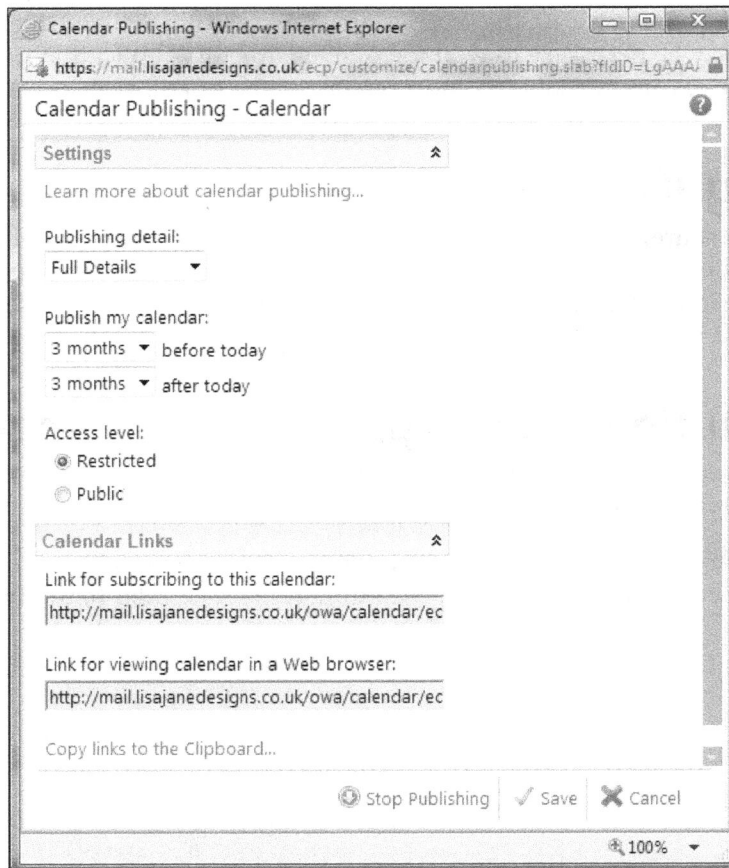

For connecting to the calendar from an iOS device, we are interested in the link to subscribe to the calendar, as this is the URL to access the calendar in iCal format.

If you are planning to use the URL with the iPhone Configuration Utility, simply choose **Copy links to the Clipboard**.

If the aim is to share an individual's calendar with another user, then click **Share** again, and choose **Send Links to This Calendar** to open a new e-mail message containing the URLs for both subscription via iCal and viewing the calendar in a web browser.

Using Outlook 2010 to publish a calendar

To publish a calendar for access from iOS devices from Microsoft Outlook, you can use the **Publish Online** option available in the Calendar view of Outlook to manage publishing settings for the calendar:

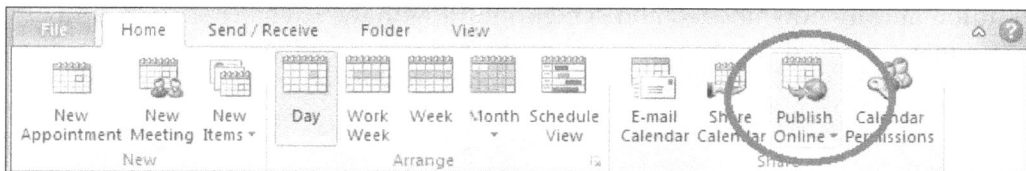

As Outlook 2010 uses the same back-end interface to configure calendar publishing, you will see the same Outlook Web App-based configuration page as shown in the previous section.

Connecting iOS devices to Shared Calendars

When adding a calendar shared using the iCal publishing features in Exchange Server 2010 to an iOS device, very little configuration is necessary on the part of the end user, or when creating a configuration profile to get access to the Calendar.

In the following sections, we'll examine how a user who has been sent links to a published calendar by another user connects to a shared calendar and also how as an administrator, it's possible to provision devices with access to published calendars pre-configured.

Adding calendars on an ad-hoc basis

As Apple devices such as the iPhone natively support iCal and can recognize the links sent in messages by other Exchange Server users, connecting to a calendar shared by the iCal protocol is very straightforward.

A user receives an e-mail containing the link to subscribe to the calendar, and by tapping the link, the iOS device automatically attempts to add the calendar, giving the option to **Subscribe** or **Cancel**:

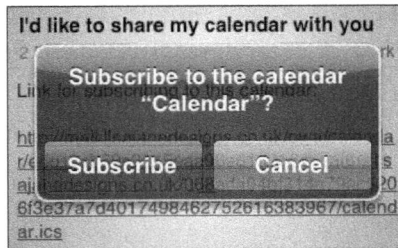

Upon successfully adding the calendar to the mobile device, the items in the calendar are automatically downloaded and synchronized with the Exchange Server, and shown in a combined calendar view. The end user can view the list of subscribed calendars within the Calendar application, under the **Subscribed** calendar list:

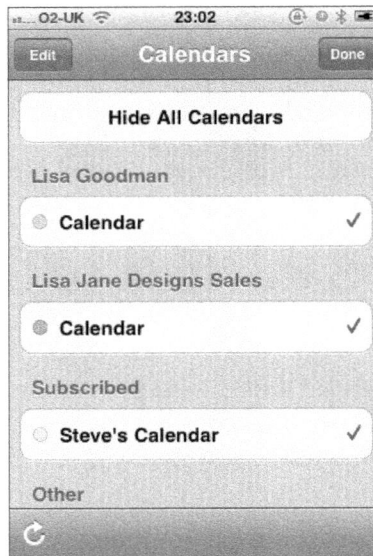

As shown in the preceding image, the subscribed calendar can be renamed from its default, "Calendar". Here the calendar has been renamed by choosing **Edit** to use a more appropriate name, in this case **Steve's Calendar**, and the color yellow chosen to signify events from this subscribed shared calendar.

Using the iPhone Configuration Utility to add shared calendars

Sharing calendars via e-mail between users isn't the only way to deploy published calendars to iOS mobile devices. There are cases where it might be desirable to pre-configure calendar subscriptions to your devices at the time of provisioning to ensure that all users have a consistent set of subscribed calendars.

The types of calendars you might want to consider deploying might include:

- Company-wide calendars showing holidays, events, and other important dates

- Team calendars to help foster better knowledge between colleagues of who is on holiday or where people are scheduled to be

- Resource calendars, such as room calendars to provide a method of checking room availability from mobile devices before attempting to book an appointment in a room

The last on the list, resource calendars, may sound controversial, as the ability to query availability information for rooms is built into Exchange Server 2010 and Office 2007 and above; however, such features are not available from iOS devices like the iPhone, so using provisioning methods to deploy access, even if it's just free/busy details, to resource calendars could be a straightforward method to extend room bookings using Calendar invitations to your mobile devices.

Configuring an iPhone Configuration Profile to include iCal-based calendar subscriptions is configured in a similar way to other items when creating configuration profiles.

Select the **Subscribed Calendars** item when creating a configuration profile and enter the **Description**, which is how the calendar will be displayed on the device, and then enter the calendar subscription URL recorded when enabling calendar publishing. The **Username**, **Password**, and **Use SSL** options should be left empty:

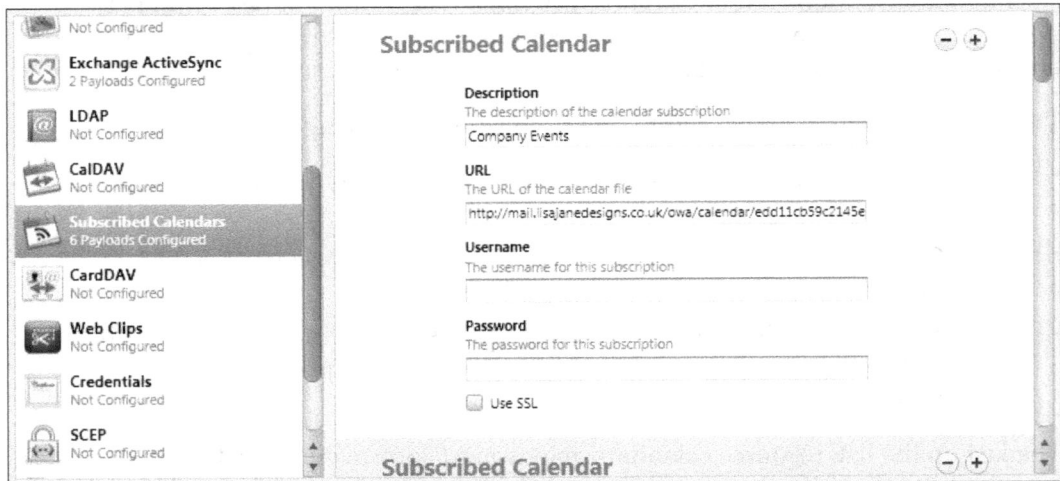

After configuration of these options, deployment follows the standard procedure for an iPhone Configuration Profile and the Subscribed Calendars should be included within a single encompassing profile that also includes all other configuration options, such as device restrictions and Exchange ActiveSync settings.

From a security perspective, it's important to consider the provisioning method used when deploying configuration profiles. If generic iPhone Configuration profiles are published via a public web server for end-users to download, the sensitivity of the calendars should be considered. This is because a generic iPhone Configuration Profile exported for general consumption by iOS devices is effectively a plain-text XML file, and as such by opening the file in a text editor the URL to each calendar can be discovered easily. Therefore, if this is a requirement, consider restricting web access to the iPhone Configuration Profile to authorized users only, restricting access to internal clients only, or deploying using direct attached devices.

Summary

In this chapter, we've explored two key features within Exchange Server 2010 for providing better collaboration facilities to users in business environments—shared mailboxes and calendar sharing.

Shared mailboxes, although a core feature of Exchange Server in the current and previous release, present a challenge when attempting to connect iOS devices to these resources, primarily due to limitations within the ActiveSync protocol.

We've looked at how Shared Mailboxes are created and access is granted to Outlook and Outlook Web App users, and then explored the methods available to connect iOS devices to the shared mailboxes by making changes to the Active Directory user that represents the shared mailbox. On the iOS device we've looked at how to configure a second ActiveSync account directly on the device, and explored how to use the iPhone Configuration Utility, covered in detail in the previous chapter, to provision multiple ActiveSync profiles at device deployment time.

Calendar Sharing is arguably more widely used within Exchange Server and the standard methods of sharing calendars with other Exchange users is unfortunately not applicable to iOS devices. We've looked at the alternative available within Exchange Server 2010, Calendar Publishing.

This technology, based on open standard, allows us to use the iCal protocol to allow users to publish personal calendars as well as general shared calendars. By default, this feature is not enabled for end user access in Exchange, and we went through the steps to ensure that the features are enabled on the Exchange Client Access Servers. We've configured Sharing Policies to enable end users to utilize the features and walked through the steps an end user needs to complete to publish and share a calendar with other users.

Finally, turning back to the iOS device we've looked at how individuals can connect to published calendars manually when they receive the location by e-mail, and we've examined some of the reasons why it might make sense to use the iPhone Configuration Utility to pre-configure end user mobile devices with subscriptions to iCal published calendars along.

In the final chapter, we'll be examining the options available for iOS device management using Exchange Server 2010's built in features including the administrative features available to understand the types of devices in use across the Exchange organization, troubleshooting features, and options for administrators and end-users when faced with lost or stolen devices.

9
iOS Client Device Management

Throughout this book, we've looked at how to set up and get users connected to and make use of different Exchange Server 2010 features from iOS devices, but so far we haven't examined the options available for management of devices once they are in the hands of users.

In the final chapter, you'll find more about how we can ensure we're able to update ourselves on the state of our ActiveSync device estate, what devices users currently have, and look at the options available to try and solve problems when they invariably occur.

We'll be tackling each of these areas across the following sections:

- Identifying iOS devices in use
- Troubleshooting connection problems for iOS devices
- Using administrator features for disabling and remote wipe of devices
- End-user features for disabling and remote wipe of devices

Before we get into how to make use of the device management features, it's worth understanding what the Exchange Server 2010 device management features offer, and how they compare in general to the competition.

The relationship between an iOS and any ActiveSync device is effectively a relationship for synchronizing Mail, Contacts, Calendar items, and Tasks. Although improved greatly in Exchange Server 2010 compared to previous releases, device management is very much light-touch.

Once an ActiveSync relationship is established, we can check if the iOS device is working, and update Exchange ActiveSync policies to define additional device restrictions, and we have the ability to wipe the iOS device if it's lost or stolen; but we aren't in full control of the device. We can address some of these issues by using the iPhone Configuration Utility, but we don't have the ability through Exchange Server 2010 to automatically push iPhone Configuration Profiles to the device and we don't have any out-of-band management ability outside of the ActiveSync device relationship.

What we can do are the most important actions, such as check that the device is still synchronizing, manage the partnership between the iOS device and Exchange Server 2010, and find out information about the device when we need to.

However, if a more complete solution is required for ongoing device management, there are Mobile Device Management solutions available that complement Exchange Server 2010 to provide this functionality, such as:

- AirWatch
- MobileIron
- Good Technology

Effectively, Mobile Device Management solutions provide the full management capability of not only monitoring devices, changing or updating security policies, but also pushing out new configuration information. These solutions could, for example, be used to streamline some of the challenges faced in previous chapters, such as pushing out new shared calendar subscriptions to devices or connections to shared mailboxes.

As the Mobile Device Management solution marketplace is a changing, competitive one, a good start when looking to select vendors to evaluate is the Gartner Magic Quadrant for Mobile Device Management Software. This report identifies the market leaders and growing competitors and provides information to assist with gaining a high-level understanding of what each vendor's solution's strengths are.

With an understanding of what we can achieve with the built-in features for managing the ongoing relationship between iOS devices like the iPhone and Exchange Server 2010, and what isn't possible without third party software, we'll move onto looking at what Exchange Server 2010 provides to help us gain a better understanding and perform basic management of our ActiveSync devices.

Identifying iOS devices in use

The first step to being able to manage your iOS device estate is to understand which devices currently have, or used to have an ActiveSync relationship with Exchange Server 2010.

In this section, we'll look at how we can find out about an individual user's iOS device and see what tools are available to allow us to understand the devices in use across the organization.

Viewing an individual user's ActiveSync devices

Each ActiveSync device relationship between an iOS device and a user mailbox is stored within Active Directory. This information allows us to examine what devices the user has attached to Exchange Server at any time, and provides us information such as the last synchronization time.

How ActiveSync information is stored in Active Directory

The information stored in Active Directory about an ActiveSync device relationship is contained with an individual user account. To gain a quick understanding of how this is stored, we'll briefly look at how this is represented when examining the user object within Active Directory Users and Computers.

To examine the ActiveSync relationships, open Active Directory Users and Computers. By default, the ActiveSync relationships won't be accessible unless we choose **View**, then select **Users, Contacts, Groups, and Computers as containers**:

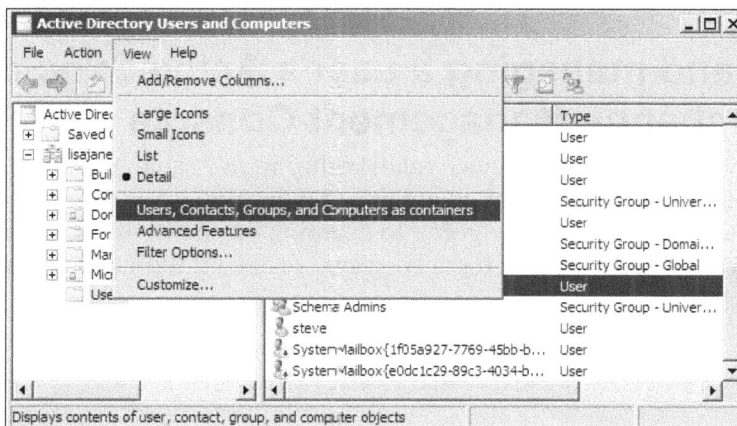

After choosing this option, Users and the other aforementioned objects now display in a similar way to Organizational Units and Containers in Active Directory Users and Computers; they can now be expanded and objects within the objects can be discovered and viewed.

To see the representations of the ActiveSync device relationships for a particular user, we'll examine the user **Lisa** and expand the user object as if it was an OU:

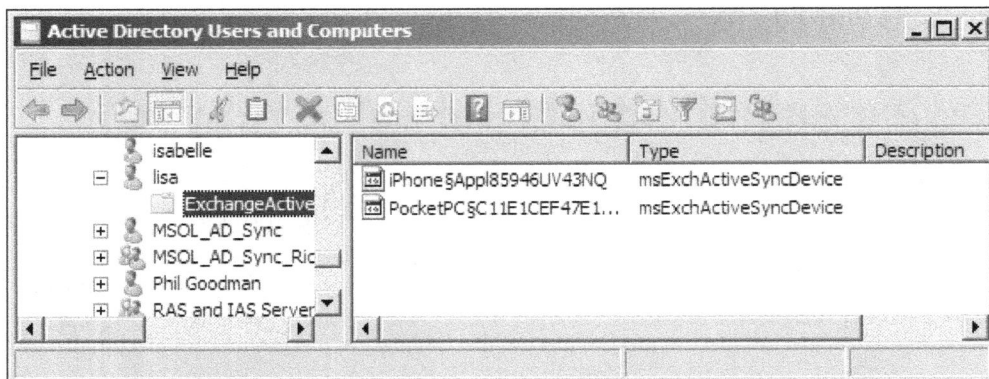

You'll see above that the **Lisa** object contains an **ExchangeActiveSyncDevices** container, and within this container we can see two objects of type **msExchActiveSyncDevice**. These objects represent the ActiveSync devices that the user has synchronized with Exchange Server 2010.

However, apart from the information we see above, we don't get to see much more information above the device. If we actually want to see detailed information about the ActiveSync device, we'll need to use the Exchange Management Console. However, it's worth seeing how the information is stored "under the hood" to help de-mystify where the actual relationship is actually stored.

Viewing and managing a user's ActiveSync devices using Exchange Management Console

When an individual user's iOS device relationship with Exchange Server 2010 must be examined, the easiest way to get this information is via the Exchange Management Console. We're now going to examine our mailbox user **Lisa** and view the ActiveSync devices that have been synchronized with this account.

To begin, launch the Exchange Management Console, and navigate to **Recipient Configuration**, then choose **Mailbox**:

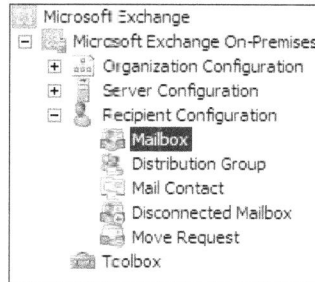

As you will expect to see by now, a list of the Exchange mailboxes within the organization is displayed.

Right click on the user from the list, and if there is an ActiveSync device relationship established the option to **Manage Mobile Phone** will be shown:

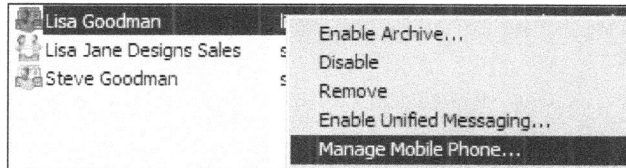

After selecting **Manage Mobile Phone**, the wizard will be displayed that initially gives us some information about the devices that the user has synchronized with Exchange Server 2010, along with some additional information including the last synchronization time, first synchronization time, and last policy update:

As a first point of call for information about the device, using the Exchange Management Console is a straightforward, easy to use method that gives us a quick summary of the important information we need to know. For example, if a user reports that they aren't receiving mails to their iPhone, we can quickly and easily see the last time the user synchronized their device.

There are also some other options available for managing the relationship between Exchange and the device, which we'll come back to later in the chapter.

Exporting ActiveSync device information

Using the Exchange Management Console is great when we know who the user is and have an idea of what to expect, but what about if we need to find out information about all of our iOS device users?

The Exchange Management Console is not a reporting utility and therefore doesn't give us the option to export information or even just filter the Mailbox list for mailbox users who have ActiveSync devices. Therefore, we'll need to resort to the Exchange Management Shell to get access to this information.

Using the Export-ActiveSyncLog command

In older releases of Exchange Server before Exchange Server 2007 Service Pack 1, gaining access to information about ActiveSync users was an arduous process, and typically involved use of the Microsoft **LogParser** utility along with some basic SQL knowledge to construct or modify example queries to find the information that was required from the Internet Information Services (IIS) log files.

In Exchange Server 2010, generating similar reports based upon IIS log files is now a built-in feature and generating a basic set of reports that provide a great overview of mobile devices is much more straightforward.

Before we attempt to generate the report, we need to know a little bit about the server we're going to run the report against, in particular the following information:

- The folder of the IIS log files for the site ActiveSync is installed within
- The folder we wish to use to output generated reports to
- Read-only or higher access to the folder containing the IIS log files
- Optionally a date range to run the report against

Armed with this information, we'll launch the Exchange Management Shell on one of the Client Access Servers and use the `Export-ActiveSyncLog` cmdlet to export log file data.

The `Export-ActiveSyncLog` cmdlet is the utility that parses the IIS log files and creates reports. We have the option to pass it a single log file (for example to look at a single day's log), or to pass it multiple log files to act upon. The date range can either be specified as a parameter to the `Export-ActiveSyncLog` cmdlet, or we can just pass it only the log files we wish to act upon.

In the example below, we'll look to generate a report against the last 90 days of IIS log files. The items in italics represent values you may need to change in your environment:

```
Get-ChildItem -Path C:\inetpub\logs\LogFiles\W3SVC1\*.log | Where-Object
{$_.LastAccessTime -gt (Get-Date).AddDays(-90)} | Export-ActiveSyncLog
-OutputPath C:\ActiveSyncReports
```

We have accomplished this using a combination of the `Get-ChildItem` cmdlet, which is a modern equivalent to `dir`, the `Where-Object` cmdlet which allows us to select a subset of the directory listing based on criteria we choose, and of course the `Export-ActiveSyncLog` cmdlet to actually do the work.

To pass the output of each distinct cmdlet to the next command, we use a technique known as **Pipelining**, signified by the | symbol which tells Powershell to use the output from the previous cmdlet as input to the next cmdlet, in a chain.

As the command is in progress we'll see information about the status of the operation, including which log file is currently being parsed:

```
[PS] C:\>Get-ChildItem -Path C:\inetpub\logs\LogFiles\W3SVC1\*.log | Where-Objec
t {$_.LastAccessTime -gt (Get-Date).AddDays(-90)} | Export-ActiveSyncLog -Output

Exchange ActiveSync reports are being generated.
    IIS log file 'C:\inetpub\logs\LogFiles\W3SVC1\u_ex110920.log' is being parse
    [                                                                           ]
```

After completion, we will be provided with a number of reports fulfilling the following purposes:

- `Hourly.csv`: an overview of the total number of devices connected hour by hour, day by day, and the synchronization requests performed.

- `PolicyCompliance.csv`: an overview of the status of Exchange ActiveSync policy compliance across the ActiveSync estate.

- `Servers.csv`: if you've copied the IIS log files for multiple Client Access Servers to a central location for analysis, this file lists the servers that ActiveSync clients connected to during the period this report was generated.

- `StatusCodes.csv`: an overview of the response codes ActiveSync devices have received from the Exchange Server. In general, nearly all of these should be 200, which signifies the request was successfully responded to by the Exchange Server.

- `UserAgents.csv`: an overview of the different device user agents that have been provided by ActiveSync clients. For iOS devices, this represents the Apple-encoded device version.

- `Users.csv`: a listing of ActiveSync users and the devices that they are using to connect to Exchange Server 2010, including information about how much data they have sent and received.

In particular, to see which users have connected ActiveSync devices, we'll examine the `Users.csv` file in Microsoft Excel, where we will see the iOS Device's **ID** and the **Type of Device** beside each user:

	A	B	C	D	E	F
	User Name	Device ID	Device Type	Items Sent	Items Receive	Hits
8	phil	Appl85946UV43NQ	iPhone	0	240	12153
10	rootuk.net\liz	Appl86952NNN3NP	iPhone	0	305	3818
12	rootuk.net\peter	Appl5U112790A4S	iPhone	0	652	17811
18	rootuk\mark	Appl88024RALA4S	iPhone	0	156	5758
19	rootuk\mark	ApplDNRGH84MDTC0	iPhone	0	178	5865
21	rootuk\sophie	Appl840233GWA4S	iPhone	0	506	8999
22	rootuk\sophie	ApplDNQGHAMTDTC0	iPhone	0	448	15971
24	rootuk\steve	Appl85946UV43NQ	iPhone	0	46	3406
25	rootuk\steve	Appl869279CB3NP	iPhone	0	185	7547
28	steve@rootuk.net	Appl85946UV43NQ	iPhone	0	24	1150
29	steve@rootuk.net	Appl869279CB3NP	iPhone	0	63	550

In our example above, you will see users listed multiple times in a number of cases. What this signifies is that over the last 90 days a number of users have had replacement or upgraded iOS devices.

Obtaining more detailed information

Whilst the information available using the `Export-ActiveSyncLog` cmdlet is great information to have access to, it doesn't provide us everything we might want to know about our device estate, as the information contained within the report is based upon IIS log files, or rather the raw connections between the Exchange Server and the iOS device itself.

If we want to find out more information, we need to examine how we can use the Exchange Management Shell to retrieve device statistics and present them in a format that's easy to examine in Microsoft Excel.

To do this, we need to look at using the Exchange Management Shell in a slightly more complicated way using the native PowerShell scripting abilities.

Before you think of PowerShell scripting and begin to worry, the important thing to remember is that you don't need to modify the script. Simply run it as is to generate the report—unless of course you wish to make your own additions or changes to implement additional features!

The reporting script is available as a downloadable PowerShell file to accompany this book. `ExportActiveSyncDeviceStatistics.ps1` retrieves this information and after correlating iOS Device information outputs the results to a CSV file.

To execute the script and generate the report, use the following parameters:

```
.\ExportActiveSyncDeviceStatistics.ps1 -OutputCSVFile file.csv
```

After using the script and exporting the report to a CSV file, open the file in Microsoft Excel where you can see detailed information about all ActiveSync clients in use, with a particular focus on iOS devices:

Upon examination, you will see the report contains the following fields, providing substantially more information than the built-in reporting capabilities in the `Export-ActiveSyncLogs` cmdlet and building upon the information provided in Exchange Server by providing information about iOS version information:

- Username
- Display Name
- Device Type
- Device Model
- iOS Version
- Device ID
- Status
- ActiveSync Policy
- ActiveSync Policy Status
- Last Sync
- Last Sync Attempt
- Last Policy Update
- First Sync

One caveat with the script is that for the iOS version to be reported correctly, the `ExportActiveSyncDeviceStatistics.ps1` script must be updated with new iOS version information as new releases of Apple's mobile device platform come out. You'll always find the most up-to-date version available on the following website:

`http://www.stevieg.org`

Troubleshooting connection problems for iOS devices

One unfortunate aspect of every system administrator's life is the adage, Murphy's law:

> *"Anything that can go wrong, will go wrong."*

Therefore with that in mind, it's essential to be prepared to understand the basic troubleshooting steps to help determine where to begin investigations when invariably an end user reports issues connecting to Exchange ActiveSync.

Mobile Devices are complex to troubleshoot as there are a lot of interdependencies that are essential for them to connect to and synchronize with Exchange Server 2010; these include:

- The iOS mobile device operating system
- Proximity to and functionality of local cell towers
- GPRS or 3G connectivity to the cell provider network
- The cell provider network's Internet connectivity
- Central Internet exchange points where Internet service providers peer or connect to transit
- The ISP providing Internet connectivity for the organization hosting the Exchange Server
- External DNS services providing name resolution for the published Exchange namespaces and intermediary DNS servers
- External firewalls protecting the organization and publishing access from the Internet to internal servers
- Hardware load balancing services providing high availability services for Exchange Server
- Availability of IIS on Client Access Servers, including Exchange Client Access configuration and SSL certificates
- Back end Exchange services, such as Mailbox servers
- Internal services including time services, DNS, and Active Directory
- Physical conditions in the organization's datacenter including hardware, cooling, or power issues

Any one of these components being subject to a failure could result in iOS devices being unable to synchronize with Exchange Server, plus a multitude of other areas including things like configuration changes.

Naturally the further removed from the Exchange Server the issue is the harder it may be to track down or isolate. The job of monitoring all these components can be daunting; however, solutions such as Microsoft Systems Center Operations Manager can be of great assistance in providing pro-active monitoring facilities to help isolate such issues even before end users report them.

If the issue is suspected to be local to the Exchange Server itself or even an isolated issue for a single user, then tools available within Exchange Server 2010 can be of assistance in providing a starting point for resolving issues.

In this section we'll examine some of the tools that will be of assistance when checking ActiveSync functionality and looking into individual iOS mobile device user issues.

Testing ActiveSync functionality

Earlier in the book, we examined using the Microsoft Remote Connectivity Analyser to verify external ActiveSync connectivity.

To recap, this tool allows synthetic tests to be performed from Microsoft datacenters against the local Exchange Server organization to verify that external clients can connect to and synchronize against Exchange Server using a variety of protocols, including Exchange ActiveSync. The Remote Connectivity Analyzer can be accessed at the following URL:

```
https://www.testexchangeconnectivity.com/
```

We can also make use of tools built into Exchange Server to make tests using Exchange's built in testing functionality.

The `Test-` cmdlets in Exchange Server 2010 rely on a dedicated Exchange connectivity test user being present within the Exchange Organization, which is used by Exchange itself when performing system tests.

If one hasn't been created, we'll need to create it using a Microsoft-provided script that resides on each Exchange Server.

To begin the process, create a test user by launching the Exchange Management Shell and entering the following command to change directory to the Exchange Scripts directory:

```
cd $ExScripts
```

After changing to the Exchange Scripts directory (typically located in `C:\Program Files\Microsoft\Exchange Server\V14\scripts` on a default installation), we can execute the script used to create the connectivity test user using the following command:

```
.\new-TestCasConnectivityUser.ps1
```

During this process, you will be prompted for initial credentials for the connectivity test user which will be periodically changed by Exchange itself, but the initial password must meet your organization's password complexity requirements. After successful creation, you should see the following results:

```
Machine: exch01.lisajanedesigns.co.uk                                    _ □ ×
[PS] C:\Windows\system32>cd $ExScripts
[PS] C:\Program Files\Microsoft\Exchange Server\V14\scripts>.\new-TestCasConnect
ivityUser.ps1
Please enter a temporary secure password for creating test users. For security
purposes, the password will be changed regularly and automatically by the syste
m.
Enter password: ***********
Create test user on: exch01.lisajanedesigns.co.uk
Click CTRL+Break to quit or click Enter to continue.:
UserPrincipalName: extest_a822c5a0bac54@lisajanedesigns.co.uk
WARNING: The command completed successfully but no settings of
'lisajanedesigns.co.uk/Users/extest_a822c5a0bac54' have been modified.

You can enable the test user for Unified Messaging by running this command with
the following optional parameters : [-UMDialPlan <dialplanname> -UMExtension <nu
mDigitsInDialplan>] . Either None or Both must be present.

[PS] C:\Program Files\Microsoft\Exchange Server\V14\scripts>_
```

Depending on your organization's Active Directory infrastructure, you may need to wait a number of minutes before the connectivity test user can be used.

After creating the connectivity test user, we can perform a test on Exchange ActiveSync to ensure its correct functionality, again from the Exchange Management Shell:

```
Test-ActiveSyncConnectivity
```

If the test is successful, you'll see output similar to the following:

```
Machine: exch01.lisajanedesigns.co.uk                                    _ □ ×
[PS] C:\>Test-ActiveSyncConnectivity

CasServer   LocalSite     Scenario        Result    Latency(MS)  Error
                                                                                
exch01      Default-Fi... Options         Success        15.60
exch01      Default-Fi... FolderSync      Success        62.40
exch01      Default-Fi... First Sync      Success        46.80
exch01      Default-Fi... GetItemEstimate Success        31.20
exch01      Default-Fi... Sync Data       Success        31.20
exch01      Default-Fi... Ping            Success      2070.01
exch01      Default-Fi... Sync Test Item  Success       109.20


[PS] C:\>_
```

If an error is shown at any stage during the process, this may not be easy to read in the table in its default format. To examine the error in greater detail, re-run the command with the following options to display full details:

```
Test-ActiveSyncConnectivity | fl
```

This time, details about the cause of the error are shown in the output, shown highlighted on the example below:

```
Machine: exch01.lisajanedesigns.co.uk                                   _ □ ×
[PS] C:\>Test-ActiveSyncConnectivity | fl

RunspaceId                   : c0f569ab-296c-4ff3-bba8-8e24addaf380
LocalSite                    : Default-First-Site-Name
SecureAccess                 : True
VirtualDirectoryName         :
Url                          :
UrlType                      : Unknown
Port                         : 0
ConnectionType               : Plaintext
ClientAccessServerShortName  : exch01
LocalSiteShortName           : Default-First-Site-Name
ClientAccessServer           : exch01.lisajanedesigns.co.uk
Scenario                     : Options
ScenarioDescription          : Issue an HTTP OPTIONS command to retrieve the Exc
                               hange ActiveSync protocol version.
PerformanceCounterName       : DirectPush Latency
Result                       : Failure
Error                        : [System.Net.WebException]: The underlying connect
                               ion was closed: Could not establish trust relatio
                               nship for the SSL/TLS secure channel. Inner error
                               [System.Security.Authentication.AuthenticationEx
                               ception]: The remote certificate is invalid accor
                               ding to the validation procedure.
UserName                     : extest_a62265a0bac54
StartTime                    : 04/12/2011 00:24:35
Latency                      : -00:00:01
EventType                    : Error
LatencyInMillisecondsString  :
Identity                     :
IsValid                      : True
```

In the example above, the underlying cause of the error appears to be due to a certificate error. This could mean that an SSL certificate is out of date. We'll have to make further investigations to understand the root cause; however, the results of the test commands have given us a direction for further investigation.

Further testing cmdlets are available with Exchange Server for testing other aspects of Exchange, for example when investigating unrelated issues with Outlook Web App. A full list of Test cmdlets is available on the Technet website:

http://technet.microsoft.com/en-us/library/aa998005.aspx

Analyzing reports

The reports generated using the built-in utility `Export-ActiveSyncLogs` and using the custom script provided in this book can be useful in examining whether the reported issue is widespread or isolated to a single user.

For example, in a case where a user is reporting that their iPhone has been unable to synchronize, it's easy to spot whether it's likely to be the Exchange infrastructure, or something local to their device.

In the following example we see that **Phil** has been unable to even attempt to synchronize, however other users are able to synchronize without issues:

	A	B	C	J	K	
1	Username	Display Name	Device Type	Last Sync	Last Sync Attempt	Last Po
2	steve	Steve Goodman	iPhone	03/12/2011 18:48	03/12/2011 18:48	03/1
3	phil	Phil Goodman	iPhone	12/11/2011 18:25	12/11/2011 18:25	10/0
4	peter	Peter Goodman	iPhone	03/12/2011 21:21	03/12/2011 21:21	10/0

Armed with that knowledge we can investigate further and attempt to rule out Exchange itself and look for another possible cause, such as a failure in the mobile network.

Enabling device-side logging

For information about issues such as sporadic failures to synchronize particular items, such as Calendar items, it's possible to remotely enable ActiveSync logging on the iOS device.

To do this, visit the Exchange Control Panel, and log in as an Administrator or a user with at least membership of the Helpdesk role-based access group. Select **Manage My Organization**, and then choose **Another User**:

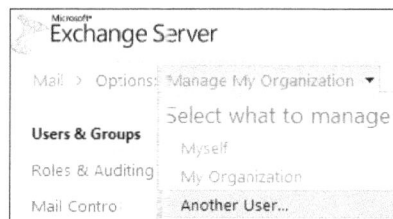

Select the mailbox user you wish to enable ActiveSync logging for, and then choose **OK**. You will now be presented with the user's options pages with full access to modify their personal settings.

From the left hand sidebar, select **Phone**, then choose the **Mobile Phones** tab. You will be presented with the list of the end user's ActiveSync devices, including the iOS device we're looking to enable ActiveSync device logging for.

To enable logging, select the correct device from the list, and then choose **Start Logging**:

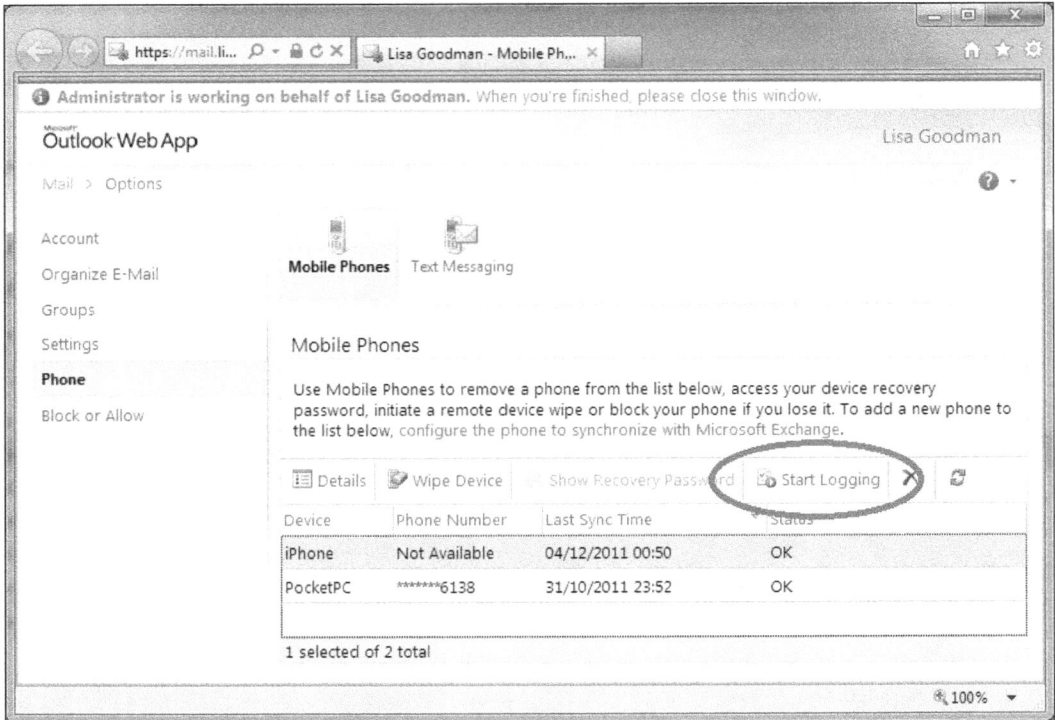

After enabling logging, ensure that the user has sufficient time to reproduce the error.

Once the user has confirmed that the sporadic error has occurred, access the user's options pages through the Exchange Management Console again, and in place of the **Start Logging** option will be the option to **Retrieve Log**:

The next time the iOS device connects to Exchange Server 2010, the ActiveSync device logs will be collected and uploaded to the Exchange Server in the form of a message in the end user's inbox.

After requesting the user to forward the message containing the logs, we should be presented with a plain-text attachment in the form of a log file with the following naming convention:

```
EASMailboxLog_username_iPhone_DeviceID.log
```

The ActiveSync device log consists of transactional information about each interaction the device has had with the Exchange Server, including detailed information about the requests that it has made to the server, and the response from the Exchange Server to those requests.

In the example below, we can see a typical section of an ActiveSync device log file generated by an iOS device:

Highlighted in the previous image, you will see by examining both the section headers and the XML contents deeper within the section that this part of the log file describes the following:

- A **Response Body** from the Exchange Server
- Containing a request to **Add** a new item onto the iOS device
- The item to add is a **Calendar** item

Therefore we can see that when a Calendar item is created by the user in Outlook Web App or Microsoft Outlook, it is being synchronized to the mobile device over ActiveSync.

In the case above, we've been able to confirm that ActiveSync isn't necessarily the problem with the calendar synchronization issue, and may need to look deeper, such as to investigate whether there is a bug in the version of iOS the end user is using causing the issue they've experienced.

Of course, calendaring issues aren't the only type of issue you may wish to use ActiveSync device logs to investigate, and the methods of verifying that the device functionality is correct are based on the same techniques—carefully examining the sections of the log file produced and attempting to correlate the requests and responses to the steps the user has taken to reproduce the issue they are experiencing.

Using administrator features for disabling and remote wipe of devices

Depending on the nature of the issue you may wish to either disable ActiveSync connectivity for a single mailbox user, or go as far as completely wiping the device.

Disabling ActiveSync for a user

If you are looking to simply disable ActiveSync for a user, but leave the items present on the Apple device intact, and without interfering with the user's access to other services such as their Active Directory account and access to their mailbox, then it's possible to disable Exchange ActiveSync on a user-by-user basis.

To disable ActiveSync for a particular user, open the Exchange Management Console and navigate to **Recipient Configuration**, then select **Mailbox** to show the list of Mailbox users.

Double-click the user you wish to disable ActiveSync access for to bring up the mailbox properties for the user. Click the **Mailbox Features** tab, and then select **Exchange ActiveSync** from the list. The option to **Disable** ActiveSync will be shown:

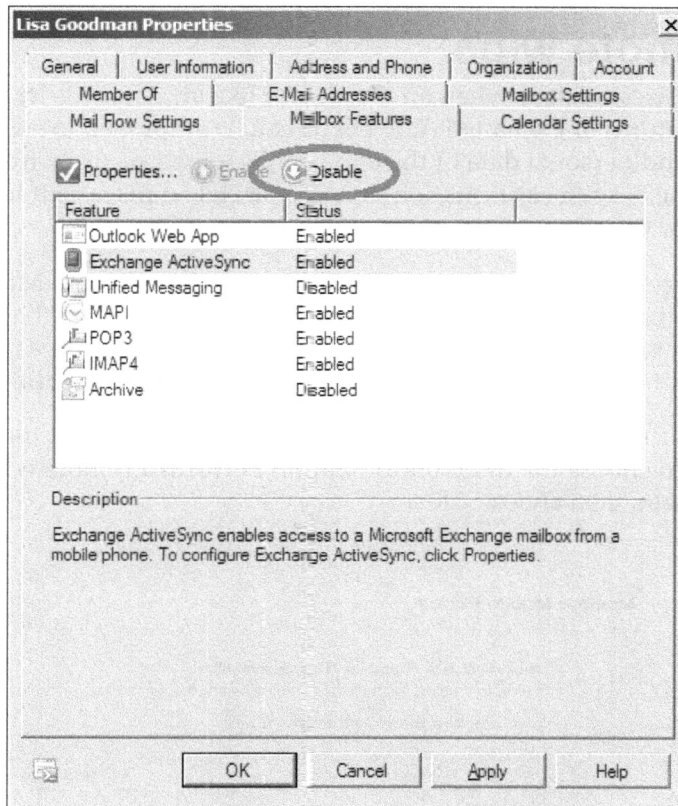

After choosing **Disable**, select **OK** to save and apply the changes to the user mailbox. The change will not take effect immediately, however after a short time the iOS device will be prevented from synchronizing with the Exchange Server, appearing to the end user as if the password entered was incorrect:

By reversing the changes and enabling ActiveSync for the mailbox again, the iOS device will be able to resume synchronization and changes made on the iOS device in the period will be uploaded to the Exchange Server mailbox.

Using remote wipe

In more drastic cases, such as when an iOS device like an iPhone is lost or stolen, the Remote Wipe features of Exchange ActiveSync can be employed to ensure that any company data, and personal data of the end user, is wiped securely from the device in a timely manner — with confirmation that this has taken place sent to the end user and displayed for the administrator to verify.

To begin the process to remote wipe an iOS device, we'll revisit the **Manage Mobile Phone** wizard we explored earlier in the chapter, by using the Exchange Management Console to list the mailbox we are looking to perform a remote wipe against, then right-clicking the mailbox and choosing **Manage Mobile Device**.

The Manage Mobile Device wizard should display. Carefully select the correct device from the list, then choose the radio button option **Perform a remote wipe to clear mobile phone data**, then choose **Clear**:

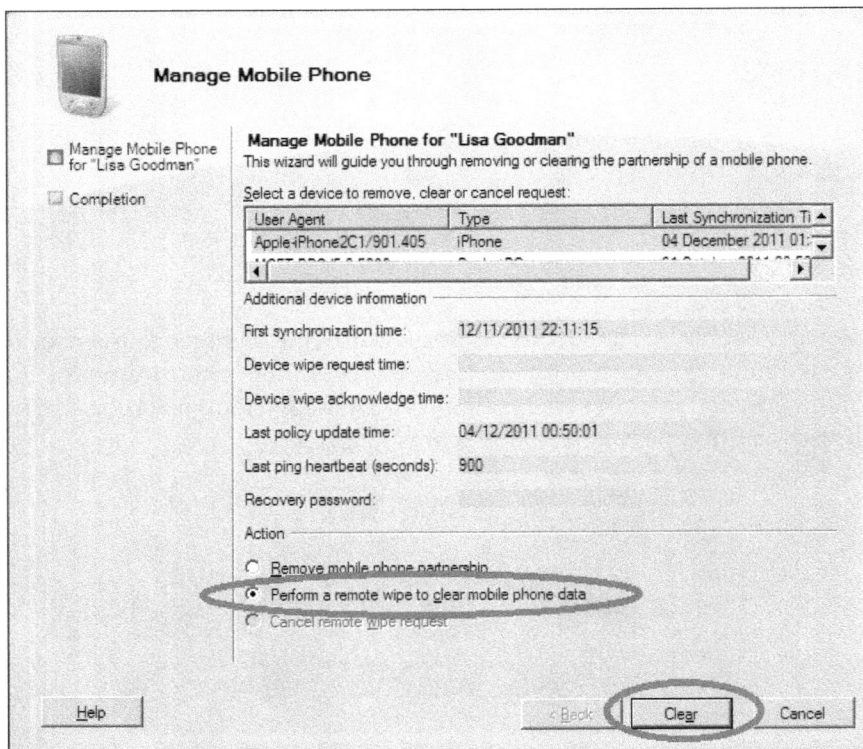

After choosing **Clear** the administrator will be asked for final confirmation that this action is definitely required, then after confirming that the device should indeed be wiped, a remote wipe notification will be pushed to the device, usually within minutes.

Once a remote wipe request has been received by the device it sends back confirmation to the Exchange Server that the operation has been successfully started. As part of this process the end user will receive a message confirming them of the action, and when re-visiting the **Manage Mobile Phone** wizard in the Exchange Management Console, it is possible to view the time the request was made and the time that the request was acknowledged by the iOS device (as shown below in the red square).

Should the device need to be reconnected to this Exchange Server organization, then it is important to ensure that the existing device relationship is removed using this wizard. To do so, select **Remove mobile phone partnership**, and then click **Remove**:

By removing a mobile phone partnership, we aren't initiating a remote wipe, which is a separate process; therefore when troubleshooting, removing a mobile phone partnership is a safe task to perform as it will not perform a remote wipe.

End-user features for remote wipe of devices

The ability for administrators to perform a remote wipe of ActiveSync devices has been available as a feature of Exchange since Exchange Server 2003 Service Pack 2, through installation of the Microsoft Exchange Server ActiveSync Web Administration Tool.

In Exchange Server 2007, the functionality to perform a remote wipe was extended to end users. However, in Exchange Server 2010 these features are easy for end users to manage and use, really putting the end user in control when it comes to ensuring that should they lose their iOS device, they can quickly and easily ensure that data on the device won't fall into the wrong hands.

For an end user to access this functionality, the end user logs into **Outlook Web App** and chooses **Options**. In the **Options** page, the user selects **Phones** from the sidebar.

After selecting the device to wipe from the list, the end user chooses **Wipe Device** as shown below:

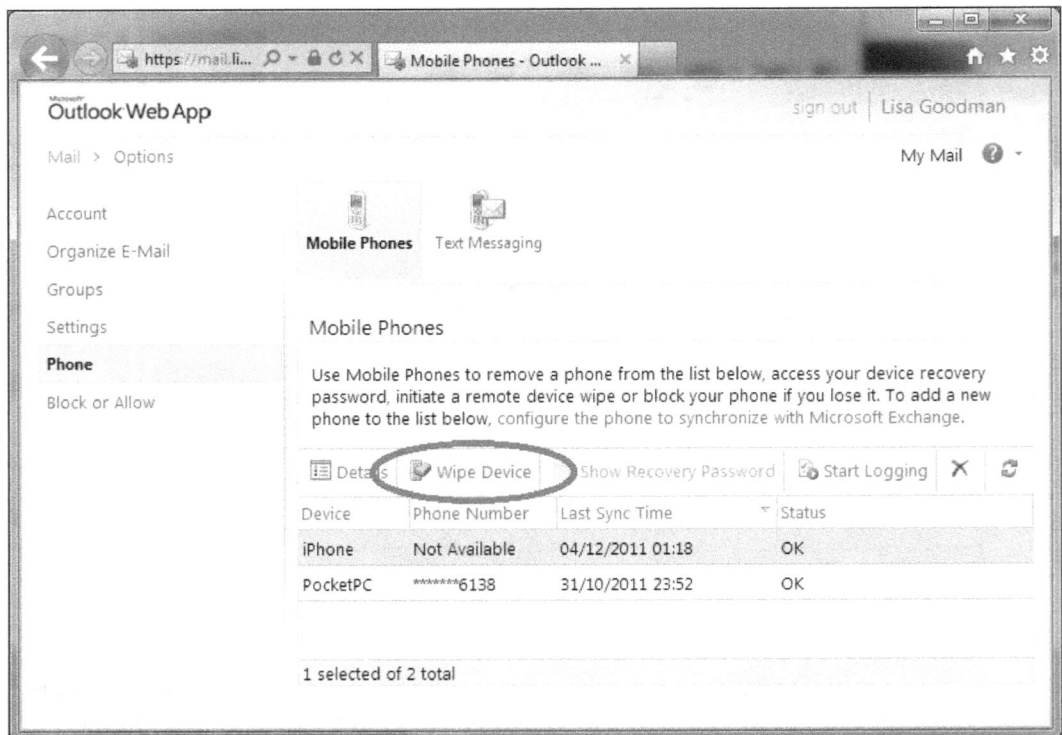

After choosing **Wipe Device**, the user is asked one last time if they are sure they want to proceed:

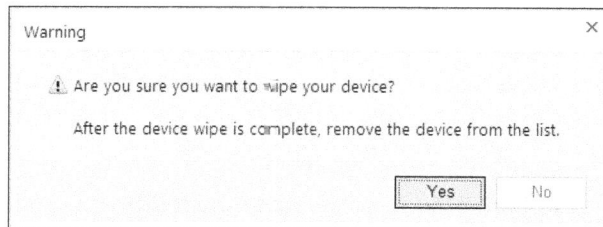

After remote wipe is confirmed, the **Mobile Phones** options page will be updated to show the end user details of when the remote wipe successfully eradicated the data on their iOS device, as well as the user receiving an e-mail confirmation that the mobile device is wiped.

The same underlying functionality as used by an administrator is used to perform a remote wipe; therefore a similar process to remove the device from the user's list of devices must be followed should the iOS device later be found; simply select the device from the list and choose the **X** button to remove the device partnership.

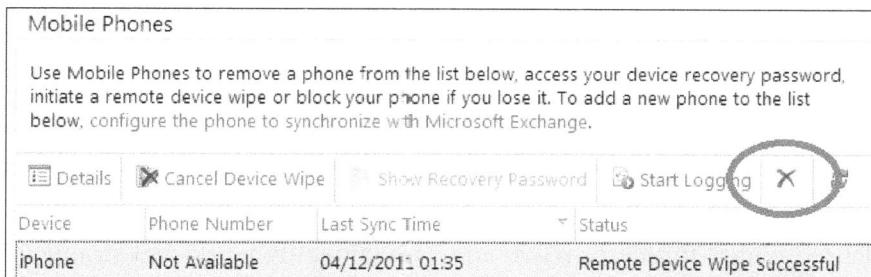

After removing the device partnership, the iOS device will be able to be reconnected to the Exchange Server, either by the user or through more advanced provisioning techniques.

Summary

In this chapter, we've covered what is possible when managing iOS devices like the iPhone in an Exchange Server 2010 environment. Early in the chapter we took a high-level view of where ActiveSync has shortcomings when managing Apple devices once they are in the hands of end users, and we briefly looked at what third party products are available that complement Exchange ActiveSync management to provide a full Mobile Device Management Solution.

We've then moved on to look at how we can use the features built into Exchange Server 2010 to view individual mobile device information, including information about when the user last synchronized their device, and then examined how we can use the Exchange Management Shell and built-in commands to parse log files on the Exchange Client Access Servers to produce basic reports about our iOS Device estate.

After looking at what Exchange can do out of the box, we've then used a custom PowerShell script to pull together information stored in Exchange Server and Active Directory for individual ActiveSync devices; this produced a detailed report that collates information about all individual ActiveSync devices, their associated users, and in particular for iOS devices, provides detailed information about the iOS software version present on the device.

In the second part of this chapter, we've moved on to look at just a few of the ways to troubleshoot issues ActiveSync clients might have, including verifying underlying server functionality is correctly functioning, and if not how to look for clues that may help us understand what may be the cause of the problem. We then touched on how we can use the reports generated in the first part of this chapter to see whether an issue is a widespread problem or localized to a couple of users.

For harder to identify problems where most functionality works but strange issues occur, we've looked at how to enable logging on the iOS device remotely from the Exchange Server, and looked at the results of a logging session so that we can see what to expect when log files are returned from the mobile device for analysis.

In the final part of this chapter we've looked at how we can use ActiveSync device management features - disabling ActiveSync for individual users and using Exchange Server 2010's remote wipe features to securely remove all data, both company and personal data, from an iOS device. We've seen that not just administrators can perform a remote wipe, but and end user can too, placing an element of control and responsibility into the hands of end users.

By the end of this chapter you should have a good basic understanding of how to manage iOS devices as they are deployed.

I hope that throughout this book you have learned not only about iOS devices, but also gained a good understanding of the core technologies within Exchange 2010. It's been my aim to help you learn how build a properly sized, high availability environment in a small to mid-size business setting, as well as help you configure all the interesting components that will make your iOS devices a useful part of your organization.

As this is the end of the book, I can only conclude by saying thank you for taking the time to read it—I've certainly enjoyed writing it. However, the journey doesn't end here -there's a lot more to Exchange than can be contained in any one book.

If you'd like to learn more about Exchange Server and Office 365, including PowerShell scripting, then drop by my website, `http://www.stevieg.org`, for regular articles including more on using iPhones with Exchange. I'd also strongly recommend following the official Exchange Team Blog, `http://blogs.technet.com/b/exchange`, a fantastic resource for Exchange Server news, advice, and tips.

Index

[PACKT] PUBLISHING enterprise
professional expertise distilled

Thank you for buying
iPhone with Microsoft Exchange Server 2010: Business Integration and Deployment

About Packt Publishing

Packt, pronounced 'packed', published its first book "Mastering phpMyAdmin for Effective MySQL Management" in April 2004 and subsequently continued to specialize in publishing highly focused books on specific technologies and solutions.

Our books and publications share the experiences of your fellow IT professionals in adapting and customizing today's systems, applications, and frameworks. Our solution based books give you the knowledge and power to customize the software and technologies you're using to get the job done. Packt books are more specific and less general than the IT books you have seen in the past. Our unique business model allows us to bring you more focused information, giving you more of what you need to know, and less of what you don't.

Packt is a modern, yet unique publishing company, which focuses on producing quality, cutting-edge books for communities of developers, administrators, and newbies alike. For more information, please visit our website: www.packtpub.com.

About Packt Enterprise

In 2010, Packt launched two new brands, Packt Enterprise and Packt Open Source, in order to continue its focus on specialization. This book is part of the Packt Enterprise brand, home to books published on enterprise software – software created by major vendors, including (but not limited to) IBM, Microsoft and Oracle, often for use in other corporations. Its titles will offer information relevant to a range of users of this software, including administrators, developers, architects, and end users.

Writing for Packt

We welcome all inquiries from people who are interested in authoring. Book proposals should be sent to author@packtpub.com. If your book idea is still at an early stage and you would like to discuss it first before writing a formal book proposal, contact us; one of our commissioning editors will get in touch with you.

We're not just looking for published authors; if you have strong technical skills but no writing experience, our experienced editors can help you develop a writing career, or simply get some additional reward for your expertise.

[PACKT] enterprise 🞥
PUBLISHING
professional expertise distilled

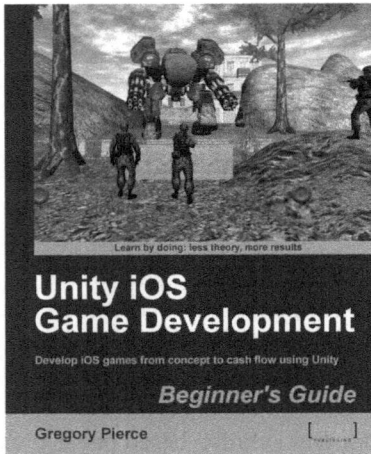

Unity iOS Game Development Beginners Guide

ISBN: 978-1-84969-040-9   Paperback: 314 pages

Develop iOS games from concept to cash flow using Unity

1. Dive straight into game development with no previous Unity or iOS experience

2. Work through the entire lifecycle of developing games for iOS

3. Add multiplayer, input controls, debugging, in app and micro payments to your game

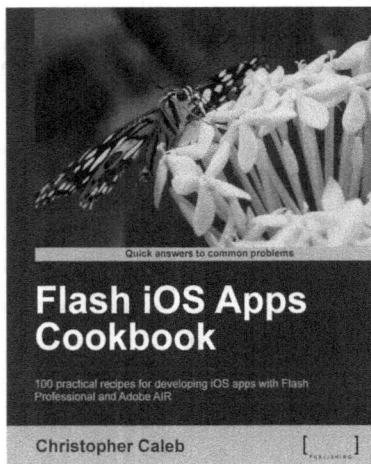

Flash iOS Apps Cookbook

ISBN: 978-1-84969-138-3   Paperback: 420 pages

100 practical recipes for developing iOS apps with Flash Professional and Adobe AIR

1. Build your own apps, port existing projects, and learn the best practices for targeting iOS devices using Flash.

2. How to compile a native iOS app directly from Flash and deploy it to the iPhone, iPad or iPod touch.

3. Full of practical recipes and step-by-step instructions for developing iOS apps with Flash Professional.

Please check **www.PacktPub.com** for information on our titles

[PACKT] enterprise
PUBLISHING   professional expertise distilled

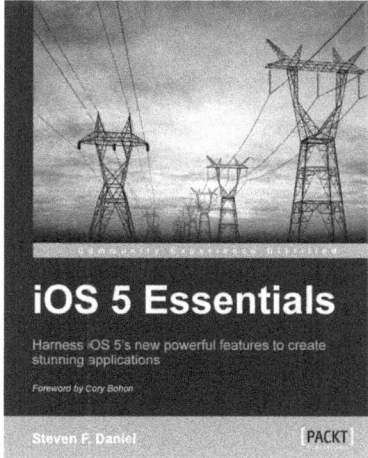

iOS 5 Essentials

ISBN: 978-1-84969-226-7   Paperback: 252 pages

Harness iOS 5's new powerful features to create stunning applications

1. Integrate iCloud, Twitter and AirPlay into your applications.

2. Lots of step-by-step examples, images and diagrams to get you up to speed in no time with helpful hints along the way.

3. Each chapter explains iOS 5's new features in-depth, whilst providing you with enough practical examples to help incorporate these features in your apps

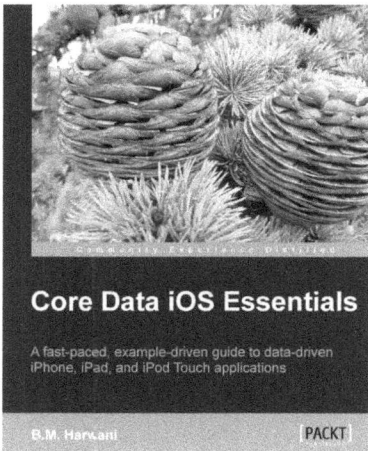

Core Data iOS Essentials

ISBN: 978-1-84969-094-2   Paperback: 340 pages

A fast-paced, example-driven guide to data-driven iPhone, iPad, and iPod Touch applications

1. Covers the essential skills you need for working with Core Data in your applications.

2. Particularly focused on developing fast, light weight data-driven iOS applications.

3. Builds a complete example application. Every technique is shown in context.

Please check **www.PacktPub.com** for information on our titles

www.ingramcontent.com/pod-product-compliance
Lightning Source LLC
Chambersburg PA
CBHW061346210326
41598CB00035B/5900

* 9 7 8 1 8 4 9 6 9 1 4 8 2 *